# *Beyond*
# INTUITION

# *Beyond* INTUITION

## A Guide to Writing and Editing Magazine Nonfiction

**Patricia Westfall**

**Ohio University**

Longman

New York & London

**Beyond Intuition: A Guide to Writing and Editing Magazine Nonfiction**

Longman, 10 Bank Street, White Plains, N.Y. 10606

Associated companies:
Longman Group Ltd., London
Longman Cheshire Pty., Melbourne
Longman Paul Pty., Auckland
Copp Clark Pitman, Toronto

Acquisitions editor: Kathleen M. Schurawich
Sponsoring editor: Gordon T.R. Anderson
Production editor: Ann P. Kearns
Text design adaptation: Silvers Design
Cover design: Joseph DePinho
Text art: Fine Line Inc.
Production supervisor: Anne P. Armeny

**Library of Congress Cataloging-in-Publication Data**

Westfall, Patricia Tichenor.
    Beyond intuition: a guide to writing and editing magazine non-
    fiction/Patricia Westfall.
        p.    cm.
    Includes index.
    ISBN 0-8013-0694-9
    1. Feature writing.  2. Journalism—Authorship.  3. Editing.
4. Journalism—Editing.  I. Title.
PN1181.W47  1993
808'.02—dc20                                              93-9958
                                                              CIP

1 2 3 4 5 6 7 8 9 10-MA-9796959493

This book is affectionately dedicated
to every writer and editor
who has hung up the phone
—wondering what the other meant.

# Contents

*Annotated Contents*    *xi*

*Demonstration Articles*    *xv*

*Preface*    *xvii*

## PART I   WORLDS APART                                                    1

### CHAPTER 1:   **ON BEING A WRITER**        3

On Perception    *3*
On Chaos    *4*
On Process    *5*
On Intuition    *8*
*For Additional Reading*    *9*

### CHAPTER 2:   **ON BEING AN EDITOR**        11

Too Much Brass    *11*
Audience    *13*
Niche    *19*
Editing for Audience and Niche    *24*
Writing for Audience and Niche    *26*
*For Additional Reading*    *28*
*Appendix 2.1:   Audience Research Methods*    *29*
*Appendix 2.2:   Demographic Terms*    *32*

**PART II    THE BASIC TOOLS**                                         **35**

CHAPTER 3:  **FOCUS**      **37**

Basic Patterns   *40*
Sophisticated Patterns   *42*
Things Best Avoided   *46*
Exploring Focusing   *47*
**The Corn**   **48**
*Raccoon Articles*   *56*

CHAPTER 4:  **FORM**      **57**

**The Linzer Torte**   **57**
A Problem of Definition   *59*
Subject   *61*
Purpose   *62*
Effect   *67*
Genre   *68*
Mix and Range   *70*
*For Additional Reading*   *85*

CHAPTER 5:  **STRUCTURE**      **87**

Elements   *88*
Mapping   *101*
**The Cold**   **103**
*For Additional Reading*   *108*


**PART III    ADVANCED TOOLS**                                        **109**

CHAPTER 6:  **AUTHORITY BASE**      **111**

**Eva's Ghost**   **112**
Strengths and Weaknesses   *116*
Writers and Authority Base   *140*
Editors and Authority Base   *141*

CHAPTER 7:  **VOICE**      **145**

The Art of Fact   *146*
The Art of Perception   *149*
*Appendix 7.1:  Selected Nonfiction Authors*   *153*
*Appendix 7.2:  Works by John McPhee*   *154*
*Appendix 7.3:  Theoretical Works*   *155*

**PART IV   BEYOND ANALYSIS** **157**

CHAPTER 8:  **TIGHTENING**      **159**

Examples of Tightening    *160*
Tightening Tricks    *172*

CHAPTER 9:  **SERENDIPITY**      **175**

Remembering    *175*
**Lists (fragments)**    **176**
Talking    *176*
Free Play    *178*

CHAPTER 10:  **EVIDENCE**      **183**

Getting Started: Do Nothing    *183*
After the Beginning    *189*
Connecting with Reality    *193*
Taking Notes    *199*
Some Final Thoughts    *201*
*Appendix 10.1:   Research Case Studies*    *203*

CHAPTER 11:  **BEYOND INTUITION**      **215**

Practical Marketing    *216*
The Editor–Writer Relationship    *219*
Recommended for the Professional Bookshelf    *220*

*Working in Groups*    *221*

*Index*    *227*

# Annotated Contents

*Preface*   *xvii*
   The love/hate relationship between editor and writer.


**PART I:   WORLDS APART**                                                                1
   Writers and editors share responsibility for producing finished articles. They
   can't live without each other. Sometimes they can't live with each other
   either.

CHAPTER 1.   **ON BEING A WRITER**      **3**
   The craft of writing has its technical side, its mastery of words and sentences,
   but at a professional level, real mastery is of *perception, chaos, process* and
   *intuition*.


CHAPTER 2.   **ON BEING AN EDITOR**      **11**
   Editors handle manuscripts, yes, but their real job is talking. Editors *explain*.
   The main things they explain are the *demographic* and *psychographic* qualities of their *audience*. They also are forever trying to get their poor dense
   writers to understand their magazine's *niche*.


**PART II:   THE BASIC TOOLS**                                                          35
   No matter how unique an article may seem, it will always have focus, form
   and structure. When editors and writers can analyze manuscripts or magazines for these three elements, they can control them too.

## CHAPTER 3.  **FOCUS**    37

Focus is the premise, angle, theme, point or message of a piece; it is the topic beneath the topic, the answer to the question "What is this about *really*?" Typical focus patterns are the *simple, traditional, bracket, tandem, complex, reverse, apologetic* and *paradox*.

## CHAPTER 4.  **FORM**    57

Form is "a literary term with a confusing variety of meanings." For sake of discussion (and of keeping the book shorter than the *Oxford English Dictionary*), form is divided into four aspects—*subject, purpose, effect* and *genre*. Three magazines are analyzed for their *mix* and *range* of forms.

## CHAPTER 5.  **STRUCTURE**    87

Every article is unique in structure, but all share common *elements* from words, to sentences, to paragraphs, from beginnings, to middles, to ends. A technique for analyzing the elements of structure, called *mapping*, is introduced.

## PART III:   ADVANCED TOOLS    109

A writer or editor could limp along with the three basic tools, but real mastery means commanding some subtleties. Authority base—or skill at signaling readings with prose devices—is one such advanced tool. Another is the mysterious quality of "voice."

## CHAPTER 6.  **AUTHORITY BASE**    111

Nonfiction must contain frequent *signals* that tell the reader a piece is true. The more skilled the writing and editing, the more subtle the signals. But every signal has advantages and disadvantages that affect *credibility* and *readability*. A demonstration article is dissected for its twenty-six authority bases.

## CHAPTER 7.  **VOICE**    145

Voice is the ineffable presence of the writer. It is mystery and yet, like an athletic talent, it can be developed through *training*.

## PART IV:   BEYOND ANALYSIS    157

Some skills essential to writing and editing are process rather than analytical. That is, no special analytical techniques are available; you just have to get out and do them to get insight into the skills. (Of course, getting out and doing focuses, forms, structure, authority base and voice wouldn't hurt either.) These process skills are grouped together in this last section even though, as with tightening, it may be the last task done in a project, or as with serendipity, it may be the first.

CHAPTER 8.  **TIGHTENING**      **159**
A totally practical look at the delicious skill of killing words—one at a time.

CHAPTER 9.  **SERENDIPITY**      **175**
How does a writer or editor get ideas in the first place? Try deliberately creating happy accidents.

CHAPTER 10.  **EVIDENCE**      **183**
Research, the foundation of all nonfiction, is a creative process. *Looking, talking* and *reading* are the basic techniques. Tips are given on where to find people, experts, things, places, statistics, chronologies and narrative detail.

CHAPTER 11.  **BEYOND INTUITION**      **215**
The editor–writer collaboration begins with a *query letter.*

*WORKING IN GROUPS*      **221**
Instructors can use the ideas in this supplement to design discussion and small group activities.

# Demonstration Articles

CHAPTER 3.  **The Corn**    48

CHAPTER 4.  **The Linzer Torte**    57

CHAPTER 5.  **The Cold**    103

CHAPTER 6.  **Eva's Ghost**    112

CHAPTER 9.  **Lists (fragments)**    176

# *Preface*

## THEORY—AND TALES

The goal of most textbooks seems to be to resolve ambiguities. The goal of this one is to raise them. I do not have answers. What I offer are ways to ask questions about writing, but readers will have to generate the answers. Obviously then, the guiding pedagogic theory here is that students discover writing. The teacher is only a facilitator. Those words *discover* and *facilitate* will be familiar to anyone in composition who uses process writing methods, but they may be new to journalism instructors.

The book grew out of a series of informal talks I gave at meetings of the Association for Education in Journalism and Mass Communications in 1988 and 1989. After one such talk, Ken Metzler of the University of Oregon and several other people persuaded me to put together a prospectus. In reality, though, the book took shape much earlier, when I began teaching—uncomfortably—at the University of Iowa. My magazine writing course was co-listed with the Writers' Workshop and the Journalism Department. I had students from both disciplines glaring at one another across a seminar table.

The workshop students felt they were slumming by taking something so practical. The journalism students were suspicious of the arty fluff I was calling journalism. Their differences troubled me at first, but the confusion I suffered would become the foundation of this book. How could these students, who wrote beautifully when the topic was themselves, be incapable of writing a piece directed toward a mass audience? How could they churn out twenty pages effortlessly, but be incapable of a coherent one-page letter to an editor? Why were they tongue-tied when the topic was writing? Why did I do all the talking in class?

Judging by rueful laughs I used to get from fellow writing teachers about that last, I gathered the problem of the silent student was not unique to me. What I began to think from talking with Metzler and others was that perhaps my solution was. This is when I appreciated what a rich opportunity sharing students from both disciplines had been. It let me combine into a single teaching strategy the fact-based, market-driven intensity of journalism with the new ideas of "writing as process" and "collaborative learning" that had been coming out of rhetoric departments. Through this pairing I came to realize that although students could write, they were not skilled readers—especially of their own writing. If they were to master the writing craft, I had to show them how to do close reading.

All this seems obvious as I put words to paper now, but it isn't. Professional writers are as handicapped by weak analytical skills as students. Editors are forever telling writers, often with exasperation weighing behind the advice, that writers should "read the magazine" before contacting editors. This advice assumes the writer knows how to read a magazine professionally or size up an audience. Few do.

Editors exacerbate the chaos when they dump responsibility for analyzing their magazines on the writers. Infuriatingly vague sentences pepper editorial guidelines. *Good Housekeeping* tells its contributors it wants "simple language with a clear narrative line." *American History Illustrated* advises "interesting topics, thorough research, good organization, clear writing, accuracy and an engaging style." *Horsemen* warns writers, "Keep your subject alive. Don't narrate. Get inside a source's head." What do any of these phrases mean? The writer who thinks "narrative" is a simple term has never written one. Is narration clear writing or purple prose?

But I admit I sympathize with these magazine editors. I've not only said such imprecise sentences; I've written them too. As a former editor for both consumer and specialty magazines, I know the frustration of trying to explain what I want. When editing, I was time and again baffled when a writer would do well on one assignment and botch another. Why were my writers so inconsistent? Why couldn't they follow simple instructions? Surely I was clear when I said I wanted short, punchy, evocative writing? So why did I get deadly, string-of-quotes stuff? I realize now that "short, punchy" and "evocative" were meaningless abstractions. No wonder my writers struggled.

When I switched to writing, the questions reversed and the pain intensified. In my editor role, I only lost time when a writer failed me. When I write, I lose money if communications founder. Once an editor asked me for a "sensitive piece" on the Sixties. I interviewed both war veterans and protesters. To me, the Sixties *were* the war. The editor rejected the piece. "Too depressing," she said. I'm angry still when I think about that assignment, but at least now I understand what happened. Writers are close to their topics, editors to their audiences. If both of us had been able to analyze topic and readers, we might have compromised, I with a more upbeat piece, and she accepting a mention or two of that war.

Fortunately, most editors I've worked with are wonderful collaborators. Ann Landi, formerly senior editor of *Savvy*, was later commissioned to edit my book *Real*

*Farm.*[1] She was always gently polite in her suggestions, but they were precisely clear—move this in front of that, expand here, delete that. She had analyzed my themes and structures and found every hole. When book reviews started coming in—and all, from the *New York Times* to the *Los Angeles Times*, were favorable—I silently thanked her again and again. Without her skill that book wouldn't have worked.

Editors with analytical skill like hers awe me as they ferret out tiny flaws invisible to me—a single word sometimes. A copy editor at *Country Journal*, whose name I've since forgotten, was editing an article of mine and was confused by my use of the word "primitive." I was confused by her confusion. We struggled for days. Then in a delightful moment of simultaneous insight, we both realized that she had heard "primitive" to mean "prehistoric" and I had meant it as "pre-Columbian." It was a few minutes' work to substitute phrases such as "before Europeans arrived." Our obsession with one word may sound demented, but in it I think both of us experienced the thrill of collaboration. I hung up the phone exhilarated; the struggle had yielded a magic moment and a better article.

As I look back over twenty years as editor and writer, for magazines as diverse as *Retail Appliance Dealer* and *Esquire*, the one thing consistent with both positive and negative experiences is analytic skill. Whenever we, editor and writer, can closely examine topic and magazine and together forge and share concrete language, the collaboration works. Whenever one or both of us is unable to deeply analyze audience or writing, communication fails. This book is dedicated to improving the collaboration. It assumes no beginning writer can master the craft without under-standing the editor's role, and no editor can get results without knowledge of the writing craft. What both editor and writer need, I argue, is a shared set of analytic tools.

## USING THIS BOOK

This text develops five analytic tools for reading and writing nonfiction: focus, form, structure, authority, and voice. The title, *Beyond Intuition*, describes the nature of these tools. The act of writing itself may begin as intuition for most writers. (It does for me. I don't think about "writing" as I work.) But writing is only a small part of the process, perhaps as little as 10 percent. The other 90 percent is prewriting, market-ing, research, revision, revision and revision. These steps are deliberate, conscious, beyond intuition. What this book argues is that deliberate, conscious analysis will enable students to unlock at least this 90 percent of their talent.

The five techniques described resemble ideas from methods used to teach process writing, but they have been adapted for mass media and the reality of editors. Freshman composition students have only earnest teaching assistants to worry about. Professional writers must deal with audiences and editors. This compli-cates the process, and my book deals with the complications.

This book can be used for either a magazine feature writing or an editing course. For writing courses, students should have had one college-level composition course (probably freshman composition) and one introductory journalism course (usually basic newswriting). But they need no other background to understand and use these five analytical tools. I supplement this book by asking students to select magazines to analyze, and I assign anthology readings.

In magazine editing courses, students also should have had a freshman composition and a basic journalism class. I recommend that editing come after the feature writing instruction, but it doesn't have to. Because this book stresses conceptual editing, it will need to be supplemented by a stylebook for copyediting drills. Most magazines use the *Chicago Manual of Style*, which I think is too expensive for students. If you use the cheaper *AP Stylebook*, be sure to point out some of the style differences—notably in numbers and commas. I have followed *Chicago* style in this book, which means numerals to ninety-nine are written out and there are far too many commas for my taste. (In my soul, I'm a comma minimalist. I hate that comma after "soul." I have defied *Chicago* and maintained AP's dropping of the final comma in a series, however.)

Whenever I quote from magazines in this book, though, I have copied their style exactly, whether or not it matches *Chicago*—or any—style. In both editing and writing classes I point out the inconsistencies among these quotations because the thesis of this book is that magazines differ—in every way, including style conventions. In a number of chapters I have boldfaced parts of the examples to help students observe the concept. A teaching strategy for using these might be to have the students first read only the boldface copy and then return to read the full text.

The book can be read and used in the order presented, but I've tried to cross-reference chapters so that instructors can reorder readings as they wish. My reason for putting discussion of query letters last and of focuses early is that this better reflects how students learn, in my experience. I used to start with query letters, but students rarely wrote good ones. Now I explain early in the course that query letters and research ideally should be done first and that this is the order mature writers use. No professional writer would waste time writing an article until it was sold. But beginning writers must first understand how an article works before they can sell one.

Focus is the most important idea to master if they hope to succeed at marketing. A focus, not a topic, is what a writer sells. A focus, not a topic, is what shapes research. So I teach focus and the related ideas—form, structure, authority base, evidence and voice—before I let students try queries. Drafts of their queries, at least for the first article, are due after initial article drafts have been critiqued. We criticize students' research strategies after these initial drafts too. This backward presentation has produced better queries and research from my students.

In writing classes I assign Chapter 2, "On Being an Editor," after we've covered most of the book. But in editing classes, I not only start with that chapter; I spend a week or two with it. Placing it early, but not first, seemed to be a reasonable compromise between the needs of these two courses.

Five of the chapters contain sample articles I wrote just for this book. All (but one) are deliberately flawed. Reading gorgeous writing in anthologies is important for a student's growth, but it intimidates as much as it inspires, I think. So less-than-brilliant pieces have an important function too. Students gain confidence, as well as awareness, if unleashed to improve writing that truly needs it. Let your students slash these pieces; this is why they're included. Suggestions for editing them are contained in the exercises.

In "Working in Groups" at the end of the book are special classroom exercises. Although the book itself speaks to individuals, working in groups is important because students need each other's help to develop the skills they will later use to collaborate as editors and writers. The subtleties of analytical reading and audience awareness are not easily discovered alone. Besides, writing is inevitably lonely work. The exercises are meant to help counter the loneliness.

Although this book is designed for journalism classes, I believe it has other applications. Writers who want to improve their marketing success could benefit from it. Professional editors who have been frustrated by the performance of their writers should consider adapting or adopting some of the vocabulary and analytical techniques of this book. Editors who wish to reposition or redesign their magazines certainly can use this book for ideas, especially the form and authority base concepts. And then, English majors may learn a good deal by studying the restraints professional writers live with. In fact, since a number of literature anthologies are basically collections of magazine articles, English students might especially benefit from this book.

## ACKNOWLEDGMENTS

On a project like this, many people help. Ken Metzler, of course, was key in my even attempting the book. The late Gordon T. R. Anderson of Longman did much to refine my thinking and shape the project. He is missed.

Betty Pytlik, coordinator of the English composition program at Ohio University, taught me more than she can realize. We worked together one insane summer to develop a writing institute for Ohio high school teachers. These teachers in turn became guides. Their enthusiasm and criticism shaped not only the content but the style of this book. Also to be thanked is Tom Engleman, executive director of the Dow Jones Newspaper Fund, Inc., for providing inspiration—and funding—for the institute.

Many students critiqued the manuscript. In particular Cary Roberts, Karen Wilk, Amy Slugg, Andrew Russ and Sara Lipowitz gave excellent advice that kept me from getting too abstruse, I hope. Tracey Modic's contributions to Chapter 10 taught me much about how students think about research. Tim Smith, instructional librarian at Ohio University's Alden Library, contributed enthusiasm and substance to the serendipity concept in Chapter 9. He still helps me with a quarterly serendipity exercise.

The comments and, sometimes, line-by-line editing of professors

Andrew Ciafolo, Loyola College (Maryland)

Gerald Grow, Florida A & M University

Sandra Haarsager, University of Idaho

Samir Husni, University of Mississippi

Jeffrey Alan John, Wright State University

Sammye Johnson, Trinity University (Texas)

Lee Jolliffe, University of Missouri

Lillian Lodge Kopenhaver, Florida International University

Marcia Prior-Miller, Iowa State University

David Summer, Ball State University

were close reading at its finest. It was thrilling to be rescued with such skill. I'd like to think I've fixed every flaw they saw, but I couldn't have, although they inspired me to try very hard. The book is better because of them.

At Longman the intense efforts of editor Kathleen Schurawich, assistant editor David Fox, production editor Ann Kearns, and production supervisor Anne Armeny insured that Tren Anderson's project reached conclusion.

I am especially grateful to my mother, who left her retirement to type, copyedit and help with the research. I'd never have finished without her. She says she will accept credit for typing and copy, but as for research, will only permit being called a junior apprentice. I disagree. She's great in a library.

Lastly, I want to thank my students. They no longer let me do all the talking.

## NOTE

1. Patricia Westfall, *Real Farm*, New Chapter Press, New York, 1989.

# Part I

# *Worlds Apart*

Writers and editors live on different planets—writers enthralled with their topics, editors cherishing their audiences. Presumably, they meet in a shared love of language. Sometimes their different worldviews make it impossible for them to understand one another. But other times their differences are dynamic, merging in prose of great craft. When the editor/ writer collaboration works, they both produce more than either could alone. Most of this book is about working through the times when communication between these professionals is difficult. But the first two chapters celebrate the differences between writers and editors. Their separate worlds are rich with creative opportunities.

# Chapter

# 1

# On Being a Writer

## ON PERCEPTION

In my town, the chief competitive sport is the potluck supper. It's genuine sport. Participants—men and women alike—spend years developing recipes for their covered dishes. Scoring in the game is subtle, as baffling as for tennis. Competitors surreptitiously eye the buffet table to see which dishes are being depleted. Points, known as compliments, are delivered with merciless etiquette. I am not interested in mastering this sport. When invited to a potluck, I go to Kroger's, buy a pound of potato salad and put it in a bowl. This is not cheating; it's indifference.

But if *Ladies' Home Journal, Better Homes and Gardens* or *Gentlemen's Quarterly* were to ask me to develop the ultimate potluck potato salad, I would scour the country for this recipe, spend hours in my kitchen testing it and deliver the article gladly because *I am a professional*. Professionals do not let something as trivial as personal interests interfere with their work. My tastes do not define me as writer. If I were to limit my work to my values, I would seldom publish. Learning to distinguish between *value judgments*, or tastes, and *critical perceptions*, or the perceived tastes of an audience, is a crucial skill for a published writer. Anyone can write for *oneself*. A professional writes for others.

There are limits, of course, to how much one should suspend values. I could not write for *Soldier of Fortune*, even if others can. Mercenaries for hire offend me. But I can—and this is the skill that matters—*read Soldier of Fortune* and dispassionately describe the values of that publication's audience. I think each writer has to decide privately where his or her limits are, but all can and should be able to describe a magazine, no matter how delightful or repugnant, without using value-laden language. This describing skill is called *critical perception* and can be achieved only by close reading.

I have had, over the years, many students who were fine writers who could not publish because they did not know how to read critically. A common failing among writers, it exasperates editors universally. "Read the magazine," editors advise in their guidelines to writers. "Read the magazine," they say in speeches. "Read the magazine," they tell writers over the phone. What they, and their writers, fail to appreciate is that telling someone to read a magazine is like telling a nonmechanic to "look under the hood." Which thingy is the carburetor and what does it do if you find it? Reading magazines, in other words, is a sophisticated skill requiring technical knowledge. This book proposes five technical tools, or analytic devices, for reading the subtleties of nonfiction prose as published.

As published.

Not "as should be." As *is*. Those five tools are focus, form, structure, authority base and voice. All come from the same toolbox, however—close reading. Word-by-word, line-by-line analysis of a target magazine is the secret to getting published; the only secret. Young writers ask what kind of paper to use for query letters, or whether letters should be sent to an editor or managing editor, or whether they can telephone instead of write. There are answers to these questions, but I've always been troubled by the spirit in which they were asked. It's as if writers were hunting for the secret handshake, the password, to give them access to print. The secret is hard, close, critical analysis. Each magazine, each book publisher, each newspaper editor has differing ideas about how nonfiction prose works. The differences must be perceived. Only close reading will permit those perceptions.

Many qualities shape prose, but taste is not one of them. What one editor considers good or bad writing is, bluntly, irrelevant outside the pages of a magazine or book. One editor's literature is another's trash. Taste is not perception but value judgment. You don't have to approve of the *National Enquirer* to understand it. And understanding is the crux of professionalism, for writers and editors alike.

## ON CHAOS

Distinguishing between personal value judgments and critical perceptions may be the foundation of professionalism, but there are, obviously, more subtle aspects to the writing craft. Mastery of three ideas—*chaos, process* and *intuition*—seems to me to be especially significant for growth as a writer.

Tolerance for chaos is one idea that I feel I've always known was important, but I must have learned it once, early, as a writer. I don't remember when, though. I do remember when I first knew, as a teacher, the importance of chaos. I was living over twenty miles from campus, so carpooled every day with a neighbor. By some cosmic coincidence, both of us had grown up in cities, were now living in the country and were beginning our first flock of chickens. Neither of us had seen living poultry before, but somehow my birds were doing beautifully. They were big, vigorous, healthy; none of them dared get sick. One chick acted wobbly for a day or two, and I nursed it back to health in my kitchen, much to the amusement of my cat. But my carpooling friend's chickens were dying left and right. They looked awful, she said, and scrawny. One morning she got in the car and announced she was now feeding them whey, and was it ever expensive.

"Whey? I said, "Don't you have goats?"

"Yes," she said.

"What are you doing with your surplus milk now?"

"Putting it on my compost heap."

"Why, why, why," I harangued her, "are you buying expensive whey and throwing milk away? Don't you know whey is a by-product of milk? Why don't you give your extra milk to your chickens?"

"I didn't know whey was from milk," she said.

"Where are you getting your information?" I asked.

"From my neighbor," she said.

"And where else?" I asked.

"That's it," she said. "Whenever I have a problem, I go ask him."

If I had spluttered before, now I practically bellowed. "Never, never, never get information from one source," I said. "If you're trying to learn anything new, get three versions. All will disagree, but that way you'll be able to invent a fourth version, yours, which works for you."

My friend hung her head in silence thinking about this. I was thinking too—but not about chickens. I was realizing for the first time that my knowing this was one thing that made me a writer. Somehow I could tolerate three versions, all different. I could study the versions, fight through the contradictions and not go crazy. I could stand chaos. People tend to be like my carpooling friend, wanting information free of stressful ambiguities. But no one has experiences like another's. My friend's neighbor told her what worked for him, not what would do for her. He could not anticipate her particular needs for information. A writer learns to respect the role of chaos in the development of articles, even if readers do not.

Some time later, I was at my carpooling friend's house, and she took me into her dining room. There stood a beautiful oak table. "I found this in a junkyard," she said, "and I did what you said. I'd never refinished a piece of furniture before, so I read three books and talked to three people. You were right, they all disagreed, but I figured out what I needed to do." She had reaped the rewards of chaos.

## ON PROCESS

Despite the reality of chaos, there persists the notion among writers, editors and professors that something exists called "the writing process." I agree there is a writing process, but it isn't a series of orderly steps. Writing is not order, but the struggle with disorder. Writers may sometimes believe they create routine (think-of-idea, go-to-library, draft-an-outline, get-a-lead, write-the-body, revise-the-text), but the truth is, routine withers in the face of chaos. Every writing project is a wrestling match. Eventually the prose is pinned down, but the process never runs the same way twice. For me, sometimes the theme is so elusive it is the last thing I control. Sometimes I can't find the lead until I've written most of the body. Almost always I must do some research after I've written parts of the article. So whatever the writing process is, it isn't orderly.

But if not steps, what is it? Thinking? Perhaps. Thinking, however, is the ultimate privacy. I hesitate to describe how it is done. Completed articles can be read, not minds. A strong piece of writing will have a thought-provoking focus, a beautiful structure, a form appropriate for its medium, good authority, a vigorous voice and unassailable evidence. But does this mean the mind that produced this order was just as ordered while working? Maybe. Maybe not. Even asking the writer produces shrugs. Writers may be willing, eager even, to talk about their mental processes, but the more I talk to other writers or read interviews with them, the more I realize how unique each of us is in the privacy of the mind. Some writers get inspiration by carefully outlining ideas; others wait for inspiration to strike; others can't think until research is done, whatever "done" means.

For myself, I usually need the prewriting process I describe in Chapter 9. If I sit down and just play with words for a while, something emerges, but the play follows no set pattern. For "The Linzer Torte" in Chapter 4, I was bored while waiting in a doctor's office; suddenly that fifteen-year-old memory popped out. To pass the time I wrote it down. "The Corn" in Chapter 3 began as a single sentence, a feeling actually. I had just moved from Iowa to Ohio and one day realized I missed Iowa's corn. The rest of the article came from hard, excessively orderly research, but the inspiration was disorderly. "Eva's Ghost" in Chapter 6 never had a moment of inspiration like the other two pieces. I'd been collecting stuff until I decided I had enough information on this woman to attempt an article about her. "Lists" in Chapter 9, which I wrote as part of a speech, was desperation, not inspiration. The publicity director for the lecture series wanted my topic right then; I pulled it out of thin air and prayed I'd find something to say about it later. (I did.) "The Cold" in Chapter 5 was assigned; an editor wanted me to write about cold as an enemy, an idea I admit I never quite understood.

I'm saying with these examples that writing has no single thought process. Each article is unique. And by extension, each writer is unique. Somehow we create order, each of us terribly alone. Craft can be improved if, *after* writing, the work is analyzed and evaluated to see whether it is indeed ordered. But I'm not sure it's possible to be so virtuously ordered while writing. I would be handicapped if I tried to think of focus, form, structure, voice *while* I wrote.

So far, all I've said is that process is not steps and perhaps not even orderly thinking. Is there something it *is*? Discipline is another idea writers seem to respect.

Perhaps when they invoke process they mean discipline. But like thinking, discipline seems overwhelmingly varied in technique. Some writers swear by keeping a journal. I've tried all my life to do this but only have managed to toss occasional clippings into a filing cabinet; then I never consult them. Other writers admonish young writers to write every day. I do not have enough to say to write so often, and I need a purpose—a deadline and an assignment—to write. Others have ideas about how much reading or traveling to do. Some tout the time they spend in bars and cafes as the source of their insights. I'm uncomfortable in bars; I can't wait to get home when I travel; I read, of course, but I'm as fond of *Star Trek* novels as I am of histories.

Do these weaknesses make me any less a writer? Am I undisciplined? With my appointment calendar I keep a list divided into four boxes labeled "Teaching," "Writing," "Play" and "Mundane." Into each box I list dozens of things I want to do, but I only have to do one from each box each week. Most weeks I do more, but I only *must* do one. In other words, I give myself permission to fail. Long ago, I decided that success is accepting failure, and because of that I write better and more often now. But this approach to discipline shows again how elusive the writing process is. If process is discipline and good discipline is failure, then what on earth is writing?

Perhaps rephrasing the question will unlock the matter. Instead of asking what the *process* of writing is, ask what the *goal* of writing is. What is it writers do for people? What is the service rendered? Forget the internal journey of learning to write; this will happen. Consider the external reality, the communication. Even if the question is still too private for answers, at least I find it easier to think about when put this way. Writers make connections, I think. Writers confront the observable world and link parts of it together in fresh ways. They describe the familiar, which readers then see as something new.

Such linkups may seem simple to the writer who makes them. When I wrote a column for *Savvy* magazine called "Modern Dilemma," I used to feel my metaphors were too ordinary. I wrote in one column that learning to handle a chain saw resembled learning confidence. Keeping a red refrigerator in my pantry, to hide it from an appraiser, was like balancing needs for individuality and conformity, I said in another. A windmill I compared to impending loss; a flock of chickens was like hunger for ideals; and so on—each column's connection seemed mere common sense to me.

But then I would get letters—wonderful letters—from readers telling me they had never seen things quite that way before, and they would tell me about the details of their lives. "My loom in the living room is like your red refrigerator," wrote one. "I defy my neighbors and plant tomatoes in the front yard because that is where the sun is, but since I give them vegetables they forgive me," wrote another. I would read these letters and wonder again, What is it to be a writer? Perhaps it is just being confident or obnoxious enough to state the obvious. But how does one do that?

When does one know what to say? How does one grow as a writer? The questions were terrifying then and are now because, whatever it is, this writing process, it is strongly intuitive.

## ON INTUITION

Yet now that I am maturing in my craft, paradoxically, the most important thing I've learned is to resist relying too much on intuition. Amateurs like to "feel" when a topic works or a paragraph sounds good, but to depend on such feelings exclusively is limiting. I may begin with intuition, but I do not stay there. If the *ideas* I write about are intuitive, the *language* that shapes them is craft, and craft is beyond intuition. It is deliberate.

Intuition is a fraction of my skill, an essential fraction perhaps, but a small fraction as well. I go from intuition to analysis. I study, at length, my target audience and the styles of the target magazine. With the aid of this analysis I can bend my style to the needs of the market but keep my voice intact as well. The problem is like my red refrigerator dilemma. I wanted a home equity loan so needed to have my house appraised. A realtor had told me to get rid of my red refrigerator because it was too eccentric. It would lower the appraised value of my house, he said. But I liked it; it was me. So I moved the refrigerator to the pantry. This seemed to appease the appraiser. Professionalism forces many compromises like this. I want to write in my style, but to be publishable I also need to write in the magazine's style. If I'm going to balance the two, I need to know as much as I can about the magazine.

Writers who simply "feel" writing are inflexible—unable to move their refrigerators, in a sense. Young writers are often misled into overemphasizing intuition because they are told their mission is to "discover" a style or "find a voice." Discovery is important, but it is not a mystical process. Discovering writing is like discovering nutritional content of food—prowl the grocery store aisles, pick up packages, read lists of ingredients, think. Work deliberately, in other words.

Discovering the part of writing that is beyond intuition is a deliberate effort to gain command of a specialized knowledge and jargon. Editors are specialists, knowledgeable about the needs and techniques of one audience, one magazine. Consequently, their language or jargon may be cryptic. An editor may say, "Give me more flair," or "Write vibrantly."

A writer who is totally intuitive will be helpless in the face of phrases like this. But a writer who is clinical, analytical, might be able to interpret these abstractions accurately to see that "flair" means details in the third paragraph for this magazine, but might mean italics and quotes for another; and that "vibrantly" means visual descriptions and no quotes for one, but short abstract labels for another. More than once I've been on the phone with an editor who, trying to explain the goals of an assignment, might say something like this: "We want it to be your story, but not your story, know what I mean?" and I, finally grown strong enough to resist intuition, reply, "Do you mean you want it to be observational, not personal?"

The relief in the editor's response can be almost palpable, as if to say, "There is language out there." Yes, there is language out there, but it takes a nonintuitive willingness to invent it and use it. Retreats into intuitive writing ("I know what's good when I write it") are the source of much weak nonfiction. There is language out there; this book is about the language out there.

## FOR ADDITIONAL READING

The first list below suggests books that offer additional views on the writing process and may be good supplemental reading for undergraduates. Some authors such as Gardner, White and Zinsser see some mystery to the writing process, as do I. Others are more concrete in their assessments of the craft. The second list presents a few of the many books on the theory and teaching of composition, plus an occasional media studies book, such as the one by Gans.

### Inspiration

Burroway, Janet. *Writing Fiction: A Guide to Narrative Craft*. 2d ed. Little, Brown, Boston, 1987.

Didion, Joan. "Introduction," *Slouching Towards Bethlehem*. Farrar, Straus & Giroux, New York, 1968.

Ferber, Edna. *A Peculiar Treasure*. Doubleday, Garden City, N.Y., 1960.

Franklin, Jon. *Writing for Story: Craft Secrets of Dramatic Nonfiction*. Atheneum, New York, 1986.

Gardner, John. *The Art of Fiction: Notes on Craft for Young Writers*. Knopf, New York, 1983.

Hall, Donald, editor. *The Contemporary Essay*. 2d ed. St. Martin's Press, New York, 1989.

Howarth, William L., editor. "Introduction," *The John McPhee Reader*. Farrar, Straus & Giroux, New York, 1984

Rico, Gabriele Lusser. *Writing the Natural Way*. J. P. Tarcher, Los Angeles, 1983.

Strunk, William, Jr., and E. B. White. *The Elements of Style*. 3d ed. Macmillan, New York, 1979.

Wolfe, Tom. *The New Journalism*. Harper & Row, New York, 1973.

Zinsser, William. *On Writing Well*. Harper & Row, New York, 1985.

### Theory

Axelrod, Rise B., and Charles R. Cooper. *Reading Critically, Writing Well*. St. Martin's Press, New York, 1990.

Berthoff, Ann E. *Forming, Thinking, Writing: The Composing Imagination*. Boynton/Cook, Montclair, N.J., 1982.

Berthoff, Ann E. *The Making of Meaning*. Boynton/Cook, Montclair, N.J., 1981.

Bloom, Lary. *The Writer Within*. Contemporary Books, Chicago, 1991.

Bomze, JoAnn W. *Reading Literature: Interpretation and Critical Writing*. Longman Group, White Plains, N.Y., 1990.

Bransford, John D., and Barry S. Stein. *The Ideal Problem Solver: A Guide for Improving Thinking, Learning, and Creativity.* Freeman, New York, 1984.

Cooper, Charles R., and Sidney Greenbaum, editors. *Studying Writing: Linguistic Approaches.* Sage Publications, Beverly Hills, Calif., 1986.

Elbow, Peter, and Pat Belanoff. *A Community of Writers: A Workshop Course in Writing.* McGraw-Hill, New York, 1989.

Frye, Northrup. *Anatomy of Criticism.* Princeton University Press, Princeton, N.J., 1973.

Fulwiler, Tober, editor. *The Journal Book.* Boynton/Cook, Portsmouth, N.H., 1987.

Gans, Herbert J. *Popular Culture and High Culture.* Basic Books, New York, 1974.

Goleman, Daniel, Paul Kaufman, and Michael Ray. *The Creative Spirit.* Dutton, Penguin Group, New York, 1992.

Kurfiss, Joanne G. *Critical Thinking.* Association for the Study of Higher Education, Washington, D.C., 1988.

Murray, Donald M. *A Writer Teaches Writing.* Houghton Mifflin, Boston, 1985.

Zinsser, William. *Writing to Learn.* Harper & Row, New York, 1988.

# Chapter

# 2

# *On Being an Editor*

## TOO MUCH BRASS

I knew I was in trouble when I saw the brass: on banisters, chandeliers, the registration desk, even on luggage carriers. The hotel was the New York Hilton. The editors of *Savvy* magazine had put me there because they wanted me in New York for a few days of "nurturing," they said. I knew otherwise. I was there for a scolding. My last three columns had been weak. I figured the glitzier the hotel, the worse the scolding. The senior editor talked with me for a day, but this was only prelude to a twenty-minute conversation with the editor, Wendy Crisp.

I asked Wendy questions I thought writers should: How old is the reader? Is she married? Does she have children? What does she do with her leisure time? What does she read? I thought my columns were failing because I didn't understand the magazine's audience. Wendy answered my questions patiently but was obviously growing more irritated with each one. Finally she exploded, "No, Pat."

She spun around in her chair, looking at the skyline a moment. Then she turned back to me. "Our reader is a woman," she said, "who is driving home alone after a very hard day. Maybe she is going home to a family; maybe not. That's not important. What is important is she's tired and she's thinking, 'Is any of this worth it? Is anything I'm doing making a difference in anyone's life?'" With that, the months of my confusion disappeared. I saw my mistake. I'd thought the reader wanted a promotion and a raise. Wendy saw her as wanting life to mean something. This editor gave me only a few words, but they made the difference between failing and succeeding as a writer for her magazine.

E. B. White once described an editor as "a person who knows more about writing than writers do, but who has escaped the terrible desire to write."[1] A charming definition, but I think it reflects a common misperception about editors. People think they fix words. True. But editors do much more. To dwell only on their manuscript handling tasks is too limited. The definition I prefer is that *editors explain*. They explain whatever needs explaining to writers, designers, photographers, artists, advertising salespeople, publishers, the general public and one another. Wendy's ability to distill her audience into a few vivid sentences is the essence of editing.

An editor is only as good as his or her ability to talk, sometimes deviously, as I learned from a staffer at *Esquire*. He was apologetic when he called about an article of mine in progress. "They want me to tell you that they are looking at that word 'lied,' " he said. He didn't explain who "they" were. I had written a quote that ended with the playful attribution, "she lied."

"No problem," I said. "Change it to 'said.' It's still clear from context what's going on."

"No," he said, "it's funnier the way you wrote it." I don't know which of us was more surprised at that moment, he that I was so cooperative or I that he would consider letting me keep a word so inflammatory.

"So you're telling me writers have to be taught to be temperamental?" I said.

He laughed. "Yes. Please don't ever tell them I helped you, either. I'm going to go back to them now and tell them you *refuse* to change it." The sentence ran as written.

This man helped save part of my style by outtalking his bosses. His use of psychology and wit, like Wendy's imaginative portrayal of a reader, was another way editors edit. But such cleverness doesn't just happen. Editors are able to outthink others because they have command of specialized knowledge that has nothing to do with commas and grammar. Modern editors are as much business managers as language experts. No doubt the old-fashioned ideal of the editor as a member of a genteel elite, passionately mourning some perennial dying of the language, standing stalwart against hordes of literary philistines, exists. But the well-paid editors who head thriving magazines are valued as much for their knowledge of how the magazine business operates as for their language skills. It is this business knowledge that lets them think quickly of solutions to situations like the two described above, although most problems editors wrestle with are far more demanding.

Editors, to survive, must study their audiences, become knowledgeable of marketing techniques and understand sophisticated statistical research. They need to know what is happening to the economy and to society so they can be poised to adapt their magazines to the slightest flicker of social change. They are psychologists and historians in addition to being grammarians. They know what psychographics, focus groups, niche and repositioning are as readily as they know what an intransitive verb is. What follows is a discussion of this business side of editing. It is technical. But it is what editors must know. If writers know it as well, the collaboration is all the better, because when an editor says, "Read the magazine," he or she is really saying read for *Audience* (the next section) or *Niche* (following later).

## AUDIENCE

*Audience:* The qualities and traits editors believe their readers possess.

Audiences are not people. Audiences are *ideas* about people. This distinction between reality and concept perhaps explains why magazine publishing is risky. Knowing what the thousands or millions of people who read a magazine think, do and want is impossible. Only broad concepts are possible. If these ideas are wrong, the magazine will not sell. Perhaps editors like to imagine they get their ideas about audience through intuition, but it's a rare magazine that functions solely on an editor's gut feelings anymore. These days, audience concepts are based on research. Lots of it. Techniques for audience research are as varied as human imagination allows, but all face the same problem: Does the research collect a true portrait of the readers? Professional researchers stop people in malls, call them on the phone, sit them around tables, spy on them from behind potted palms, even sift through their garbage, all in hopes of getting enough data to get beyond *guessing* what a reader wants to *knowing*. (See Appendix 2.1 for more detail on research methods.)

What do researchers learn when they tackle people in shopping malls or sort through garbage? That, of course, depends on what they ask. A 1984 study by the Home Testing Institute surveyed men who enjoyed buying tools. Among the thirty-eight questions asked were, Did the men like to save money? to shop around for a good price? to go to different stores? to do projects slowly and carefully? to have their shops neat and tidy? to stay home instead of go out? to feel creative? to keep busy? to learn something new? to relax? to be with people? to get away from home?[2]

Answers to these questions could be enormously valuable to an editor of a woodworking magazine. The reader who makes things to save money is not like one who wants to be creative. If readers prefer saving money to being creative, then the editor knows to feature simple and practical projects. And if readers are neatness nuts instead of slobs, the editor knows to run regular articles on how to build shop cabinets and drawers.

Another example of research that could be useful to a magazine editor comes from a garbage study. Researchers studied several families' garbage for five weeks looking for consumption of cat food. The trash revealed that most cat owners used several types of cat food and that dry food users switched brands less often than canned food users. The study also indicated that in homes with both cats and dogs, cats got better treatment. If cats got canned food, the dog got dry. Some other bewildering patterns: cats ate about six grams of table scraps a day, dogs about sixteen grams; homes with only cats tended to read *TV Guide* and *National Enquirer* more than did families with only dogs.[3] The editor of *Cat Fancy* could get a whole year's worth of article ideas from this one study:

- Don't feel guilty for feeding your cat dried food.
- Cats: The aristocrats of house pets.

- Some table scraps may be good for your cat.
- Do cat owners watch more TV than dog owners?

Specific information like this about readers can mean the difference between survival and failure in the fiercely competitive magazine market. This is why audience research has become a multi-million-dollar industry. The January 1992 issue of *American Demographics* featured the top 100 organizations that conduct some sort of research.[4] These firms uncover delightful things. For example, one study by Young & Rubicam suggests that Boston is as snobbish as its image. Boston families tend to put the *New Yorker, Atlantic Monthly* and *Gourmet* on their coffee tables, but Pittsburgh homes will display the *Star, National Enquirer* and *Parade*.[5] And a study by the University of Maryland shows that, although the total amount of time people spend reading has fallen 30 percent in the last fifty years, their time with books or magazines has increased. The drop in reading time has hurt newspapers, not magazines.[6] This is information editors and publishers can take to advertisers. Rare is a magazine today that doesn't use professional research. In 1988 *Journalism Quarterly* published a survey of 223 magazines about the ways they use commissioned research. There were eighteen categories, from reader profiles to cover evaluations. Editors don't guess much anymore.

As Table 2.1 reveals, a lot of data exist out there. Too much sometimes. To make sense of these data, they are usually grouped into two categories—demographic and psychographic.

**TABLE 2.1**   Medium and large-sized magazines using various studies ($n = 223$)

|  | Percentage | | |
| --- | --- | --- | --- |
|  | *Total* | *Business* | *Consumer* |
| Reader profile | 79 | 70 | 88 |
| Market studies | 58 | 54 | 61 |
| Buying influence and intention | 57 | 55 | 58 |
| Surveys for article and feature ideas | 50 | 54 | 43 |
| Editorial effectiveness | 51 | 52 | 52 |
| Syndicated readership studies | 40 | 35 | 44 |
| Reader traffic studies | 34 | 36 | 33 |
| Competitive readership analysis | 47 | 49 | 46 |
| Market and circulation profiling | 53 | 53 | 54 |
| Brand awareness/preference | 39 | 43 | 38 |
| Product ownership and usage | 49 | 36 | 60 |
| Advertising/agency perception of media | 23 | 19 | 25 |
| Competitive publication analysis | 50 | 47 | 52 |
| Acquisition launch analysis and appraisals | 18 | 20 | 15 |
| Studies for individual advertisers | 44 | 54 | 34 |
| Cover analysis | 19 | 18 | 19 |
| Art and design studies | 15 | 18 | 13 |
| Other | 5 | 5 | 4 |

SOURCE:  Thomas Jacobson, "Research Activity of Magazine Publishers," *Journalism Quarterly*, v. 65 Summer 1988, p. 513. Reprinted by permission of AEJMC from *Journalism Quarterly*.

## Demographics

Demographics are the *characteristics of a population*. These include such familiar census categories as age, sex, marital status, number of children, occupation, income, education level, number living in household, ownership of homes or other durable goods, geographic region, size or type of community, religion, political affiliation and membership in organizations. For example, a "demographic portrait" of a magazine's audience might show that the readers are 18 to 35 years old, female, single, working in white-collar jobs, earning under $30,000, and college educated; they live in apartments in medium-sized cities, own cars, and were raised Protestant but are not currently church members. Obviously, not all readers of a magazine would fit that profile. But enough would that editors of that magazine could use it to make decisions about content.

Demographic terms are often confusing. What is a "household" or a "medium-sized city?" (See Appendix 2.2 for detailed definitions of official and unofficial census terms.) Because demographic terms are quite subtle and bewildering, it's important that editors and writers who use them discuss the definitions first. Take the familiar demographic idea of religion. Should distinctions be made between being raised in a religion and practicing it? Is a person who was raised Catholic but has fallen away still Catholic? Is a person who goes home for Yom Kippur just because his mother would be hurt if he didn't a Jew? If religions are thought of as ethnic groupings, maybe nonobservers are still members. But if religion is a freely chosen commitment to a belief system, then nonpractitioners do not belong in the demographic groups that name religions. Either definition is acceptable, so if an editor and a writer are discussing a feature on the stress of going home for the holidays, both had better be using the same definition.

## Psychographics

Despite the abundance of demographic data, none of them reveal a thing about how people *feel*. One 25-year-old woman may prefer to host quiet dinners, go for walks and read *Victoria*. Her friend in the apartment next door, who is the same age, making the same income and working in a similar job, may like to give big parties, hike on the weekends and read *Outside*. Demographics doesn't explain these differences. The two women are demographically identical but nothing alike. *Psychographics* is the research tool that attempts to decipher baffling personality differences.

The formal definition of psychographics is the *measurement of attitudes and values of a population*. "Measurement" is the controversial word in that definition. Market researchers are confident they can measure *opinion*, but why people hold their opinions, or the *values* that shape opinions, were thought to be too complex to accurately measure for a whole population. Personal values are an intricate blend of childhood experiences, formal education, peer pressures, media influences, life experiences and occasionally common sense. A person may buy a brand of margarine because his mother did or his friends approve, or because he likes those sexy, young TV margarine eaters or because he thinks it's good for his health. Or for all these reasons. If deciphering "why margarine?" for one person is this complex, can any of the rest of it—commitments to community, environmental attitudes and ideals about relationships held by millions of people—be measured? More significantly, can predictions about the future be made from measuring this melange of values?

Predictions are the primary goal of audience and marketing research. Demography is useful, not for what it tells us about today but for what it reveals about the future. If there are 3.8 million 18-year-olds now,[7] then we know, with a little help from insurance mortality tables, that in ten years almost that many 28-year-olds will be wanting cars, houses, families, babies—and magazines about these things.

Could psychographic data be equally useful? Could knowing how people feel about margarine or buying tools or feeding cats *now* produce clues to future trends? In 1971 the marketing research firm Yankelovich Skelly & White (YSW) examined changing American values and developed a trend-spotting tool they called *Monitor*. Annually they questioned 2,500 people on how they felt about nondemographic essentials such as "novelty and change," "anti-bigness," "blurring of the sexes," "responsiveness to fantasy" and "environmental concerns." People reacted to these concepts, and the sum total of their reactions was supposedly a portrait of American values. One amusing trend the *Monitor* recorded was "personal identification need" or whether people needed monograms on their towels.

Over fifty trends were monitored, some playful like the monogram mania, others more serious, like environmental worry. But in that form—as trends—the data were no more innovative than past opinion surveys; YSW's innovation was to cluster the response patterns into six "lifestyle groups." They gave these fanciful names: New Autonomous, Gamesmen, Scramblers, American Dreamers, Traditionals and Aimless.[8] YSW would put the two identical young women above in different groups: the party-hearty one in New Autonomous; the quiet-dinners one in Traditional. Instead of trying to make sense of hundreds of surveys, *Monitor* subscribers could watch the six groups. If there are fewer Traditional women this year, it may be time to invest less in homemaking magazines and start titles for working women. The potential usefulness of this information excited editors greatly. Demographics revealed only how many potential readers there were. Perhaps psychographics could tell what those people wanted. *Monitor* had no trouble attracting subscribers, despite its $15,000 to $25,000 annual fee.

As a prediction tool, *Monitor* was far from perfect. It did predict the trend to high-priced shampoo and the wine fad. But it didn't reveal the careerism of the Eighties or the emerging conservative activism of the Nineties—trends that from an editor's point of view are more important than feelings about hand cream. Critics dismissed *Monitor* as just another consumer survey, despite the addition of lifestyle groups. Others complained that it wasn't solidly based on psychological theory.

In 1980 a California research firm, SRI International, developed VALS—short for values and lifestyles. Using theories of psychological development, they created an eighty-five-page questionnaire that approximately 2,900 people completed. From the one million data bits they gathered from these surveys, SRI decided there were four value systems in America: the Need Driven, or people whose economic and social straits were so desperate that every choice they made was determined by requirements as basic as food and shelter; the Outer Directed, or people who tended to need the approval of others for their actions; the Inner Directed, who used an internal code of values to make decisions; and lastly the Integrateds, who were, like Mary Poppins, practically perfect. These four value systems broke down into nine lifestyle groups. The Need Driven could be either Sustainers (deeply desperate) or Survivors (broke but clever). The Outer Directed could be Belongers (salt of the earth types), Emulators (buy a flashy car to impress the guys at work) or Achievers (work until midnight to get that promotion). The Inner Directed divided into I-Am-Me's (risk-taking youth), Experientials (just do it) and Societally Conscious (on the picket lines). Integrateds were, well, integrated personalities—fully mature, wise, deep—and very rare. The VALS system, although complicated, seemed to describe just about everybody.[9]

VALS, with its nine lifestyles and four value systems, captured the imagination of marketers and advertisers—and editors. Its categories seemed to be stable. Wouldn't there always be Survivors, Belongers and Achievers, just as there would always be 18-year-olds? If so, then, as in demographic work, researchers could follow the changes in these lifestyle groups and make predictions about coming years. If more people were Achievers than last year, or if the Belongers were declining, didn't we know the future?

If predictions are the primary goal of research, here was a tool that could finally predict feelings, editors thought. Since magazines are in the business of serving feelings, at last editing could become science. "We're very big on psychographics," an editor at Whittle Communications told me once. Editors in scores of companies were saying the same thing.

## Uses and Misuses of Audience Research

The popularity of VALS stimulated a rash of imitators. Most such studies were narrowly designed and seemed to be competing more for "cleverest name for a lifestyle" than for success as a predicting tool. A study of outdoor enthusiasts decided that nature lovers had five lifestyle segments: Excitement Seeking Competitors, Get Away Actives, Fitness Driven, Health Conscious Sociables and Unstressed Unmotivateds (the Unstressed Unmotivateds preferred playing bingo).[10]

Another company "discovered" four lifestyle groups: Analyticals, Drivers, Amiables and Expressives.[11] A lifestyle analysis published in *Journalism Quarterly* divided readers of tabloids into three categories: Interest Diversion Seekers, Distracted Information Collectors and Selfish Believers. One group read tabloids to make fun of them; the second wanted the truly informative articles that came after the outrageous headlines; and the third group actually believed the stuff.[12] Fortunately for the future of civilization, the Believers were few in number. In 1990 an advertising company entered the field with the "New American Grownup," which it divided into two lifestyle groups: Vanguards and Rear Guards.[13] Rear Guarders were overwhelmed by the Nineties, but Vanguarders were doing it all—career, family, fun, social causes and, oh yes, reading serious books.

Obviously, if research had to tell us that some of us were grownups, then psychographics was getting silly. As one critic said, "If a bag lady lives in a low-rent hotel room, do we need a battery of lifestyle questions to label this consumer as a light user of Gucci shoes, Jordache jeans, Chivas Regal and Godiva chocolates?"[14] Psychographics was beginning to be seen as a fancy way to describe the obvious.

Another frustration with psychographic categories was people might fit into several groups at once, making nonsense of the categories. A 35-year-old is a 35-year-old demographically no matter what he or she likes to do on the weekend. But what about a 35-year-old tool user? In the Home Testing Institute's survey of tool users mentioned above, researchers divided the data into four psychographic groups: Frugal, Traditional, Innovative and Sociable men. A high percentage of the Frugal men said they valued saving money; but so did a high percentage of the Innovatives, who mostly liked to be creative. Thirty percent of the Frugals said they liked to relax and be with people—just like the Sociables. The Traditional men tended to be the ones who liked things tidy and neat, but so did some of the Innovative, Sociable or Frugal men. Innovative men tended to own more tools than any other group, and they valued skill, creativity and new ideas.[15] But if a woodworking magazine stressed creativity alone, it would lose the interest of the Frugal, Traditional or Sociable men in the audience, and even the Innovatives would like ideas for neatness once in a while. In other words, these psychographic groups were too vague to be useful for editing a hobby magazine. Editors and advertisers were beginning to see psychographics as a can of worms, as likely to confuse as to reveal.

As more and more research firms started to build lifestyle models, more and more users of psychographics began to doubt their value for making predictions. Psychographics told how people were *now*, but didn't tell much about what they would be like five or ten years from now. With growing skepticism, there began what *Business Week* called a "bloodbath in marketing research." The industry that had been growing at a fantastic 8 percent a year began declining in 1990. The huge advertising agency J. Walter Thompson and the Gallup polling organization both slashed staff and budgets.[16] SRI International came out with VALS II in an attempt to restore confidence of clients. (VALS II had only three value systems and just eight lifestyle groups.)[17] But the damage was done. Companies still pay big fees to YSW, SRI, Gallup, J. Walter Thompson, Grey Advertising and the other big research firms. But they use the studies more cautiously.

Does that mean that editors are returning to intuition to explain their audiences? Whether they do or not, the language of psychographics will probably remain. It has added much to an editor's ability to talk about readers. Wendy's portrayal of the *Savvy* reader may or may not have been based on statistical research, but it was purely psychographic in language.

# NICHE

*Niche:* The unique qualities of an audience that distinguish a magazine from its nearest rivals.

*Mademoiselle* is not *Glamour*.

*Bon Appetit* is not *Gourmet*.

*Esquire* is not *Gentlemen's Quarterly*.

Nicheing is why not. Every magazine tries to create subtle differences between itself and competitors so that advertisers and readers will prefer it, or at the very least feel they have to buy it in addition to its rival. Editors and writers who can't detect niches don't last very long in magazine journalism. Magazines live and die by niches. A niche is usually a distinction in audience rather than content, however. *McCall's* covers many of the same topics as *Ladies' Home Journal*, but both magazines survive because advertisers think readers are different.

In this era, when it is not uncommon for the same model or the same photo of Princess Di to be on the covers of half a dozen magazines at once, it is not easy to create believable niches. One technique is to emphasize minor psychographic qualities of an audience. For example, one cooking magazine might imagine that its readers cook for cooking's sake. Its rival, next to it on the newsstand, with just as pretty a pie on the cover, will argue its readers cook for the pleasures of eating. A subtle difference, but enough to make an advertiser hesitate to exclude either. A magazine for young women might aim toward readers who "need guidance," while a rival might believe its readers "make up their own minds." Again, a small difference, but enough to create separate niches as well as to confuse writers. The writer who writes a step-by-step advice piece for the make-up-their-own-minds magazine is going to get a baffling letter back saying "Although the research was good, the writing just isn't us." Why? Wrong niche.

Careers of editors rise and fall by their skills in creating subtle niches. Advertisers were excited when *Self* magazine was launched in 1980. The ad director for Sally Hansen nail products told a *Magazine Age* reporter, "It's not that we expect to get a totally different person from the one we could have reached before but that we expect to reach this woman in a new and more contemporary environment."[18] Another ad director for another product, Kahlua coffee liqueurs, said the woman who read *Self* was

a rather aware person and trying to get a better handle on what her life was all about. She's probably a more active person just in the way she conducts herself; she has a very healthy and confident approach. She feels good about herself and the life she leads.[19]

Notice how all this gushing is about a reader, not articles. Somehow editors of *Self* had persuaded advertisers like Kahlua that they had a unique niche. It would be obvious to anyone who could look at a magazine cover that the *Self* reader is much like *Glamour* and *Mademoiselle* readers. So why were advertisers excited? The magazine's editorial suggested a "fresh niche." Editor Phyllis Starr Wilson described *Self*'s editorial niche this way:

> *Self*'s subject is self-development and it covers physical fitness, beauty and fashion, health, nutrition and diet, and emotional well-being—whatever affects our reader emotionally and whatever affects her body. It has a slant built into its subject; for example, when it covers food, it covers nutrition. But what distinguishes *Self*'s approach is its "psychological slant." Its subject is self-development or self-improvement, and the approach is through self-knowledge. We try to give our reader enough information to make up her mind as an individual to do what's best for her.[20]

Because Wilson is an editor, some of her comments are about articles. But notice how much of what she says describes the readers' state of mind—a fantasy unless Wilson is telepathic, yet believable enough for the magazine to work.

Niche marketing has been the trend in magazine editing for over a quarter of a century. With general magazines, such as women's homemaking, young women's beauty and men's lifestyle magazines, the strategy has been to do as *Self* did—create a psychographic niche within an existing audience. But many new magazines have made their fortunes by carving out totally new audiences. A scan of *Standard Rate and Data Service* (SRDS) turns up some amazing niches:

> *Basically Buckles*. This magazine from LaMoure, North Dakota, circulation 1,317, is for collectors of belt buckles, watch fobs, key rings and related paraphernalia—but not suspenders. A popular column is "The Silver Buckle Collector."
>
> *Your Prom*. To quote the editor's statement: "Edited for teenagers preparing for the prom. Its articles feature fashion, beauty, checklists and tips on aspects of this rite of passage in the life of teenagers." Published by a big company, Cahners, New York; 600,000 copies are printed each year.
>
> *Snow Goer*. Snowmobilers, 75,000 of them, call this magazine bible and devour it for its tips on new machines, new products, performance, personalities and do-it-yourself projects—whatever a do-it-yourself in the snow might be. From Wayzata, Minnesota.
>
> *Turkey & Turkey Hunting*. Over 53,000 people want to shoot their own wild birds. The editorial description says nothing about plucking or cooking turkeys, just hunting them. From Iola, Wisconsin.
>
> *Twins*. For parents and children who live with copies of themselves. Triplets and quadruplets read this too, to share "feelings, expectations, myths and realities about being and living with multiples." Circulation: 29,000; from Merriam, Kansas.

*Doll Reader.* Doll collectors, doll makers, doll artists and doll manufacturers read this magazine for news of auctions, shows and projects, according to the editor's statement. Even paper dolls (with patterns) are covered. Circulation: 93,000; from Cumberland, Maryland.

*Teddy Bear Review.* Not everybody wants a doll. A New York publisher caters to teddy bear collectors, teddy bear artists, teddy bear manufacturers and teddy bear dressers (we hope these are people who make clothes for teddy bears, not people who dress like them). There's even an astrological column on famous teddy bear people. Circulation: 45,000.

*Creative Loafing.* Not what it sounds like; this Atlanta-based investigative reporting magazine covers environmental law and other social issues. Circulation: 99,000.

*Harley Women.* Not for women who sit on the backs of motorcycles behind their boyfriends, but for women who have their own Harley Davidsons and know what to do with them. Circulation: 15,000; published by Asphalt Angels, Streamwood, Illinois.

*Better Beagling.* From Essex, Vermont, comes a magazine for people who believe in beagles as hunting hounds. Circulation: 6,000.

While an initial reaction of people who don't believe in beagles might be to laugh at some of these niches, they are no laughing matter to the bankers and editors of the magazines that serve them. They not only survive but thrive financially. I first saw *Harley Women* when a student brought it to class as part of an assignment to select an "ugly" magazine for discussion. My student thought she wouldn't like *Harley Women*, but the more she looked at it, the more she respected it. Articles affirmed the desire of these women to be independent, self-reliant bikers and feminine at the same time. The only difference between Harley women and my student was choice of hobby. She preferred hiking and read *Outside*. In fact, *Outside* irritated her because it wasn't focused toward women. She began to envy women Harley owners for having their own magazine and wondered why women hikers didn't have a magazine too.

All the magazines above are serious magazines with serious purposes, even *Basically Buckles*. Still, there is something funny about the trend toward ever narrower and narrower niches, and so it was inevitable that a humorist would become alarmed. Roy Blount, Jr., author of *One Fell Soup* and *Crackers*, satirized modern niche marketing in a *Columbia Journalism Review* essay:

We had just finished packaging *Knock and Twinge: the Magazine for People with Psychosomatic Car Trouble*, and Hepworth could have been forgiven a few moments, even a whole afternoon, of complacency. But that wasn't Hepworth. Hepworth was looking off into space. He was *glaring* off into space.

"It's out there," he was saying. "There's something else out there. I can *feel* it. I can almost *read* it. *Fever! the Newsletter for People Running More*

*Than 101 Temperature*—no, too ephemeral. *Deep End, the Depressive's Companion*. No . . ."

"Hepworth! Let up!" I expostulated. "You have tested the very limits of the special-audience concept with *Illiterate Quarterly*. *Protective Coating Annual* is a hot book, as is *Chainsaw Times*. Not to mention *The Earthworm Breeder*, which thrives despite a slump in the earthworm industry itself. Why can't you take a week or so and just lay back . . ."

"*Layback, a Guide to Unobsessive Living*. Unh-uh,"

"Hepworth!," I cried. "Listen to me . . ."[21]

Most new magazines in any given year are launched to fill new niches. In 1989 some of the new titles spotlighted by *Folio* magazine[22] included

*Connections*, for traveling senior citizens

*Country America*, for country music fans

*Emerge*, for middle-income blacks

*First for Women*, for women

*Frisko*, for active San Francisco residents

*Garbage*, for people interested in waste management

*Hook, Line & Sinker*, for keepers of ponds

*Laugh Track*, for comedy club patrons

*Newlywed*, for newlyweds

*Quality Living*, for aging baby boomers

*Rug Hooking*, for rug hookers

*Shaker Spirit*, for Shaker lifestyle enthusiasts

*WHY*, for people interested in hunger/poverty issues

Of the titles above, only *First for Women* could be said to aim at a general audience. All the other titles identify some narrow specialty. *Frisko*, for example, was not for plain old, everyday San Franciscans, but for active ones; this is nicheing with a passion. Because finding a good niche is so crucial to magazine success, editors pay a lot of attention to niche forecasters. In 1989 *Adweek* predicted[23] that the hot niches for the Nineties were going to be

The Overstressed

The Romantics

Heavy Metal Kids

The Downwardly Mobile

New Parents

Natural Disaster Victims

Desperate Singles

Proud Singles

Sensitive Men

Maybe Blount's humor wasn't so far off after all. *Advertising Age*'s predictions[24] of hot niches for the Nineties included

Older Women (*Lear's, Mirabella*)

Trendy Lifestyle (*Vanity Fair, Spy*)

Country (*Country America*)

Travel (*Condé Nast Traveler*)

Parenting (*Healthy Kids, Today's Family*)

Celebrities (*Premiere, Entertainment Weekly*)

*Advertising Age* also predicted that lustful men (*Playboy, Penthouse*) was going to be a cold, cold niche. But they also cautioned that every niche has now been exploited: "More publications are going out than going in." Yet hundreds of new titles started up anyway.

## Repositioning

Editors of established magazines pay attention to niche forecasts too. Even if a magazine is decades old, demographic or psychographic changes could send it into decline. *Whenever a magazine adapts to changes*, it too is recognizing niche trends, but *the term for the adaptations is repositioning*." To reposition, a magazine changes its design or its editorial direction or both. Sometimes magazines make abrupt changes. Others gradually introduce new elements. When *Nation's Business* repositioned itself in 1990, it made almost unnoticeable changes. It shrank its logo, placed it in a black bar, repeated the bar inside on department heads and put colored initial caps into the copy.[25] Few readers have the graphics sophistication to even notice such minor changes, and yet advertisers (and critics) could, and they praised the "modern" new look.

America's magazine with the highest circulation, *Modern Maturity*, simply changed its long horizontal rules to short ones and increased the weight of some of the headings on the table of contents pages when it repositioned. These were not major changes, but the editors and designers probably discussed them at length before risking them.

A more dramatic repositioning was the 1981 change of *Apartment Life* to *Metropolitan Home*. Everything was changed in that makeover, from topics to size of page. As editor Dorothy Kalins put it in an interview, *Apartment Life*'s emphasis on do-it-yourself decorating had become dated because the baby boomer audience had become busy and rich. "The only thing our readers seemed interested in making themselves was money."[26]

Because repositionings are often subtle—editors want to attract new readers without alienating current ones—it takes close observation to see the changes. Writers must spot those changes to succeed. A cursory glance at a 1950 *Glamour* and a 1990 *Glamour* doesn't show much change, but as Donna Fenn, a writer for the *Washington Monthly*, said:

> When you put a 1950 *Glamour* next to a 1981 edition, you do see changes. Women don't always wear hats and white gloves now, jobs are not exclusively secretarial or assistant something-or-other, birth control is not only advertised but advocated, and, for good or ill, psychological advice is dispensed routinely. In the 1950s there were certainly no articles like the December 1980 "Why My Affair with a Married Man Was One of the Happiest Loves of My Life." (The "one of" sense alone would have counted that headline out in earlier years.) Now it's okay to wear revealing clothes, take the pill, and be assertive.[27]

"One of." Such a small change. But it reflects major upheavals in social values over the past forty years.

## EDITING FOR AUDIENCE AND NICHE

If demographers are right, repositionings at most magazines are going to be needed to reflect changes in the family, the ethnic diversity of this country, the changing roles of women, declining affluence and the aging of the population. Of these trends, none is as dramatic as the last. On July 20, 1988, the Census Bureau announced that middle-aged Americans equaled young Americans for the first time.[28] Never before in our history had there been more graying heads than heads to cause gray hairs. While few editors noted its passing, the date is significant for the magazine industry because magazines, perhaps more than any other product except diapers, are affected by people's ages. It is good news for the industry. People aged 25 to 55 are most likely to buy magazines.[29] But how are the other demographic trends affecting magazines?

### Changes in the Family

Women are having fewer babies. By 2000, women will average 1.8 children per family—less than zero population growth.[30] There already are more blended families, that is, families with stepchildren or stepparents, and this will continue. More women are waiting until their thirties to have children. For magazines, this does not mean less interest in families and children, but more. Fewer children mean more intense attention from parents. But more than half of all children will spend part of their lives in single-parent homes.[31] This is not because divorce rates continue to increase—in fact, they are leveling off—but because more babies will be born to unmarried mothers. Magazines will focus more on parents, women heads of households and older first-time parents.

## Ethnic Diversity

Already white men are less than half the labor force. By the end of the century, thanks to the low birthrate, immigration will become an important source of population growth. Asian and Hispanic immigration will continue to lead, but Middle Eastern immigrants will also contribute to the diversity. Immigrants are expected to account for 33 percent of population increase. An editor of *American Demographics* commented on the trend: "By 2010 everyone will belong to a minority group."[32] The most diverse counties in America will be in the South and the Southwest; San Francisco is already and should continue to be the most ethnically diverse county in the country.[33] Look for new magazines for minority groups and increasing coverage of ethnic issues in established ones.

## Changing Roles of Women

Fewer babies and work are changing the roles of women, yes. But the real impetus for change is the great number of women who choose or are forced to be heads of households. In 1980, 18 percent of women said they worked to support a family (compared with 43 percent who said they worked just for extra money). By 1990, 32 percent of women said they worked to support a family. Necessity was forcing women to be serious about their work. Forty-five percent of women think of their work as a career instead of "just a job." This almost matches the number of men—57 percent—who think of their work as a career, not a job.[34] The pressure on women to both support and care for a family is bringing women's issues into focus in the workplace. Increasingly, a woman's problems at home are an employer's problems too. Look for business magazines to cover women's issues more.

## Declining Affluence

Opinions vary. The doom-and-gloom set argues that despite two incomes, families will find it increasingly harder to stay in the middle class.[35] Other demographers think the middle class will probably adjust to energy shocks, continuing inflation, recurrent recession, growing global competition and corporate restructurings. Though real income has declined, if a family can find housing and if the woman in the family can find a good job, it usually is insulated against the worst of these shocks.[36] Career opportunities for women have improved and housing prices have fallen, so younger families have a fighting chance to be middle class. Even so, housing continues to take so large a chunk of family income that the home is not the protection against economic forces it once was. Look for more magazines on family finance.

## Aging of the Population

With the baby boomers reaching middle age and retirement age, and their parents living longer than anyone ever imagined, pressures on the Social Security system will obviously grow. But the aging of the population will have subtle effects as well. More people in their forties and fifties will find fewer top management positions available. They will push for and get career tracks other than management. Some workers will find technical or research jobs outside management in big companies. Others will start their own businesses. Many will go back to college—just for fun.[37] Look for new magazines to help baby boomers shift careers.

How many of the foregoing predictions are going to be true? That's anybody's guess. *Forbes*, in an article in February 1989, bragged that it had successfully predicted trends when it picked *Vanity Fair*, *U.S.A. Today* and *M* as "hot" before these publications made it. The same article then went on to predict that *Condé Nast Traveler*, *Memories*, *7-Days* and *Fame* would be the next hot books. Of these, only *Traveler* survived.[38] So much for predicting the future.

And yet trying to edit without attempting to predict demographic and psychographic trends is even more hazardous. The editor who "edits for himself" is an endangered breed. Just as professional writers must write for others, professional editors must edit for others. *Advertising Age* frequently interviews editors of new magazines that it thinks might make it. Here's what Terry McDonnell, the editor and president of *Smart*, said (emphasis mine):

> When I decided to start *Smart* I wanted to edit a magazine that would appeal to *what I saw* as a growing number of sophisticated readers who had a complicated new mix of cultural interests.[39]

And here's what Alexander Kaplen, the editor of *Wigwag*, said:

> I also have wanted to see a magazine that gave readers a sense of what it's like in all sorts of towns around the country, encouraged story-telling in its reporting, was beautiful and spoke casually, gently and directly to its readers. But the most important reason I started *Wigwag was to please myself.*[40]

Both magazines were widely praised by critics. Both folded in about a year. It's the potato salad syndrome of Chapter 1 again. Just as writers must write for others, editors must edit for others. Editors must shape their magazines for people as they are and not as the editors wish they were.

## WRITING FOR AUDIENCE AND NICHE

The more writers understand of editors' ideas about audience and niche, the easier it is to break in and get published. But there is only one thing they *have* to grasp from the preceding discussion of demographics and psychographics, niche and repositioning. This is that *reader concepts are complicated*. The one- or two-sentence descriptions of audience in *Writers' Market*, or SRDS are too superficial to help a writer accurately target topics and prose to magazines. Writing a magazine to request a copy of its editorial guidelines may give a little more audience data, but again not enough. A request for a media kit (the materials publishers use to sell advertising) may result in even more research data, but magazines are often reluctant to give out these expensive kits.

The best source of audience and niche data is the magazine. Look first at the ads. What products are advertised? What sorts of people populate the ads? What are they doing, besides enjoying the product? These images are clues to advertisers' beliefs about readers.

Then study the editorial content. This is skilled work. The next five chapters are in part on how to write, but also in part on how to read a magazine to uncover clues about readers. The words and images in a magazine are portraits of its readers.

## NOTES

1. Quoted by William Leary in "Jean Stafford, Katharine White, and the *New Yorker*," *Sewanee Review*, Fall 1985, p. 585.
2. Alfred S. Boote, "Interactions in Psychographics Segmentation: Implications for Advertising," *Journal of Advertising*, v. 13, no. 2, 1984, p. 46.
3. Michael D. Reilly, "Household Refuse and Market Research," *American Behavioral Scientist*, September/October 1984, pp. 121–126.
4. "The Best 100 Sources for Marketing Information," *American Demographics*, Special Supplement, January 1992, pp. 3–46.
5. Brad Edmondson, "What's on the Coffee Table?" *American Demographics*, October 1989, p. 15.
6. John P. Robinson, "Thanks for Reading This," *American Demographics*, May 1990, p. 6.
7. U.S. Bureau of the Census, *Statistical Abstract of the United States: 1991* (111th edition), Washington, D.C., p. 12.
8. Summarized from Landon Jones, *Great Expectations*, Ballantine Books, New York, 1980, and from Daniel Yankelovich, *New Rules: Searching for Self-Fulfillment in a World Turned Upside Down*, Random House, New York, 1981.
9. Summarized from Arnold Mitchell, *The Nine American Lifestyles*, Warner Books, New York, 1983.
10. Barbara Everitt Bryant, "Built for Excitement," *American Demographics*, March 1987, p. 41.
11. Robert Kriegel, "Does Your Ad Talk the Way Your Prospect Thinks?" *Business Marketing*, July 1984, p. 86.
12. Eileen Lehnert and Mary J. Perpich, "An Attitude Segmentation Study of Supermarket Tabloid Readers," *Journalism Quarterly*, Spring 1982, pp. 104–111.
13. "How to Market to 'New Grown-ups,'" *Advertising Age*, April 16, 1990, p. 54.
14. Bickley Townsend, "Psychographic Glitter," *Across the Board*, March 1986, p. 45.
15. Boote, "Interactions," p. 48.
16. Mark Landler, "The Bloodbath in Market Research," *Business Week*, February 11, 1991, p. 72.
17. Judith Graham, "New VALS 2 Takes Psychological Route," *Advertising Age*, February 13, 1989, p. 24.

18. Stewart Alter, "*Self & Omni*: Two New Viewpoints," *Magazine Age*, May 1980, p. 56.
19. Ibid.
20. Ibid., pp. 57–58.
21. Roy Blount, Jr., "The In-House Effect," *Columbia Journalism Review*, October 1980, p. 42.
22. "New Magazines: 1989," *Folio*, January 1990, pp. 107–116.
23. "Hot Markets," *Adweek's Marketing Week*, November 13, 1989, pp. 14–28.
24. Laura Loro, "Media Experts Pick Hot, Cold Niches," *Advertising Age*, October 23, 1989, pp. S12–S14.
25. David Merrill, "Change by Design," *Folio*, May 1990, pp. 123–124.
26. Stuart J. Elliott, "How Editors Keep Their Magazines Fresh," *Advertising Age*, October 31, 1983, p. 58.
27. Donna Fenn, "99 Ways to Increase Your Insecurity," *Washington Monthly*, April 1981, p. 29.
28. Christine Donahue, "America's Date with Destiny," *Adweek's Marketing Week*, July 11, 1988, p. 2.
29. "The Magazine Audience," *American Demographics*, October 1989, p. 23.
30. Kate Ballen, "How America Will Change Over the Next 30 Years," *Fortune*, June 17, 1991, p. 12.
31. Judith Waldrop, "You'll Know It's the 21st Century When . . . ," *American Demographics*, December 1990, p. 24.
32. Ibid., p. 23.
33. James P. Allen and Eugene Turner, "Where Diversity Reigns," *American Demographics*, August 1990, p. 36.
34. Bickley Townsend and Kathleen O'Neil, "Women Get Mad," *American Demographics*, August 1990, p. 32.
35. "The Way We Are Now," *Harper's*, November 1991, pp. 34–37. Excerpted from an introduction by Alan Wolfe to *America at Century's End*, University of California Press, Berkeley, 1991.
36. Louis S. Richman, "The New Middle Class: How It Lives," *Fortune*, August 13, 1990, pp. 104–113.
37. Doris Walsh, "Who Will Your Readers Be in the Next Decade?" *Folio*, January 1990, p. 84–89.
38. "Trying to Pick Winners among New Publications," *Forbes*, February 6, 1989, p. 20.
39. Joie Davidow, "Industry Still Has Room for Dreamers," *Advertising Age*, October 23, 1989, p. S6.
40. Ibid.

## FOR ADDITIONAL READING

Jones, Landon Y. *Great Expectations: America and the Baby Boom Generation*. Ballantine Books, New York, 1980.
Lazer, William. *Handbook of Demographics for Marketing and Advertising*. Lexington Books, Lexington Mass., 1987.
Mitchell, Arnold. *The Nine American Lifestyles*. Warner Books, New York, 1983.
Naisbitt, John. *Megatrends Two Thousand: Ten New Directions for the 1990s*. Avon, New York, 1991.
Yankelovich, Daniel. *New Rules*. Random House, New York, 1981.

# *Audience Research Methods*

## BASIC RESEARCH METHODS

It's every researcher's dream: to invent a method that can cheaply and completely measure human beings. But people refuse to be easily measured. Nine methods are described here; none is perfect.

*Personal interviews.* Sitting down, one-on-one with readers, sometimes in their own living rooms, is an effective but expensive form of research. Its advantages are completeness and accuracy. It's hard to lie when a skilled interviewer is looking you in the eye and asking follow-up questions to expose contradictions in your answers. But it's possible. Even in interviews, people will lie about sensitive topics, such as sex, drugs or alcohol. At other times they'll try to give the answer they think is expected, such as saying they go to church more than they do. Most inaccuracies, though, occur because people simply don't remember.

*Shopping mall intercepts.* Stopping people in malls to ask them "just a few questions" is much cheaper than doing full-length interviews, but it gathers less information per interview. Also, because people tend to be with friends in shopping malls, they may say what the friends expect instead of what they actually believe.

*Focus groups.* A group is formed by carefully selecting people who will meet together to discuss a single topic. Sometimes the participants are paid. A trained moderator guides the discussion. A disadvantage of this research is that very strong personalities in the group may bias the conversation. Others start thinking what a "leader" thinks. But the advantage is that the researchers have the complete attention of the subjects for a while.

*Telephone interviews.* While much less expensive than other forms of interview, the telephone interview is more likely to be seen as intrusive or annoying by subjects. They hang up. Since accurate research depends on getting an accurate sample of a population, every hang-up can distort the results.

*Consumer panels.* Some companies organize more or less permanent groups and regularly ask for their opinions. Sometimes, though, panel members begin to see themselves as guardians of society and may give untrue answers with high social ratings: "I read Shakespeare, not romance novels."

*Consumer diaries.* These are records of purchases or activities. Most famous are the Nielsen diaries for television ratings, but magazine and advertising audience research uses diaries too. Anyone who has tried to count calories knows why data from diaries are suspect—despite good intentions, few people can keep records for very long. Increasingly, data from electronic scanners at checkout counters in grocery stores and convenience marts are replacing diaries.

*Self-administered questionnaires.* Perhaps the least expensive form of research, questionnaires are mailed to people in hopes they will mail them back. Errors arise with this method because it misses subtleties. One-word answers, such as "always," "sometimes," "rarely" or "never" don't explain "why."

*Direct observation.* When a researcher simply watches behavior but doesn't talk with the subjects, this produces some honest behavior since the people may not know they are being watched. But like the questionnaire, this method misses the "why," and it raises some troubling ethical questions. Is it right to spy on people in a store? Does this invade their privacy?

*Experiments.* An experiment is a designed, controlled situation for observing people. In the magazine industry a common experiment consists of trying two different covers on newsstands in a given city and seeing which one sells better. A weakness of experiments is that they must be done on a small scale. If the city chosen for a cover experiment is not "typical," the results are skewed. (See demographic terms in Appendix 2.2.)

## FIGHTING DISTORTION

People's ability to distort answers poses a problem in most of these methods. Researchers call the sources of these inaccuracies biasing behaviors. One behavior, the outright lie, is rare though. Usually something in the design of the research causes people to say something untrue. Most of the time they will not know they're speaking falsely. People are suggestible, as psychologists have often demonstrated.

In a famous experiment two psychologists had students read a pamphlet on sleep. Some students were told the pamphlet had been written by a YMCA director and others were told the author was a Nobel Prize winning physiologist. The pamphlets gave advice ranging from outright crazy (zero sleep a night) to practical (eight hours). The more ridiculous the advice, the more likely students were to accept it if it came from the "Nobel Prize winner." Just the suggestion of "expertise" was enough to confuse the students. This shows how easily the results of studying people can become distorted.

Biasing behavior isn't the only problem researchers worry about. Failure of people to respond causes huge headaches for data gatherers. When people selected for a study don't respond, it can throw off the results either by leaving out too many of a group (such as when men are 49 percent of a population but only 39 percent of the respondents) or by getting too many of a certain personality trait (such as "people who like to get and reply to junk mail"). Of the preceding research methods, mailed questionnaires have the highest nonresponse rate (31 percent average) and personal interviews have the lowest (22 percent). Researchers try to improve response by giving premiums, using famous sponsors, promising anonymity, setting deadlines or even paying. One study measured how much payment it took to get the chosen subjects to answer; it took about five dollars.

An increasingly prevalent type of nonresponse is deliberate refusal to participate. The public is getting fed up with surveys. *American Demographics* magazine once commented that the transformation of America into an "information society" has made information and the research that gathers it valuable. By the late 1980s, 36 percent of Americans had been asked to participate in a survey, compared with 19 percent in 1978. So in just one decade, double the number of Americans had been interrupted at dinner, distracted from their favorite television show or delayed on their way to a shopping mall sale. No wonder a record 34 percent won't talk. They're annoyed.

Some people refuse because of the inconvenience. But an increasing number fear that a survey is going to be followed by a sales pitch, or worse, that whatever they say will be put in a data base and sold to the highest bidder. Fear of invasion of privacy is growing. In 1991

Congress briefly considered setting up a Data Protection Board to monitor privacy issues. Nothing came of this idea then, but it made marketing research firms nervous. One of the largest, Lotus, killed a plan to sell "MarketPlace," a data base on 80 million households. Lotus received over 30,000 complaints when they announced the project, *Advertising Age* reported. Lotus's chief executive, Jim Manzi, described the uproar as an emotional storm. "We could not ignore the volume and tenor of response from consumers," he said.

## THE ULTIMATE RESEARCH METHOD

Undeterred by all this, researchers continue to invent creative ways to observe the elusive American. One of the most controversial (if not the silliest) is garbology. This is the study of refuse. Yes. Trash. Dedicated scientists collect trash bags from a carefully selected sample of households and they measure the contents. Wearing gloves and masks, these seekers of truth pick over the tissues and table scraps, empty cans, and used diapers of the American family.

Garbologists are ecstatic about the advantages of their technique. They argue that it's unobtrusive because people don't have to know their garbage is under scrutiny; that it solves the nonresponse problem because no one can refuse to create refuse; that it solves inaccurate response because an empty tuna fish can neither lies nor forgets; and that the method is complete—even illegal behaviors show up in the garbage. The only serious bias, claim garbologists, is occasional missing evidence such as when table scraps are put in compost piles or fed to pets.

# Appendix 2.2

# *Demographic Terms*

Here are some official Census Bureau definitions plus unofficial demographic terms in common use. "Unofficial" does not mean unusable. The unofficial terms are needed because census terms aren't always specific enough. But whether using official or unofficial terms, use them precisely. Don't say family when you mean household, for example.

*Housing unit.* A dwelling that has its own entrance inside or outside and has basic bathing and cooking facilities. A room rented in a boarding house is "separate living quarters."

*Household.* A housing unit with people in it. An empty apartment is not a household, just a unit. Most Americans live in households, but others live in group quarters such as college dorms, military barracks, prisons or nursing homes. Households come in two types, family and nonfamily.

*Family household.* This has at least two people, a *householder*, the person who owns or rents the unit, and a relative by marriage, blood or adoption. Seven out of ten American households are families.

*Nonfamily households.* Unrelated groups such as roommates or cohabiting couples. If a woman is living alone with her child she is a family, but if she moves in with her boyfriend, the Census Bureau calls the household a nonfamily; the kid becomes a subfamily.

*Subfamilies.* Related subfamilies are assortments of relatives who live with a householder. Unrelated subfamilies are people who may be related to each other but are not related to the householder. For example, if a grandparent lets a married child and his kids live with him, this mob is a related subfamily. But if the old man takes in his butler's family, these people are an unrelated subfamily.

*Family groups.* There are two ways to describe a family group in census Bureau lingo. First is by who heads the house: a married couple, a man without a spouse or a woman without a spouse. (In the United States 56 percent of family groups are headed by married couples.) The second way of describing a family is according to whether children are present. If they are, the Census Bureau divides these children into two groups: those under age 18 and those over. Increasingly, grown children do live with their parents.

*Traditional family.* The Census Bureau does not define a traditional family. If *traditional* is simply two parents with children under 18, then 26 percent of all households qualify. If it means husband and *nonworking* wife and some kids, only 9 percent of households are traditional. But if "traditional" means husband, nonworking wife and *two* kids, barely 3 percent of American households fit the pattern.

*Race.* The Census Bureau identifies four major groups and only four: white, black, Asian (including Pacific Islanders) and Native Americans (including Eskimos and Aleuts). Americans can choose their racial category on census forms.

*Ethnic group*. The correct census term, "ancestry group," refers to cultural, not racial background, although the two terms are often confused. For example, Hispanics are an ethnic category, not a race, even though increasingly the Census Bureau lists Hispanic data with race—but always with a footnote explaining that Hispanics can be of any race. Ethnic origins have many footnotes in census tables. For example, French origins, footnotes explain, exclude French Basques and Soviet origins include Georgians but exclude Ukrainians.

*Income*. The Census Bureau defines income as total annual cash accumulation from all sources, including stock dividends, welfare and child support. Money from a job is just "earnings." Only when money from *all* sources is added together does the Census Bureau consider it income. Noncash benefits such as food stamps or housing subsidies are not income according to the Census Bureau, but many other government offices do see these as income. (See why demographic terms are confusing?) To make it really complex, the Census Bureau likes to think of the imaginary rent a home owner pays to himself or the vegetables a gardener eats as income; but don't worry, the IRS doesn't—unless that produce is *swapped* for rent or another good or service.

*Disposable income*. This is earnings *after* taxes.

*Discretionary income*. A term the Census Bureau doesn't define but one that's important in creating a demographic portrait of people. It means the money left after housing, food and other necessities are paid for. But what are necessities? A person with an office job may make more than a blue-collar worker but have less discretionary income because buying business attire is a necessity.

*Poverty*. An annual index first designed by the Social Security Adminstration in 1964. It is based on money income, not noncash benefits. In 1989 a single person was poor if he or she was under 65 and making less than $6452 annually. A household of four was poor if it took in less than $12,675 annually.

*Wealth*. Again a word the Census Bureau is reluctant to define, but it is important for understanding people. It is not income but assets, such as house, stock holdings, land. These things, accumulated over time, make up wealth. But debt diminishes wealth, as a certain leveraged billionaire discovered when banks made him cut expenses and scrape by on $400,000 a month. Older people whose homes are free of mortgages are often quite "wealthy," but because of low "income" they must live frugally.

*Affluence*. Also an unofficial term but one demographers use to get around the anomalies of wealthy people who are cash poor and seemingly wealthy people who are debt ridden. Most researchers define affluence as income (not assets) of at least $50,000. Some, though, use $75,000 or even $100,000 as a minimum.

*Community type*. There is no such thing as "medium-sized city" in census jargon. There are only "metropolitan regions" and "nonmetropolitan regions." Metropolitan areas or MSAs (for metropolitan statistical areas) are not cities but counties (except in New England, where they are cities, not counties—why make this easy?). MSAs must have an urbanized area of at least 50,000 people, but if they have a million or more, they may be termed a CMSA, or consolidated metropolitan statistical area, which is made up of PMSAs, primary metropolitan statistical areas. (Isn't this fun?) There are twenty-one CMSAs. For example, the CMSA for my hometown is called the "Chicago–Gary–Lake County (IL) IL-IN-WI" CMSA, but the PMSA that houses my particular suburb (Crystal Lake) is "Chicago."

*Typical city.* Obviously if cities don't exist in census terminology, then neither does a typical city. To fill this gap, private research firms have developed profiles. Saatchi & Saatchi publishes a *Guide to Test Market Media Planning and Market Selection*, which identifies fifty-four cities as "marketing barometers," meaning they're typical enough to serve as stand-ins for the whole country. Saatchi is serious about this list. They rudely dropped Fargo, North Dakota, when it gained too many people over 65. And Springfield–Decatur–Champaign, Illinois, was dropped because it had too many people under 25. The most popular typical city is Minneapolis–St. Paul; in 1990, 112 new products were tested there. Other highly regarded ordinary towns are Denver, Colorado; Portland, Oregon; and Columbus, Ohio. The most famous typical city, Peoria, Illinois, is not as popular as it used to be; only eleven products were tested there in 1990.

To be typical, a city must closely match the national profile. Median income should be about $29,000. Racial mix should be 84 percent white, 12 percent black and 4 percent other, and there should be more than 125,000 households but fewer than 1.5 million. The town must also be reasonably isolated from broadcast signals of other, larger cities.

# Part II

# *The Basic Tools*

$S$ pread a few magazines out on a table. Open at random. Study the headlines and layouts. They differ so radically, how can they be considered one medium? One will be splashy, with teasing, cryptic heads; another formal, austere. One will exist to help, splaying advice on every page; another is argumentative, reveling in controversy. The diversity seems too chaotic for anyone to understand, let alone master, but there are three main concepts or patterns common to every article. Focus—or the themes within articles—follows predictable patterns in magazines. Forms—or the range of editors' expectations about article treatments—may be complicated in magazines, but likewise they are predictable from issue to issue. Structures—or the organization within individual articles—also form patterns. But before any of these patterns can be imitated, it must be first observed. These next three chapters, on focus, form and structure, are as much about analyzing patterns as they are about creating them. Your tools for analysis will include charts, graphs, and—yes—even maps.

# Chapter

# 3

# *Focus*

I've had my share of encounters with raccoons. Just before dawn once, I was sitting on a screened porch when a mother raccoon stopped by with her five cubs to let them splash in a tub of rainwater kept just outside. The cubs tumbled less than a foot from where I sat. Didn't they know I was there? I held my breath for fear of startling them.

Another time I was walking through a woods and saw movement in the gully below. A mother raccoon was napping on a log while her three cubs played about her.

Yet another time I was driving home when a neighbor flagged me down. "Do you want some sweet corn?" she asked. Of course I said yes. "Follow me," she said and led me into a stand of field corn. "Let's see, three to the north, five to the west . . ." she muttered aloud to herself as she worked her way through the rows.

"What are you doing?" I said.

"I've hidden my sweet corn in the field corn."

"Why?"

"To keep it from the raccoons."

"Does it work; do you fool the raccoons?"

"Oh no," she said, "they always find it."

What you have just read are three anecdotes about raccoons. No doubt you noticed that. In fact, it's possible you would prefer to continue reading about raccoons, but I can't keep writing about them just now because all I have are these three anecdotes. They are a string of facts, nothing more. If I have raised your desire to read about raccoons, I will have to disappoint you (again for now) because I have not yet thought of some way to link those anecdotes so that they proceed to a point or message. I have not thought of a *focus*, in other words. I have a topic, but this is not enough for nonfiction writing.

This reality, that a topic is not enough, is most baffling for novice writers. Thinking of topics appears easy for beginners. I give my students just five minutes to produce a list of topics; no one yet has turned in a blank sheet of paper. But the next step, shaping those topics into well-focused articles, is so difficult and elusive that many of these same students will still be struggling after weeks of intensive writing practice. Focusing is the basic task of writing and may be the central talent. It is also the hardest of skills.

Editors use a host of words for focus: angle, slant, thesis, premise, theme, point, message, idea. Webster's defines it as directed attention or center of attention, but this is like calling a raccoon cute. It says nothing about the problem at hand. I like to define focus as a promise. *A focus promises a reader that the writer will deliver a certain message about a topic*. The writer will give more than mere information. There will be something deeper—a meaning to this topic. Another way to say this is that there are two questions every writer must answer in beginning a piece of nonfiction. The first is, "What is this article about?"—that's the topic. The second is, "What is this article about *really*?" That's the focus. The "really" is the reach for insight, the attempt at freshness, the stretch for language, the connection with readers, the—well—point, premise, theme, angle, slant, idea, message or promise. It is the genuine subject beneath the surface. Focus is what makes an article a joy to read.

Usually even the simplest article has a focus. In a women's service magazine the topic "cake baking" could have dozens of focuses over several years. One might be "Cake baking is easy—try it." Another might be "Why do cakes rise?" Another: "Children can bake cakes." Another: "Cake recipes differ around the world."

A popular history magazine might also cover cake baking, but there the focus might be "Cakes have not always been a symbol for celebration." A literary magazine might publish something on cakes, too, but the editors might expect an evocative piece on the ways cakes bind families. One topic can be focused in thousands of ways and the best focuses are usually far more subtle than these six cake ideas.

The topic "raccoons" is a good example of this potential for subtlety. Between 1983 and 1991 there were thirty-three articles on raccoons listed on the computerized version of the *Readers' Guide*. Two of these appeared in regular columns (the *New Yorker*'s "Notes and Comments" and *The Nation*'s "Uncivil Liberties," by Calvin Trillin), so were not given titles. But the titles for the remaining thirty-one raccoon articles suggest how intricately varied approaches to a single topic can be (full citations for these and the untitled pieces are listed at chapter's end):

"Coon of the Yellow Moon"

"One Paw ahead of the Law"

"Greatest Hound That Ever Lived"

"Rabies Claims Another Wildlife Victim in New York State"

"Jimmy Kimmery and the Saddle Horse"

"The Raccoon and the Hummingbird"

"Virginia OKs Rabies Vaccine Test"

"South Carolina Blocks Test of Rabies Vaccine"

"A Hound's Start in Life"

"Listening in the Dark"

"Help! There's a Raccoon in My Chimney"

"The Raccoon Unmasked"

"Starting Coonhounds the Easy Way"

"The Raccoon Coat"

"Raccoons and Rabies"

"Backyard Bandits"

"Raccoons and Rabies: An Eastern Urban Threat"

"Old Dogs, New Treks"

"Vaccine Sandwich to Go"

"Panda Pedigree: Giant and Lesser"

"Raccoons Live It Up in Town"

"Rocky Times for Rocky"

"Night Stalker!"

"Masked Survivor"

"Raccoons Harbor Lethal Parasite"

"An Epizootic of Rabies"

"A Vermont Corn Cage"

"Computer Coonhunting"

"A Taste for Raccoon"

"Raccoons to Remember"

"The Trapper's Larder"

In that mix of titles is everything from the cuteness of the critters, to their nuisance qualities, to the disease danger they pose to humans and pets, to their evolutionary heritage (dogs, bears, pandas and raccoons are thought to be descended from the same ancestor), to ways of keeping them out of sweet corn (none of which seem to work), to techniques for hunting them. The stretch—from hummingbirds to computers—only begins to hint at the variety of focuses any topic contains.

Titles alone do not reveal the actual focuses, however, because focuses develop slowly as an article progresses. While there are no "rules" for how a focus should develop, there are some common conventions. The most common of all these conventions is use of the *focusing statement*. Virtually every nonfiction article has one. This is the first time in an article when the idea or theme appears. Sometimes it comes after the topic is mentioned; sometimes before. It may be as short as a phrase or a sentence or as long as several paragraphs. Usually it comes near the beginning of the article, but not always. In some cases it merely hints or *foreshadows* what is to come and is so well disguised that only on a second reading can an editor detect it. ("I was hiking one day.") At the other extreme, a focusing statement can be utterly blunt. ("Raccoons are cute.")

A second important convention in building a focus is the use of *refocusing statements*. These also can be subtle or blunt. Their function is to repeat the focus idea. Sometimes a refocusing statement is used as a transition; other times it is buried as a phrase within a paragraph. Sometimes it develops the ideas. ("A raccoon's cuteness is an evolutionary defense mechanism.") Other times a refocusing statement just repeats the focus unchanged. ("Another way in which raccoons are cute . . . ")

The last refocusing statement in an article is the *transformation*. It is the moment when the focus appears fully developed. This finished focus, if the article has progressed successfully, is changed into a complete idea. No more hints; no more games; the author must tell us what this article is really about—or we may never understand the message.

Sometimes the transformation is narrow, with very little change from the initial focus statement. ("So those are the ways raccoons are cute.") Other times the transformation is deep, leaping over great philosophical distances. ("Blindness to the charm of the raccoon is blindness to our own humanity.") Only by retracing the article can a reader see how the writer made the leap.

Magazines differ as to how much transformation they think their readers can handle. Some editors expect articles to always reach for insight. Others want articles to stick to business, to not get too subtle. The degree of transformations a magazine likes is something a writer needs to think about when proposing topics.

Although every successful piece could be said to have a unique focus, there are broad patterns that, conveniently enough, these raccoon pieces illustrate. The main differences among patterns are the placement of focusing statements and degree of transformation. Basic patterns with fairly narrow transformations are Simple, Bracket and Traditional. Sophisticated patterns, requiring more skill from the writer because of their ambitious transformations, are Tandem, Complex, Reverse, Apologetic and Paradox. Undoubtedly there are other patterns, but these eight will illustrate how a focus develops and transforms. They will also show why it is a major skill to control a focus.

## BASIC PATTERNS

### The Simple Focus

The simple focus is just that: the focusing statement appears very early in the piece—sometimes in the first paragraph. And the transformation at the end is very slight. The conclusion is almost identical to the opening promise. It's the what-you-see-is-what-you-get school of journalism. What it lacks in subtlety, though, it makes up for in ease of reading, so it is a very popular focusing style. "Masked Survivor," by Harry Middleton in *Southern Living*, is an example of a simple focus.[1]

The lead is a short single paragraph that describes a neighbor who had a family of raccoons move into his dead oak tree. They immediately raided his garbage cans and he had to chase them away. The focusing statement is the first sentence of the second paragraph:

"After buttoning down the lids of his garbage cans, our friend gladly accepted his new four-legged neighbors." This article, this focus suggests, is *really* about enjoying nearby wildlife.

The development simply describes all the natural habits of raccoons in general, with an occasional reference to the specific raccoons in that oak tree. The ending describes the mother raccoon who is about to have her babies. The friend, in other words, is still enjoying his nearby raccoons. The promise is unchanged—the transformation is slight—but a lot of information about raccoons has been imparted along the way. This is a pattern that lends itself to packing a lot of facts into a small space because little space is needed to flesh out the promise. But—an important "but" here—the focus is still present. The author doesn't just plunge into a discussion of raccoons. He focuses first. It is the focusing that distinguishes this material as an article instead of a file of facts.

## The Bracket Focus

One of the greatest challenges facing any writer in managing a topic is control of wildly unrelated subtopics. A focusing technique that helps control such material is to begin and end a piece with almost the same exact focusing scenario. Then, within the piece, minor focus statements enclose or bracket each subtopic. An article that does this is "Backyard Bandits" by David Petersen for *Mother Earth News*.[2] The opening focus statement at the end of the second paragraph says, "The raccoon is possibly the most adaptable wild mammal in North America." The first major subtopic the author labels "The Great Coon Quandary," which asks why raccoons wash their food. He opens with a question, discusses what scientists have thought, and ends by repeating the question, noting that nobody really knows. Then he launches into a long discussion of the havoc raccoons wreak on gardens.

He bridges the leap from these two vastly different subtopics, washing and gardening, by saying "There's no doubt about *what* a raccoon washes and gobbles down." The "why" may be a mystery but the "what" is not. It's not a subtle transition, but it does the job. It links the two sections. To return to his adaptable theme, he simply says that raccoon cleverness at raiding gardens makes it easy for the animals to enter suburbs and stay. Then he takes that adaptability theme to another level with his transformation sentence: "Eventually, of course, humanity being even more adaptable and occasionally more clever than the raccoon, will get the upper hand." The focus, adaptability, brackets an in-depth discussion of the topic: raccoons. But adaptability is the real issue, not washing food and wrecking gardens. This author's message is that we are the more adaptable species.

## The Traditional Focus

A *Country Journal* piece, "The Raccoon Unmasked," by John Yurus,[3] begins with a four-paragraph anecdote. The author and his wife are sitting in a restaurant when she notices a raccoon peering through a laundry chute. He walks over to the chute; the raccoon and he stare at one another for a moment, and then finally the raccoon backs down and leaves. Yurus concludes his anecdote with this sentence: "No other wild animal I know would be bold enough to poke its pointy nose into a room full of people." This is the focusing statement.

Here the focusing statement, a full sentence, directs our attention to something more than just the topic, raccoons. Raccoons are wild animals; but they behave in a nonwild way around people. That's the promise: this article is *really* about raccoons and people.

In his development, the author immediately reinforces the promise. ("*Procyon lotor* knows how to make itself at home among people.") But then he raises a question, his first subtopic: Why? He gives two answers. The first, that the animal's body makes it especially adaptable, takes five paragraphs. His second four-paragraph answer is the paws. We people identify with those handlike feet. "A raccoon can no more keep those hands to itself than a duck can learn to blow a kiss."

He moves from this into his second subtopic, a general natural history of the raccoon—its hibernation, mating, rearing of young, and foraging skills. The piece becomes in this section a typical "our friend the raccoon" article. But toward the end of his foraging discussion Yurus returns to the "hands" idea. "It's the nature of *Procyon lotor* to explore, to touch, to try whatever is in front of it, and retain from it any new information that helps fill its belly, protect its young, or cover its backside." With this sentence he has delivered his promise, but it's been transformed since the lead. He began by promising to explore the relationship of raccoons to people. But he ended by saying raccoons are somewhat like people.

The pattern in this article—long opening scene, fairly late placement of a generalized focusing statement and moderate transformation of the focus—define the piece as "traditional." But the change in the idea from simplistic "raccoons and people" to the more subtle "raccoons are like people" is the real tradition. Magazine articles traditionally are vehicles for ideas, not conveyors of facts alone.

## SOPHISTICATED PATTERNS

## The Tandem Focus

The tandem focus is an ambitious focus pattern in both structure and level of insight. In it the writer seizes two or more ideas—beyond the topic—and develops both fully without getting lost, tangled or confused. That's not easy in a world where communicating even one idea is a major accomplishment. The writers who can perform at this level of skill are rare and wonderful. Calvin Trillin is such a writer.

One of his "Uncivil Liberties" columns in *The Nation* is an essay on raccoons.[4] The lead contains two focuses: raccoons in the garbage and the local know-it-all Trillin asked for help. "When the raccoons started getting at the garbage cans this summer, I naturally consulted the man in our town we call the Old Timer." That opening sentence sets up two thoughts, which will be developed simultaneously. First, Trillin portrays the uselessness of the Old Timer's advice. ("Have you tried red onions?") Then he switches quickly to describing the brilliance of the raccoons who ate the onions, "except for the skins, which they mixed into some coffee grounds and spread on the rose bush." He alternates from the obnoxious Old Timer to the all-powerful raccoons and ends the essay with his problem unresolved. So he follows the Old Timer's advice to lock the cans with a combination lock because "a raccoon's cunning but he's got no head for figures."

The humor of the article rests on its style—exaggeration. No raccoon I know would help me fertilize my roses. But style is not focus. The meaning of this piece is more than mere joke. The piece is about raccoons as a nuisance. But what is it about *really*? It's first an attack on all human beings who use a pretense of knowledge to bludgeon the rest of us. And it is *also* really about how unbelievably complicated solving life's simple problems can be. Both focuses, developed in tandem, reach beyond the topic to confront us readers in our daily lives. We may not have to padlock our garbage cans, but we deal with obnoxious people and daily frustrations. This is the power of focusing; it gives any topic potential to explore deeper truths.

## The Complex Focus

The complex focus is also an ambitious form of writing. The writer deliberately looks for symbol, metaphor, philosophy or insight beyond the surface topics. "Notes and Comments" in the *New Yorker* ran a piece on raccoons that illustrates this pattern.[5] Its lead doesn't mention raccoons at all; instead it serves more to set a literary mood than define a topic. The author writes there is truth in Stendhal's comment that with every hundred miles of travel there is material for a new novel. The author has left Manhattan and gone upstate where "the talk is of Governor Cuomo, agriculture and drought." So far no topic. So far no focus either.

The second paragraph begins with a sentence that establishes both the topic and focus: "In the area where I've been staying everybody talks about raccoons." This article is about raccoons but it is *really* about people talking.

The writer begins development with a string of anecdotes on the outrageous feats of these small cousins of bears. Listening to her neighbors catalog their defeats at the paws of raccoons, she writes, is like listening to the *Iliad* from the Trojan side. She concludes this narrative of woe with the story of a neighbor coming home to find a raccoon trying to open the refrigerator.

This is followed by a refocusing statement, a device much needed in complex prose: "I wonder why we brag about our raccoons instead of our children. At the very moment of telling, all our raccoon stories, implausible and veracious, seem to turn into folklore."

With the second sentence the author is reminding us that the topic is not just the things raccoons do, but people talking about these things. Having clarified that, she moves on to the insight she had in mind all along: "I suspect that we exchange these narratives as a way of acquiring the animals' wildness for ourselves."

In one sense the "message" of this piece is very much like the "Masked Survivor" piece above. Both writers are telling us to enjoy nearby wildlife. But the *New Yorker* writer has taken a more complex line of thinking. It's not the animals alone we enjoy, she observes, but the sharing of our experiences. Through sharing, these stories become like folklore and literature, infused with a power for moral instruction.

## The Reverse Focus

An *Organic Gardening* article, "A Vermont Corn Cage," by Eric Frederick Jensen[6] is similar to the traditional *Country Journal* piece discussed earlier in that it starts with a lengthy anecdotal lead before giving a focusing statement. The lead tells how humans are not the only creatures who like sweet corn; raccoons love it so much that not one edible ear may be left in an unprotected field. "That's what happened to our first Vermont garden," the author concludes his lead, which he follows with this focusing statement: "And then we started to think about ways of beating them off next year."

This sounds like the author is going to tell how to keep raccoons out of the corn, but instead his development gives all the tricks he tried that didn't work—noisemakers, pumpkin vines, hot peppers, sleeping in the field. This technique of following a focus with an exactly opposite development is an old and honorable and usually entertaining technique. The author does discuss one thing that did work, a cage, but gives it only one paragraph and does not describe how to build it. Rather, he goes on to comment that instead of keeping raccoons out of the corn, maybe we ought to share it with them. "I sympathize with any creature to whom sweet corn means so much."

His pattern, which began by following the traditional model, instead produced an article that completely reversed from the opening premise. The "transformation" is a 180-degree turn. It can be a risky pattern to use. If readers feel cheated ("Where's my information on how to keep raccoons out of my corn?"), the article could disappoint them. Most times, though, the surprise delights.

## The Apologetic Focus

As with the reverse focus, sometimes a little guile can give a routine set of facts intrigue and depth. Lee Eisenberg used an apology in "The Raccoon and the Hummingbird" in *Esquire*.[7] Then editor-in-chief of the magazine, Eisenberg devoted one of his monthly columns to thinking about raccoons in the garbage. (City folks seem to be fascinated by raccoons' adeptness with garbage.) Eisenberg begins with a shrug. "Bear with me, this is my first attempt at fable." He follows with a straight description of his sufferings from raccoon raids, including all the trips he needed to the hardware store for elaborate but ineffective solutions. In mid-essay, he refocuses: "I assessed my alternatives, not rationally, *wrathfully*." He is saying this is not beast against garbage but beast against man. Note how this refocusing transforms the piece, making it not one man's struggle but all humanity's and not just against garbage predators, but against all of nature.

After the refocusing though, he switches and tells of buying a plastic hummingbird feeder at the same hardware store. He hung it out filled with a nectar of sugar-water dyed red. Then he discusses the similarity of a raccoon stealing garbage from a garbage can and a hummingbird drinking red glop, or as he put it, "Raccoons eat our pasta; hummingbirds drink our Kool-Aid." He then bluntly explains the meaning of his tale, that our relationship with wild animals could not exist without hardware stores and consequently, "We lose our ability to write fables." Eisenberg is saying we must enjoy animals as they are, but he adds to this an urgency. If we don't take them as they are, we lose ourselves as we are too. We are a fable-making species. We need our wild animals to be wild so we can continue to create fables. His apology lets him take a more audacious leap than would the reverse or traditional approaches.

## The Paradox Focus

Information is the foundation of all nonfiction, but rarely are facts unambiguous. Gardening, cooking, dieting, hunting, politics, history, science, sports, business—all are full of divergent and contradictory realities. Sophisticated writers exploit the paradoxes of a topic rather than avoid them. One such article, which rests its focus on paradoxes, is a hunting essay, "Listening in the Dark," by Bill Tarrant, for *Field & Stream*.[8] The author begins with a seemingly simple paradox. He and some cronies are hunting at night. "It's a perfect night for stepping into a hole and breaking your neck. Which means it's a perfect night for running coons." This focus sentence foreshadows that more contradictions will follow.

The next paradox is broader in scope. Coon hounds are best if they have a good loud voice, but most other gun dogs, he says, are better if silent. His next paradox ups the stakes to reach into the psyches of the hunters. He quotes one hunter who says, " 'I don't know what I'd rather do—breathe or hunt coons.' 'Well,' I reply, "that would take an understanding wife.' 'I ain't married,' the hunter told him, 'I get married Saturday night.' " Through this humor the author is revealing the paradoxical choices hunters have to make. Which passion is more important? His next paradox is about the raccoons themselves, which obviously the hunters and the author admire even though they're all trying to kill them.

From there, he leaps to his concluding paradox, the relationship of humans to hunting: "From far down the hollow, I hear the coon dogs bawl. It is a lonely, eerie thing—a melody and a mystery. A call to something unknown that lies deep in a man's soul." The paradoxes are left as they are. His "transformation" is not to resolve the puzzles, but to offer readers increasingly more subtle dilemmas as the essay progresses. A skilled writer recognizes when it is enough to leave a mystery alone. The power of paradox is that through it an author can sometimes get close to the unknown that lies deep in all our souls.

## THINGS BEST AVOIDED

Editing is not a perfect science, not a science at all, actually. It is possible to get an article published that doesn't have a focus or is written with a very limited news focus. If editors are desperate enough for a topic or careless enough in their reading, they will let a no-focus piece slip through. And some magazines that cover news aspects of an industry or field prefer news style over the focus patterns discussed earlier. These no-focus and news-focus patterns are rare in magazines, but I did find them in this raccoon collection.

### The News Focus

The news focus pounces immediately on the news value of a topic rather than on an idea or theme. An example in this raccoon collection is "Raccoons and Rabies" by Robert Cooke in *Technology Review*.[9] The lead is the focus in this case. No warm-up anecdote, no preamble, no philosophy. Just who, what, where, when and why: "Scientists are trying to control rabies in wild animals by redesigning the virus that conquered smallpox."

That's the first sentence and that's the focusing statement. The development, too, follows news style in that its information is arranged in descending order of importance. There's a discussion on how rare it is for raccoon rabies to spread to humans; then details on rabies prevalence in wild raccoons; then facts on the vaccine; then a long digression on experiments in Argentina (including some local political resentment of the experiments). The ending is a discussion of an untried idea for dropping bait laced with vaccine from airplanes. It's not an ending at all; the article merely stops.

This sort of structuring and focusing, or rather, nonstructured, nonfocused writing, is common in newspapers but is usually resisted by magazines. For that reason, journalists trained in newspaper style often have difficulty switching to more tightly focused writing. However, the existence of this piece proves that news style does get published in magazines. Science and business magazines use news focuses most.

### The No Focus

While most nonfiction writing is carefully crafted around a focus, there are exceptions. In unfocused pieces not only is it impossible to tell what the article is about *really*; it's impossible to tell what it's about *period*. An example of this hodgepodge journalism is "An Epizootic of Rabies," by Alan M. Beck, in *Natural History*.[10]

The article begins with a rambling discussion of the 2,000-year history of rabies in dogs and cats. (The topic is rabies in raccoons, remember?) Finally, the author mentions the first cases of raccoon rabies spotted in the South and speculates about movement into the Mid-Atlantic region. Next comes a complete topic (and style) change as the author tells how to avoid contact with rabid raccoons (vaccinate your dogs). Then comes a philosophical discussion on the cuteness of raccoons, with a reminder that they're wild animals. Next is another short essay on how cat owners resist vaccinating their pets. Then a few paragraphs on difficulties in immunizing animals in the wild. The end is a return to the sermon tone, advising people to enjoy wild animals at a distance and to, of course, wash all bites thoroughly.

If writers take this unfocused, but published, reality as proof that they do not have to master focusing to succeed, they should look at the fine print at the end of the article. Beck is a veterinarian, and no doubt the editors welcomed him for his expertise, not his craft. That the editors had difficulty working with this piece is hinted at in the headlines. Editors write headlines at most magazines. The main head for Beck's piece is simply "An Epizootic of Rabies," a topic that isn't introduced until after all that history. The secondary head, or deck, says "Raccoon rabies has surged into the Mid-Atlantic region, spilling over into the dog and cat population. Will humans escape a summer outbreak?" This head summarizes a subtopic that doesn't come up until halfway through the piece and is one the author barely develops. The editors felt *they* had to focus on something, even if the writer did not. This absence of control was probably tolerated only because of the author's reputation as a veterinarian.

## EXPLORING FOCUSING

In general then, a focus expands the reach of the topic. There are many tools for focusing, but the four main ones are, first, the *focusing statement*, a device near the beginning that reveals the promise. This was present in every article (except in the no-focus disaster). Second is the *refocusing statement* used most often in complex pieces. Such statements are placed throughout or near the end of the articles to remind the reader of the deeper level as well as to develop that depth. A third technique is *foreshadowing*, used by authors to reveal intent but not too clearly so as not to spoil the ending. Foreshadowing is important when a focus undergoes a major transformation or when paradoxes are explored. The final technique is *transformation* itself—letting the focus change as the piece progresses.

A reason for studying the focus patterns of so many articles is to discover if there are any remaining opportunities with the topic. Remember that I began this chapter wanting to write about raccoons myself. With thirty-three articles covering just about every focusing nuance to the topic, was there anything left for me? Editors study their niche rivals. If another magazine has recently covered a topic (and "recent" can mean anything from last month to within the last five years), then the editor probably won't welcome a proposal from me on the same topic unless it really has a unique focus.

I'll confess that after reading so many raccoon articles, I was depressed. Top-notch writers had explored this topic with subtlety, facticity, grace and complexity. How could I top what had already been done? My three anecdotes looked limp compared to some of the others I'd read. Still, no topic is ever exhausted. There had to be an angle in it for me. I rejected a hunting focus right away simply because I'm neither qualified for nor interested in hunting. The "our friend the raccoon" theme had been done to death as had the "clever bandit" idea. I had nothing to add on raccoon diseases with so many recent articles having discussed this. But I noticed that all the articles seemed to link the raccoon with something: raccoons and people; raccoons and dogs; raccoons and cities; raccoons and disease. Were there any linkages missing from that lineup?

Corn. Only one article dealt with raccoons and corn. So I went to the library and looked at corn. In the process, I stumbled across a fact I'd never known before, that there is no such thing as truly wild corn. That intrigued me so much I changed topics and wrote "The Corn," the article that follows, for *Country Journal*.[11] Raccoons are still a factor in the article but are mere supporting details now, not the focus.

The focus pattern I used for "The Corn" was the paradox. How could something so familiar be such a mystery? How could something so common be missed if absent? How could something natural be a human artifact? Ordinarily, when reading a manuscript, an editor (and a writer too) should read it at least twice. The first reading is the "laundromat" reading, when your goal should be to read as sloppily as a real magazine reader would—while sitting in a doctor's office perhaps, or while passing time in a laundromat or when a radio is blaring in the background. The second reading—after you know how the piece ends—should be a hunt for the focusing statements. But for "The Corn" I've highlighted (set in boldface type) all the focusing, refocusing and transformation statements. So read these statements first and then go back and read the whole essay. Notice how few focusing statements there are. Focusing should never be intrusive. It may be the most important element of nonfiction, but it is also the most subtle, a brush stroke. Sledgehammer focusing dulls reader interest. Better to hint at messages rather than blare them.

## *The Corn*

### I. May

**I miss the corn.**

I spent so many years griping about field corn that it's embarrassing to miss it, but I do. The chunk of Appalachian Ohio I live in now has little corn. Flowers, wild and otherwise, bloom in profuse variety, but whenever I drive north to Columbus and encounter flat, corn-chocked fields, I feel an odd relief which is more than nostalgic; it's visual. It is good to *see* the corn stretching mile after monotonous mile.

This is corn country: Iowa and Illinois and Nebraska and Minnesota and Indiana, and almost all of Ohio. That is what I seldom saw when I lived there, and now that I seldom see it, I miss it.

**I miss soil being prepared for seed.** In spring, nightly television promised bumper crops if only this or that chemical were applied. The tractors pulled aerators and hoppers then, so I knew the ads were heard, but no chemical or machine ever altered the blackness of the earth. It is so dark that newcomers to the Midwest mistake it for asphalt. Seed is planted in May, more or less, depending on each farmer's estimate of the latest possible moment to plant for highest yield. May 10 was the date in my area.

When the corn emerged about 10 days later, it was as illusory as the soil itself, its tracings faint, mere pulses of color. Individual plants weren't distinguishable at first, but the green rows were visible, precise, controlled and irrevocably human.

**The corn we know is a human creation.** There is no wild corn. There has been no wild corn for thousands of years. Volunteer corn, or plants that grow from spilled seed, is a nuisance but is not wild. Humans, not the plant itself, dispersed the seed.

Charles Darwin was the first to puzzle over the absence of wildness. Corn defied his theory that plants evolve only if they survive. In all its modern-day varieties, corn cannot plant itself. Seed kernels are firmly anchored upon an ear which is in turn tightly wrapped in a husk. Unless the husk is peeled away and the seeds separated from the ear, the plant cannot develop. Even if the seeds should push through a fallen husk to germinate in soil, the mass of seedlings clustered on one ear would strangle themselves.

Scientists assumed early growers must have crossed two grasses to get corn. But in 1950, building excavations in Mexico City yielded 80,000-year-old soil samples that predated agriculture, or for that matter humans in the area, containing actual corn pollen. It *must* have grown wild.

Indeed, experiments to reverse-breed corn—to deliberately create its ancestors—eventually produced a plant with tiny ears, few husks, and even some pollen-bearing male tassels on the ears. In short, the experimental corn could sow itself, though modern husked corn cannot. When archaeologists found tiny, 5,400-year-old cobs of corn in New Mexico that were less than a thumbnail long, that clinched it.

Botanists have investigated two possible points of origin for corn: Peru, which has most corn varieties, and Mexico, with its abundant wild corn relatives (not wild corn, but wild relatives). The origin is hard to deduce because corn was fully dispersed throughout the Americas when Columbus first saw it in Cuba.

Those who accept that the ancestor of corn is corn believe bands of nomads moved into valleys in Mexico (or Peru) 12,000 to 20,000 years ago and collected corn. Perhaps by tossing corn into fire the nomads discovered kernels would pop into a delicious food and began to value its seed. They might have carried seeds with them, planting them along the way.

Columbus thought the Indians called this unknown grain meys, mays, or maize. There were four groups of corn then—popcorn, flint (a smooth, starchy kernel), dent (a pitted, sweeter, thinly cased grain) and flour. All four were grown from Maine to Tierra del Fuego. A fifth group of corn, sweet corn, was not cataloged until about 1830. It was a mutation, a happy accident, with a gene that inhibits corn's natural tendency to convert sugar to starch. The gene is recessive; sweet corn crossed with other types would have starchy offspring. Still, to the first explorers, even starchy corn was a wonderfully delicious new delicacy. Columbus reported he was especially fond of Indian porridge (probably grits).

Native Americans said the gods had given them corn, and it must have seemed a miracle grain to the Europeans. Conveniently bunched in ears, adaptable to pine or rain forest, able to pollinate itself from its tassels, it clung to life on less than 10 inches of rainfall a year. It also stored well inside its husks, and if kernels were kept dry they didn't even need husks for protection. Thousand-year-old corn found in archaeological digs in Mexico was edible—much to the discoverers' dismay, who almost lost it to their burros. Corn 900 years old, found in Peru, popped when heated.

When pollen from the eared corn crossed with remaining wild corn, over thousands of years, it yielded offspring which could not seed itself. In effect, corn must have killed its ancestors, leaving behind a human-dependent plant that has filled the horizons of the world. Because man favored it, more acres today are planted in corn than in anything else, and every single grain is planted by someone.

**The May I miss is a human thing.**


## II. July

**I miss tasseling time.** For one brief, spectacular moment each year, tassels are pure gold and leaves are pure green. Corn—ordinary, controlled, rigid, economic corn—explodes with color. Before that, tassels are spindly and bland. After, leaves are brittle and brown. But for one short moment the corn is thrilling.

These days the moment is supposed to happen in July. The saying, "Knee high by the Fourth of July" is obsolete. Nowadays if corn is not head high or higher at July's end, something is wrong.

Something was wrong last summer, although to an untrained eye the drought's effects were invisible in the cornfields. Despite daily temperatures of well over 100 and no rain for weeks, the corn stood green. Cotton, soybeans, and wheat wilted or browned, but not corn. That's because the plant has some gimmicks for resisting water stress. If denied rain in the early stages of growth (the knee-high phase), it will send deep roots searching for water and produce fewer, but green, leaves. This means a short stalk but a plant still capable of photosynthesis. A field can produce some ears even during a dry summer. Water-starved leaves wilt and wrinkle into that familiar curlicue, but still carry on up to a point.

Corn is most vulnerable to drought during its reproductive phase— tasseling time. The time only lasts about ten days. It must rain then for the silks to emerge and the kernels to fill. Even without rain, some kernels will fill. Farmers' decisions not to harvest their stunted ears of field corn last summer had more to do with the cost of gasoline and their debt burdens than the lack of corn. If they had been hungry, they would have had corn to eat. What they didn't have was enough corn to pay their bills. The despair and pain of the drought was economic; as human a creation as the corn.

At tasseling time, the farmer wants one good rain. After that, the leaves of the corn will touch in the rows—*canopy*—and shelter the soil. Then the farmer need not worry again for a year about weeds or water. The corn will mature.

Until that moment, though, raising the corn will have been a trial. It can falter before weeds and pests and flop at the mere mention of hail or wind. (Later, of course, the corn's root braces, a circle of tendrils at its base, will grow stronger, and better able to hold up the plant.) Crabgrass, morning glory, honeysuckle, jimsonweed, nightshade, foxtail, pigweed—corn can be smothered by anything.

Until the advent of herbicides, there were few efficient ways to curb weeds in corn rows. Strips or blocks of a dozen or more rows were usually planted six to eight feet apart. Between strips a horse- or tractor-drawn cultivator would slow weeds. But in the rows themselves anything mechanical would disturb the shallower roots. Only a hoe could get the weeds. For generations, hoeing corn was a childhood reality, day after day, for boy or girl, rich or poor. Corn demanded hoeing.

Corn demanded guarding, too. Sparrows fed at dawn, deer, woodchuck, and squirrels raided by day, the raccoons struck at night. Farm families protected their crops by sleeping in the fields at night: dogs, kids, mom, dad, and sweethearts. It didn't help.

Raccoons in particular were legendary for their thefts and still are. They outsmart electric fences, snares, blaring radios and flashing lights. Fortunately for field corn's modern farmers, raccoons prefer sweet corn to starchy field corn. A neighbor of mine once stopped me to give me some fresh sweet corn. "Follow me," she said, and walked into a large stand of field corn. She walked through the field muttering numbers to herself. "Three to the north, five to the west, two to the east . . ."

"What are you doing?" I asked.

"I've hidden my sweet corn in the field corn," she said.

"Why?"

"To keep it from the raccoons," she said.

"Does it work—do you fool the raccoons?"

"Oh no, they always find it."

No matter how corn is grown and protected, reality is the same for every farmer: lots of work. But after the corn canopies, there is August. For the most part, all a farmer has to do is sit and listen to the corn grow, except perhaps spray for ear and stalk larvae. The time before harvest is traditionally **a time of doldrums. I miss that, too.**

## III. October

I didn't appreciate this until recently, but every field of corn I've ever seen has been hybridized. The hybrid corn revolution took place the decade before I was born. It was a true revolution, changing agriculture more than even the plow did. In a scant 10 years, hybrid corn plantings went from less than 1 percent in 1934 to 60 percent by 1944. Today hybrids account for more than 90 percent of corn acreage.

Visually, hybrids changed little. Rows are closer together. The cornfields are larger too, because the vast improvement of machines and methods since the 1930s means one farmer can do more work. But the appearance of the corn plant itself has changed little. For most of the year, a hybrid plant looks pretty much like a standard or open pollinated plant—until October.

In October, the browned corn stands tall, stalks unbroken. Before hybrids, *lodging*, or the tendency of stalks to weaken and fall, prevented harvesting by machine. The fallen ears had to be picked up by hand and tossed into a cart, one ear at a time. Later the ears would be husked and *shelled*, a word that may have come from the Indian practice of using mussel shells to pop kernels from the ears.

Shelling was often done by husking bees. Young men would hide ears with red kernels in the unhusked piles because a red ear gave the finder the right to kiss a girl. (On second thought, perhaps it was the women who hid the ears.) Huskings were friendly events; hard work, too. Hybrids changed that. If corn could stand in the field, a machine could cut it. Hybrids eliminated the red ear and the rest of it—husking, shelling, bees, and much of the labor.

Now harvesting is done by one machine. The combine cuts the stalks, shreds them, husks the ear, and shells the kernels—in seconds. In big fields at harvest time, a semi-truck keeps pace with a combine as both creep slowly up and down the field, stubble to one side, tall stalks to the other. The grain flows like liquid into the truck bed. The combine pauses only to let an empty truck pull up and the full one leave. The combine and trucks rumble from dawn until late at night, their headlights eerie as they crawl in the darkness.

A hybrid is essentially a crossing of seed from two or four varieties of standard corn (a four-way cross is a double cross, naturally). The seed produces unusually vigorous field corn which grows quickly, with greater yields, and resists heat and disease. But offspring of hybrid corn do not breed true, so seed has to be recrossed every year. If a farmer is to use it, he has to buy it from a dealer who does the crossing. Thus, the change to hybrids meant thousands of independent, stubborn, can't-even-agree-how-to-hoe-the-stuff farmers had to be persuaded to pay cash for seed they'd always gotten for free.

What convinced farmers to change so rapidly were those standing, tall stalks. A farmer who struggled to pick up 80 bushels a day by hand was a quick convert after he saw a neighbor pick 80 bushels in an hour or two. Seed dealers hardly had to talk to sell their products.

Yield levels were impressive, too. In the 1930s, hybrids gave about 25 bushels an acre; by the 1950s yields were around 50 bushels an acre. Today yields average 80 to 90 bushels an acre, even more in some places or in good weather. With 25 percent of United States cropland in corn, that equals eight billion bushels a year.

Hybrid seeds also changed adolescence. Farmers' sons and daughters, for about $7 an hour, spend their summer days detasseling seed corn. Seed companies produce their special crosses by removing the pollen-bearing tassels from stalks before they ripen. Then silks in the ear are dusted with pollen the breeders choose. The labor for the detaseling is supplied by heat-resistant, tall-standing, rural high school students, most of whom are saving the money for college and an escape from farming. **They'll miss the farm when they are gone.**

## IV. February

I almost bought a pair of cross-country skis when I first moved to Iowa. I thought that with the open country I'd have room and opportunity for the perfect exercise. I'm glad I waited to buy them. There's snow enough. In some parts of corn country, there's snow from November to March. But these days wise farmers leave a formidable, foot-high stubble in their fields. Stubble holds soil from wind and water erosion during the winter. But it makes skiing tricky to impossible. I'm not complaining. Stalks through snow are like stitching on a quilt—delicate, subtle in pattern.

I used to think when the snow quilts appeared, the corn was gone, but after time in corn country I realized most corn never leaves the farm. The silver bins or blue towers beside every barn hold most of the corn I'd seen growing in summer. Why grow it if it only sits in bins, I'd ask my neighbors. They'd say they were waiting for the price to change.

Yields have become so bountiful that productivity has long outstripped human or even animal needs. Half the crop, at least in this country, is unprocessed animal feed. When Indians were first asked by settlers for grain for horses, it was given as a courtesy only. To Indians it was an insult to give the grain of the gods to mere beasts of burden. Today beasts eat half of it. One 48-pound bushel of corn equals about 10 pounds of hog.

Droughts may have some impact on that bounty, particularly if, as some climatologists predict, they become more frequent. Yet hybrid breeding and growing techniques are already offsetting the change in climate. Crossing deep rooting varieties with large-eared ones shows promise. Another idea is to breed for changed leaf shapes. A more upright posture reduces the amount of water loss.

One technique that's worked is to spray corn with a growth retardant early in the season. This, in a sense, fools the plant. It grows shorter, with deeper roots as if it were suffering from drought, so that later, when it really is dry, the plant is tougher. Another experimental method is to spray the leaves with anti-transpirants, chemicals which slow water evaporation from leaves. **Corn is a human creation. Its problems may have human solutions.**

Once, 90 percent of corn went to feed, but the last 20 years have changed the ratios. Twenty-five percent now goes to export—the dollar, climate, and geopolitical shenanigans permitting. Export corn has lately spent much time in those bins. It'll keep—a thousand years if it has to—and there are some farmers, I think, stubborn enough to wait that long.

Thirteen percent of the annual crop goes to industrial uses. Industry means food, but it also means fuel, consumer products, and novelties (yes, there is still a market for corncob pipes). The remainder, about 12 percent, is euphemistically called carryover. That means it, too, sits in bins waiting for a drought and an accompanying price jump.

There is an abundance of ideas for what to do with the abundance. Take corn starch. A 48-pound bushel, when processed, yields 31.5 pounds of starch, 12 pounds of processed feed, three pounds of meal, and 1.5 pounds of oil. The 31.5 pounds of starch in turn can be processed into 33 pounds of sweeteners or 2.5 gallons of ethanol (plus 17 pounds of carbon dioxide to become carbonation in beverages or dry ice). The sweeteners are dextrose, used in cake mixes or to feed yeasts for baked goods; syrups, used in canned fruits and ice cream; and fructose for soda pop. Over 300 million bushels a year go into soft drinks. The beverage industry's switch to corn sweeteners means that, in 1981, for the first time in history, corn as human food surpassed wheat.

Americans annually swallow about 650 million bushels of wheat but 880 million bushels of corn in ice cream, donuts, jams, chewing gum, peanut butter, instant tea, marshmallows, gelatin, wine, processed cheese, medications, vitamins—and soda pop. One American, the United States Commerce Department estimates, annually consumes 73 pounds of corn sweeteners, but only three pounds of corn flakes.

While the food industry accounts for two thirds of corn's industrial use, the remaining nonfood uses of starch can get pretty exotic. One of the new uses for starch has been in the disposable diaper. Those babies on television, cooing with dry delight, are sitting on several million bushels of corn.

Paper production is the biggest single use for starch, but the most familiar is probably ethanol, an additive to gasoline. Researchers have been trying to figure how to make ethanol desulfurize coal, a technology that would radically change both industries.

Another new industrial application is to process starch into methylglucoside, a plastic. Enthusiasts think corn plastic can take over the trash bag industry. Methylglucoside bags are thicker than conventional ones and feel silky, not sticky (touching one is like rubbing corn starch). But they are also biodegradable. Corn plastic breaks down after being buried for seven months, petroleum-based plastic never disintegrates. Farmers with full bins have high hopes for methylglucoside.

Summer sweet corn is such a small fraction of the corn industry that corn producers don't bother to keep statistics on it. Most sweet corn isn't grown in corn country, anyway. It's grown on small truck farms in California, Texas, and New Jersey. The corn I miss is the starchy kind, but I'm told if you pick it just before it's ripe and roast it, it's as sweet as sweet corn. I've never tried this, and **now that there are woods, not fields, outside my window I'm sorry I missed that.**

## NOTES

1. Harry Middleton, "Masked Survivor," *Southern Living*, February 1985, p. 22+.
2. David Petersen, "Backyard Bandits," *Mother Earth News*, January/February 1987, pp. 66–69.
3. John Yurus, "The Raccoon Unmasked," *Country Journal*, July 1988, pp. 34–40.
4. Calvin Trillin, "Uncivil Liberties," *The Nation*, September 7, 1985, p. 168.
5. "Notes and Comments," *New Yorker*, September 30, 1985, pp. 25–26.
6. Eric Frederick Jensen, "A Vermont Corn Cage," *Organic Gardening*, February 1984, pp. 144–145.
7. Lee Eisenberg, "The Raccoon and the Hummingbird," *Esquire*, October 1989, p. 43.
8. Bill Tarrant, "Listening in the Dark," *Field & Stream*, January 1989, p. 94+.
9. Robert Cooke, "Raccoons and Rabies," *Technology Review*, May/June 1987, pp. 15–16.
10. Alan M. Beck, "An Epizootic of Rabies," *Natural History*, July 1984, pp. 6–8+.
11. Patricia Westfall, "The Corn," *Country Journal*, July 1989, pp. 20–26.

## RACCOON ARTICLES
## (In Reverse Date Order)

Tarrant, Bill. "Coon of the Yellow Moon." *Field & Stream*, May 1991, p. 80+.

"One Paw ahead of the Law." *Newsweek*, May 27, 1991, p. 66+.

Tarrant, Bill. "Greatest Hound That Ever Lived." *Field & Stream*, November 1990, pp. 104–105.

Kadlecek, Mary. "Rabies Claims Another Wildlife Victim in New York State." *The Conservationist*, May/June 1990, p. 54.

Tarrant, Bill. "Jimmy Kimmery and the Saddle Horse." *Field & Stream*, December 1989, pp. 102–103.

Eisenberg, Lee. "The Raccoon and the Hummingbird." *Esquire*, October 1989, p. 43.

Sun, Marjorie. "Virginia OKs Rabies Vaccine Test." *Science*, July 14, 1989, p. 126.

Sun, Marjorie. "South Carolina Blocks Test of Rabies Vaccine." *Science*, June 30, 1989, p. 153.

Mueller, Larry. "A Hound's Start in Life." *Outdoor Life*, February 1989, pp. 43–44.

Tarrant, Bill. "Listening in the Dark." *Field & Stream*, January 1989, p. 94+.

Hershey, Daniel L. "Help! There's a Raccoon in My Chimney." *The Conservationist*, November/December 1988, pp. 34–39.

Yurus, John. "The Raccoon Unmasked." *Country Journal*, July 1988, pp. 34–40.

Mueller, Larry. "Starting Coonhounds the Easy Way." *Outdoor Life*, March 1988, p. 46+.

Berendt, John. "The Raccoon Coat." *Esquire*, January 1988, p. 22.

Cooke, Robert. "Raccoons and Rabies." *Technology Review*, May/June 1987, pp. 15–16.

Petersen, David, "Backyard Bandits." *Mother Earth News*, January/February 1987, pp. 66–69.

"Raccoons and Rabies: An Eastern Urban Threat." *Mother Earth News*, January/February 1987, p. 69.

Ikeda, Hiroshi. "Old Dogs, New Treks." *Natural History*, August 1986, pp. 38–45.

Freiherr, Gregory. "Vaccine Sandwich to Go." *Science 86*, July/August 1986, p. 68+.

"Panda Pedigree: Giant and Lesser." *Science News*, October 5, 1985, p. 216.

"Raccoons Live It Up in Town." *National Geographic World*, October 1985, pp. 24–29.

"Notes and Comments." *New Yorker*, September 30, 1985, pp. 25–26.

Trillin, Calvin. "Uncivil Liberties." *The Nation*, September, 1985, p. 168.

Lipske, Mike. "Night Stalker!" *National Wildlife*, June/July 1985, pp. 20–24.

Moser, Penny Ward. "Rocky Times for Rocky." *Discover*, May 1985, pp. 72–77.

Middleton, Harry. "Masked Survivor." *Southern Living*, February 1985, p. 22+.

"Raccoons Harbor Lethal Parasite." *Prevention*, February 1985, p. 11.

Beck, Alan M. "An Epizootic of Rabies." *Natural History*, July 1984, pp. 6–8+.

Jensen, Eric Frederick. "A Vermont Corn Cage." *Organic Gardening*, February 1984, pp. 144–145.

Mueller, Larry. "Computer Coonhunting." *Outdoor Life*, October 1983, p. 142+.

"A Taste for Raccoon." *FDA Consumer*, October 1983, p. 37.

Mueller, Larry. "Raccoons to Remember." *Outdoor Life*, April 1983, pp. 93–96.

Bashline, Sylvia. "The Trapper's Larder." *Field & Stream*, February 1983, p. 74+.

# Chapter

# 4

# *Form*

## The Linzer Torte

This is the difference between New York and San Francisco.

In New York on the East Side in Little Hungary there used to be a bakery which displayed among its black pumpernickels a confection; no, a creation; no, ambrosia itself: a cookie. As a Chicago native, I may have been wise in the ways of pizza, but I was innocent of this milieu. It was a cookie, yes, but lushly smothered with powdered sugar and filled with—what?

"Raspberry," the baker said.

"Wonderful," I said. "May I have one of those raspberry cookies please?"

"No," the baker said.

"No? What do you mean 'no'?"

"No. I mean 'no.' "

"Why not?"

"Because they are not raspberry cookies."

"What are they?"

"Linzer tortes. Can you say that?"

I glared at him. No one had spoken to me in that tone of voice since the third grade. How badly did I want a—whatsit.

"Linsi tart?" I said.

"No, lin-zer-torte."

"Lin-zer-torte."

Apparently I wanted it badly. For weeks I struggled with the phrase. Linda's tart. Linley tech. Lindar touch. When I finally learned it, the baker seemed sad. He had enjoyed our language lessons.

New York insisted on teaching me lessons in particulars: the right word, the right museum, the right restaurant, the right wardrobe, the right wall decor, the right junk foods (hot dogs with sauerkraut, bagels with cream cheese). One must have taste, the right tastes, to be a New Yorker.

In San Francisco, the bakeries were as lushly endowed as New York's, but different.

"Order a bagel," my friend and host advised. I did and it arrived drenched in alfalfa sprouts.

"What's this?" I said.

The waitress was puzzled by the question. "That's how they come," she said.

I looked at my friend. He smiled. "Welcome to San Francisco," he said.

Sprouts on a bagel? To a New Yorker, even a Chicago New Yorker, this was not right. Interesting, yes, but not right. Nothing about San Francisco was right. My host took me to Coit Tower on Telegraph Hill where we admired the murals and read plaques as tourists should. Then we left, exiting the hilltop by slipping through a gap in a stone wall onto a path of wooden steps. Down we walked until we reached a platform, a boardwalk, complete with green street sign. When I looked to either side, I could see door fronts peeking from among the vines and shrubbery.

"Is this a street?"

"Yes."

"How do people get in and out?"

"See that?" Two men went by struggling with a dresser. "That's how."

We descended to another "street" and turned left. My friend chose a door, then knocked. When a woman answered, his face fell.

"Where's Barbara?" he said.

"She moved about three weeks ago."

"Oh no. I wanted to show Pat the apartment."

To my astonishment, the woman invited us in where we were treated to an expanse of windows and an extravagant view of the Bay. I glanced behind me, back toward the door, and a calico cat walked through a sunbeam among the flowers.

None of this was quite right. It was perfect, too perfect—the view; the cat; the utter impossibility (at least to a Chicago New Yorker) that someone would risk strangers in her apartment. I was overwhelmed by the moment and asked to stop a while. We settled into a coffee shop/bakery, and there—as if I had not had enough perfection for one day—was a linzer torte beyond description.

"May I have a linzer torte, please?" I asked the baker.

"What?" she said.

"That, the linzer torte," I said.

"Ah, you mean the raspberry cookie," she said.

"Yes," I said, "the raspberry cookie."

I live in Ohio now.

## A PROBLEM OF DEFINITION

What is this story about? Differences among places. What is this story about *really*? How wrong a place can be for a person. How someone might not belong in a place. When I wrote the first draft, I didn't know any of this. I discovered the focus, the *really*, as I wrote the last sentence, "I live in Ohio now." The sentence popped out and I thought as it did, "That's it; I'm writing about how much I hated New York." Until then I thought I was writing about linzer tortes.

So, I've written a piece with a clear topic and focus. I'm ready to publish, right? I wish. Still ahead is the problem of form. If the story above is ever to be printed, it must be reworked into a form liked by the editor of a target magazine. But what is form? The *Concise Oxford Dictionary of Literary Terms*[1] defines "form" as a term "with a confusing variety of meanings." If august Oxford dons are intimidated by the word, no wonder writing and editing are elusive crafts. Form will take some time to explain.

Roger Fowler, editor of *A Dictionary of Modern Critical Terms*, is more daring than the Oxford crowd. He defines "form" as "the *way* something is said in contrast to *what* is said":

> Even though form and content may be inseparable for the "full meaning" of a work, the paraphrasable content may nevertheless be used to enable the concept of form to be discussed.[2]

In that muddy sentence, Fowler is trying to say content is anything that can be paraphrased, and form is anything that would be ruined by paraphrasing. He means form and content are inseparable, but a rational mind can pretend they are separate. We are smart enough, he is saying, to ignore the *topic*, "linzer tortes," and examine the *form*, "narration." The limitation of Fowler's definition is that it leaves out the reader. It assumes that we can study language without considering the people who use it. But readers experience reading. Form must have something to do with readers reading.

A definition of form that does include readers, and one of my favorites, is by W. Ross Winterowd, who begins with the playful description of form as "the alligator-infested morass of making sense." Then he goes on to write in *Composition/Rhetoric: A Synthesis*:

> What you derive from a text as a reader is, in a sense, its form. That is, you usually don't remember the details but retain something of the general tenor and perhaps the structure of the plot or argument. The form of the text for you, the reader, is what you retain in memory.[3]

While this idea, that a reader's memories are form, is beguiling, and though it does allow for reader impact on form, it's not practical enough for a working writer. Readers may experience reading, but writers experience editors. Editors hack and slash, move and meld, mangle and patch copy, and no writer experiences it as "being read." It's called "being edited" and it's a far more aggressive process than being—in Winterowd's gentle phrase—"retained in memory."

The definition I prefer is that form is *"a set of expectations."* For example, if I write:

> This is the
>
> Difference
>
> Between New York and San
>
> Francisco

the opening words from "The Linzer Torte," the content is the same, but the form has changed. In this case the form change is structural, from paragraphs to lines, but a host of new expectations arises because of that change. The work has become a poem (even if a bad one). Readers thus assume its meaning is larger than the words. New York must be a metaphor for something and San Francisco for something else and that word "difference" no doubt contains clues to the meaning of life. The words are identical, but in poetry form they raise reader expectations. The form, not the meaning or the merits of the language, does this.

If I had written the same sentence as the ending or final sentence of the story, another set of expectations would come into play. Readers know from experience that the ending of a story limits meaning. This sentence could be ironic ("These cities are virtually the same if all that differs is the name of a cookie"), or comic ("How silly to limit perception of something as complex as a city to a cookie") or informational ("Travelers, be aware that food and culture change within countries as well as among countries"). The exact meaning of the sentence would depend on what had preceded it, but its placement at the end will shape readers' interpretations. The ending is a point of emphasis so the sentence will be assumed to be important.

Since the sentence is at the beginning of the story, the actual expectation aroused is that the word "this" will be clarified. Readers don't know if the clarity will be comic or serious, but they can be confident an explanation will follow. They know from years of reading that a beginning is a promise of what is to come. Form, not content, has shaped these expectations.

This idea of form as expectations can be thought of as something like conventions in sport. A football field is similar to, but different from, a hockey rink, as are the equipment, scoring and strategies of the games. Fans know this. They do not expect a hockey player to pick up the puck and throw a forward pass or a football tight end to trot out on the field in ice skates. Form restrains the players but within these restraints are an infinite number of possibilities. Hence the fascination of the games.

For writers, form is less restrictive than it is in sports. Language has no official umpires or rule books (although there are many unofficial or self-appointed ones).

Despite the absence of umpires, the fans—the readers—exert considerable control over writers. Or rather, editors acting on their behalf do. The cynical view might be that form is "editor tyranny," but editing is too complicated an intellectual process for cynicism. More accurate might be that form is an editor's *interpretation* of readers' expectations.

Sometimes that interpretive process is intuitive or even egocentric. Other times it is intensely researched, using every demographic and psychographic tool available. Most editors seem to operate between those two extremes, with intuition and research being equally important to them. But however editors may edit, the consequence for writers is that the forms expected are complex and subtle. If a writer is to figure them out, the task of analysis can't involve just a glance at a magazine. To sell my linzer torte piece, I must intimately know a magazine's forms. As with focuses, the burden is on me to figure out what options I have. When I know what forms a magazine wants, I will know what to do with my linzer torte idea.

To analyze form in a magazine I study four things—*subject, purpose, effect* and *genre*. I need all four because none alone tells me enough about what editors expect. Each can be thought of as an aspect of form. When I study the four aspects, I am trying to determine the *mix* and *range* for each.

When I finish an analysis, I will have a portrait of the magazine's forms— literally, because I chart and graph my observations. Charts? Graphs? Yes. Form is complex. Only a sophisticated analytical device will unlock it. Before describing how to do the charts and graphs, though, I need to explain those six terms—subject, purpose, effect, genre, mix and range.

## SUBJECT

"Subject" means the topic categories a magazine expects. A professor of composition wouldn't consider subject an aspect of form at all. "Science" is a subject, but a science article could be "remembered" by a reader as "funny," "informational," "full of people" or "argumentive." So calling "science writing" a form is too casual for serious scholarship. Few composition scholars study "subject" as an aspect of form. Subject is *content* to them. Professional magazine editors, however, disagree. Subject matter is very much a part of reader "expectations." Consequently, many journalism (as opposed to composition) textbooks have chapters that explain the science or business or sports or travel article as if each were a distinct form.

There are a few stylistic differences among these subject groups that could be considered "nonparaphrasable form." Sports articles tend to be nimble with verbs. ("Braves bag big one in ninth.") Science articles tend to always explain how the experiment was done, not just what was learned. Travel articles tend to have lush descriptions.

Except for those stylistic conventions, it's difficult to find qualities of "subject" forms that are unique to the form. Science articles can be as lively as sports pieces, if the editors choose. Yet, even so, subject as a concept for describing form is a pervasive way of thinking in the magazine business. Common subject categories covered in journalism textbooks include

travel (places)
history (events)
biography (profile, interview)
autobiography (personal narration)
nature (animals, gardening)
culture (media, music, pop culture)
business (finance, industry)
science (technology, computers)
law
philosophy (morals, theology, inspiration, ethics)
political science (government)
criticism
social issues (environment, women, minorities)
lifestyle (health, home, food)
sports (fitness)

When analyzing subject expectations of a magazine, I don't limit myself to "textbook"-approved categories. Magazines do have a limited palette of subject matter, but they're subtle. No magazine fits purely into any one of the above groups. For example, *Sports Illustrated* does sports. But it also does nature and lifestyle, some business, some ethics. Magazines do try to limit the range of their subject matter, but even with limits, the range of their coverage is far broader than any list I've yet to find in a textbook. While analyzing, you need to keep your mind open, alert to the opportunities of a magazine's subject range. *Sports Illustrated* does sports, right? It will never do raspberries, right? But while researching the linzer torte piece, I discovered that grouse hunters in Scotland stuff their birds with raspberries. With a little creative focusing maybe I could get a linzer torte piece in *Sports Illustrated* after all.

## PURPOSE

"Purpose" means that the *writer's intentions* shape the style—or form—of the article. Purposes of writers differ. Sometimes the writer wants to persuade, sometimes to warn, sometimes to contrast, sometimes to describe. Writers *create* and editors *select* purposes. The purposes editors prefer or expect determine a magazine's identity.

In theory there could be millions of purposes, since there are millions of writers, each with a private agenda. But in reality, there are only a few traditional purposes, long recognized by scholars. Plato was the first thinker to argue for a limited number of rhetorical purposes or reasons for writing. He identified—or at least only admired—three. These were to generate understanding, to stimulate recollection and to elevate the soul. Aristotle, history's first genius at one-up-manship, argued for *four* purposes of composition: to make truth prevail, to instruct others, to debate issues and to defend a point of view. Not much has changed in the intervening 2,300 years, except that thinkers have found a few more admirable purposes for writing. Some of them are the following, commonly taught in freshman composition courses—and easily found in magazines too:

*To Inform.*    Information about a subject is used to shape and limit the content. Facts, facts, facts. For example:

> Linz, for which the linzer torte is named, is a city in Austria.

*To Explain.*    Telling the "why" behind the facts becomes the intent:

> Hungarians believe they must have invented the linzer torte because they produce more raspberries than Austria. In fact, they are the world's second largest producer, after the former Soviet Union.

*To Share an Experience.*    Information also matters in a piece that has sharing as the goal, but this form uses private experiences to unveil the facts:

> It was a cookie, yes, but lushly smothered with powdered sugar and filled with—what? "Raspberry," the baker said.

*To Describe.*    Colors. Sensations. Shapes. Again, information is important in a descriptive piece, but sensory details are the mechanisms for revealing the information:

> The cookie I remembered was daisy-shaped; it had two layers of pastry with the jam between. A hole was cut into the top layer to let the jam peek through. Powdered sugar drenched the whole.

*To Analyze.*    "Analyze" means to break a whole down into component parts and examine each part one at a time. Usually, the writers of freshman textbooks intend something quite intellectual. (What are the roots of the American Civil War?) But the following is an analysis, too. It examines component parts:

> *Linzer Torte*
> 1. Beat together until light and fluffy 1¼ c. softened margarine, ¾ c. sugar, 1 tsp. lemon juice, ½ tsp. ground cinnamon and one egg.

2. Stir in 2½ c. flour and ½ c. ground almonds. Chill one hour.

3. Set aside ⅓ of dough. Press remaining dough into jelly roll pan (approx. 16 × 10 × 1) or into two 8-inch pie plates. Spread preserves evenly in pans. Roll out remaining dough; cut into thin strips; arrange over jam in lattice pattern.

4. Bake at 350 degrees approx. 30 minutes or until golden brown. Cool before cutting.

***To Tell a Story.***    "Once upon a time," or narration, may be the world's oldest form. It, too, details information and issues but these are secondary to character, plot or theme. Nonfiction can be in narrative form; in fact, some magazines specialize in narrative or "literary" nonfiction:

> "Order a bagel," my friend and host advised. I did and it arrived drenched in alfalfa sprouts.
> "What's this?" I said.
> The waitress was puzzled by the question. "That's how they come," she said.
> I looked at my friend. He smiled. "Welcome to San Francisco," he said.

***To Define.***    This, perhaps the most difficult of purposes, is illustrating an idea in terms of other ideas. It is difficult because the terms that explain the idea have to also be clear. Does a reader, in this era of the Pop-tart and Eskimo Pie, really know what a pie or cookie is? If not, the example below makes no sense.

> In Europe, a torte is similar to a pie, and a biscuit, if sweet, is like our cookie.

***To Give Examples.***    This is to illustrate an idea in terms of concrete realities instead of abstract terms:

> Americans use three words for the European biscuit. A biscuit in America is bread made with baking powder or soda. A cracker is also made with baking soda, but flattened and heavy with salt. A cookie is yet another baking powder flat bread but laden with sugar. Sometimes a cookie is more than a cookie, however. Nabisco Foods recently aired a television commercial in which a child was about to be scolded by his mother for eating cookies in bed. When he said it was a Fig Newton, she said that was all right.

***To Classify.***    This means to organize facts into naturally related groups. The groups then control all further discussion. This chapter on "forms," since it's organized, in part, around the six ideas of subject, purpose, effect, genre, mix and range, is an example of this form. Here's another, simpler example:

1. Biscuits: corn bread, plain biscuits, blueberry muffins, hush puppies, bran muffins.
2. Crackers (usually machine-made): soda, Wheat Thins, Triscuits, graham.
3. Cookies: sugar, icebox, macaroons, spice drop, chocolate chip, peanut butter.

***To Compare and/or Contrast.***    To illustrate an idea, using realities that are strongly similar or strongly different. Analogy is a special kind of comparison that uses something unlike the subject to illustrate some ineffable quality of the topic:

> *Comparison*: A linzer torte tastes like a turnover;
>
> *Contrast*: although it does not have the yeasty or flaky feel that a turnover does;
>
> *Analogy*: but the way the raspberry flavor bursts over the taste of the pastry is something like the surprise of a jack-in-the box—expected, but not expected.

***To Show Cause and Effect.***    Here, the purpose of the writer is to argue that there is a connection between one set of facts and another set. This is similar to explanation in that the why matters more than the facts themselves. But now the writer's claim is more audacious. Something caused something. Cause and effect is a form peculiarly prey to fallacy because it might be based on speculation. Is the following cause/effect relationship true? I don't know. All the facts cited are true, so perhaps it's true:

> Few raspberries grow in Austria, so the claim of the Austrian city, Linz, to the linzer torte may have more to do with a bridge than with raspberry fields. Linz for many years had the only bridge over the Danube for hundreds of miles. The bridge, built in 1497, made the city a center of commerce attracting vendors from all over the region including, no doubt, from the raspberry-choked plains of Hungary. People buying their tortes in Linz probably mislabeled them "Linzer tortes," even though technically they were "the tortes brought to Linz."

***To Persuade.***    The writer wants the reader to believe as he or she does. This form goes beyond fact, beyond information to reveal the writer's heart and soul:

> Some swear by the chocolate chip. Some live their lives by the vanilla wafer. But I have seen the linzer torte and I have much to tell.

***To Praise (or Condemn).***    The writer wants the reader to know his or her values:

> The best linzer tortes are made not in Austria but in New York on the East Side near 86th Street.

**TABLE 4.1**  Example of a record: Annual production of raspberries by country (top 10)

| Country | Thousand Metric Tons |
|---|---|
| U.S.S.R. | 120 |
| Hungary | 25 |
| Yugoslavia | 24 |
| West Germany | 22 |
| United Kingdom | 17 |
| Poland | 14 |
| U.S.A. | 12 |
| Bulgaria | 9 |
| Canada | 7 |
| France | 5 |

SOURCE: *Food & Nutrition Encyclopedia*, Pegus Press, Clovis, Calif., 1983, p. 1909. Copyright 1983 by Pegus Press.

***To Record or Report.***     These forms are particularly important in news or trade magazines. Both forms give facts for the sake of general knowledge, but a record is information preserved or recorded as it happens, while a report gathers facts after they happen or have been recorded. Table 4.1 is an example of a record, whereas an example of a report would be this:

> Hungary is the second largest producer of raspberries in the world. Austria's berry production is so low it doesn't even place among the top ten.

There are many more purposes like these: to ask questions, to answer questions, to respond, to inspire, to characterize. It's not important to memorize some list of three, four or forty approved purposes. Instead, understand that purpose helps create form. Tone of language, types of facts (i.e., content), style, even focus or theme (content again) can yield to purpose. All magazines have some purposes they prefer. All writers have some purposes they do best. The goal should be a good match. This is important because the differences in form caused by purpose are extreme. All of the examples above are about linzer tortes or raspberries, but matter-of-fact tables on Hungarian raspberry yields bear no resemblance—in form—to the passions of that chocolate chip hater. If purpose can shape such extreme differences in just sentences, imagine the differences in whole articles or magazines. This is why understanding a magazine means trying to get a feel for the purposes it usually selects.

## EFFECT

Effect, in a sense, is the opposite of purpose. Instead of emphasizing the writer, it emphasizes the reader. An effect is a description of *impact on the reader*. When Winterowd described form as "what you retain in memory," he was trying to discuss this idea. It is rare, however, for a scholar or textbook writer to risk making lists of approved effects. Scholars, from Plato on, are bold when enumerating *purposes* writers should emulate but less venturesome in asserting what *effects* readers are supposed to feel—with good reason. Who could know? Unless one hears the reader laugh, sees the reader cry, how can a piece be labeled humorous or sad? The *intent* may have been to entertain or move the emotions, but the *effect* of felt humor or pain is unmeasurable unless the reader is assertive enough to write the editor.

Scholarly reluctance to describe effects is recent. Nineteenth-century composition books did promote effects as realizable goals for writers. An 1875 text, *Advanced Course of Composition and Rhetoric: A Series of Practical Lessons,* by G. P. Quackenbos,[4] lists these effects as worthy ideals in its table of contents:

The Sublime (four chapters)

The Beautiful

Gracefulness

Wit

Humor and Ridicule

Purity (two chapters)

Precision

Harmony

I think Quackenbos's list is charming, and I'm sorry such thinking is out of scholarly fashion, yet I sympathize with modern scholars who find using such terms too risky. These ideals can have meaning only if the reader truly responds to The Beautiful as beauty, Wit as funny and Harmony as harmonious. These are emotions to be felt by the readers, not facts to be communicated by writers.

But, if scholars are timid, editors constantly talk about effects. They calculate whether readers will enjoy a piece or learn from it, laugh at or be stirred to action by it, admire it or become outraged. Judging effects is crucial to editing, even if most editors experience it as an intuitive process. Emotions as felt by readers cannot be checked like facts, yet predicting those emotions accurately is the secret to editorial job security. Scholars may be cautious about describing effect, but not so editors. If editors cannot calculate effect, they don't last long in the game.

Because judging effects is almost entirely subjective, using effect as an analytical tool is essentially guesswork. Effect is best gauged if you use it as an idea when reading. Ask, while reading, what effect you *think* a piece of writing was supposed to have on the reader. Don't ask, "What effect did the writing have on *you*?" You are not the reader, but a writer. If you resemble the reader personally, perhaps the task is easier, but if you limit yourself to analyzing only magazines you personally like to read, you will publish very little. Imagine the experience of the article from the reader's point of view. Was the reader supposed to

- do something (try a recipe, make a workbench, stop a bad habit, lose weight, try a wild lipstick)?
- feel a mood (nostalgia, happiness, pride)?
- affirm or challenge a value (save the ozone layer, feed the homeless, improve the schools, cherish families)?
- worry about a problem (will the deficit be controlled, can the gypsy moth be eradicated, will scientists find the cause of multiple sclerosis, will Di and Charles get back together)?
- stop worrying about a problem (fat in moderation is good for you, alcohol in moderation is good for you, you don't need as much exercise as you think, it's normal to feel blue on the holidays, your 2-year-old will outgrow those tantrums)?
- accept things as they are (learning to live with the death of a loved one, learning to love a companion's bad habits, seeing retirement as the beginning of a new life for you)?

Your trying to deduce effects of an article may be subjective, but it is still analysis. That is, to do it, your reading must shift from passive to active. The list above is much shorter than the one for purposes because, in reality, you are on your own to think of effects. Selecting your own verbs, creating your own catalog of effects, is the best way to read actively. It may seem idiosyncratic to invent your own textbook this way, but doing it gives you information about the magazine that will help you forge a topic into a form an editor will like. The value of reading for effect is, as with subjects and purposes, that all magazines have effects they prefer, and all writers are more adept at creating certain ones. Understanding a magazine means trying to get a feel for the effects it usually selects, and then deciding whether you can or want to match those preferences.

## GENRE

Genre, French for "kind" or "type" or "category," refers to the tradition of formal, codified (i.e., cast in stone) patterns for organizing writing (or in magazines organizing pages). In compositional theory, the main structural ideas, of course, are poetry and prose. Poetry presumably has lines and prose has paragraphs (although the danger of coding by structure is immediately obvious with a prose poem). Prose genres recognized in composition theory include drama, the short story and the novel. Some theories recognize the expository essay as a genre as well.

Journalism codifies its genres far more strictly than these but, ironically, rarely calls them genres. They're called styles sometimes, as in "the inverted pyramid style" or the "I-style." But mostly they're not labeled at all. Textbooks will discuss "the photo essay" or "the sidebar" or "the spread" and never mention that these could be considered genres, even though much is said about how to create the form. For example, the inverted pyramid idea is described as putting important ideas in the first paragraph and then arraying ideas of decreasing importance in later paragraphs. Another familiar genre is the news feature, usually described as an "hour glass"; this means it has a big splashy opening pegged to a current news story; a quieter middle; and a splashy ending, which echoes the opening. The magazine article genre, when codified in how-to books, is supposed to have a hook opening with a focus state-ment; then development, usually with several subtopics; and a forceful conclusion.

One weakness of journalistic models like these is that they tend to ignore reality. Rare is the news story in a pure pyramid, or news feature in an hour glass, or magazine article with tidy beginning, middle and end. There are hundreds more possibilities, few of which have ever been named or described in textbooks but many of which are familiar to any working editor. Some are

- the picture story (photos with captions)
- the picture text or index (photos with very long captions)
- the sidebar or box (charts or text accompanying a main story)
- the spread (an article placed on facing pages to maximize impact of text, display type and images)
- the dot piece (typographic devices put in front of every point; this list you are reading is in dot style; other terms for the dots are bullets, deltas and dingbats; the devices can be anything—dots, stars, asterisks, squares, hearts, bars)
- The how-to or recipe (step-by-step organization, often with numerals or deltas)
- the BME, or traditional (for beginning, middle, end)
- the classic (a BME with elegance)
- the short (a little BME)
- the item (just facts, no real organization)
- the digression (a complete little article buried within an article)
- the department (meaning it matches the *form* of other departments in the issue)
- the feature (it deliberately varies in *form* from other articles in the issue—meaning textbooks that try to describe "feature writing" as having

some kind of formula miss the reality at most magazines, that the "features" are the ones that *don't* follow a formula)

- the Q/A (questions and answers; a variation is the advice column)
- the pro/con (both sides are presented, sometimes in separate articles)
- the special section (a group of related articles)
- the "just us" (something the magazine has invented and probably tried to register as a trademark so no one can steal it; *Harper's* has its "Index," *Newsweek* its "My Turn," *Spy* its reviews of reviewers, *Glamour* its "Do's and Don't's")

A purist, the sort who thinks things have been going downhill since Plato, would argue that an idea that is unique can't be a genre. Genre implies a group; it is a class or category of something. But the "just us" items form a category because all have the same function—to set the magazine apart from its rivals. Every magazine has to have a gimmick. Understanding a magazine means trying to get a feel for the gimmicks—er, genres—it usually selects.

## MIX AND RANGE

Form, then, is a set of editor expectations. The four concepts described so far—subject, purpose, effect and genre—are aspects of those expectations. But you cannot make sense of the aspects unless you can detect patterns. The secret for observing patterns is to look for mix and range.

*Mix* is just that: subject, purpose, effect or genre will be mixed in predictable amounts in every issue. There will always be so many features, so many helping articles or so many beauty pieces. Mix is usually easy for editors to describe. Some editors can tell you down to the inch how much of any given element will be in their mix. Here would be some typical descriptions of their mixes:

*Subject mix.* No talking animals. Adventure stories are what we want, the more outdoorsy the better—camping, fishing, hiking. We will do one or two sports items per issue, but we're not a sports book. Lots of regional flavor. No history.

*Purpose mix.* We like about a third of our pieces each issue to be straight reporting—just the facts, and in depth. Occasionally we run opinion or instructional pieces, but no personal narratives.

*Effect mix.* Our goal is to help the reader realize her potential. Articles should never talk down to her, but always treat her as a thinker, someone who makes up her own mind. She has fought hard for her independence and our articles affirm her achievement.

*Genre mix.* We do about 30 percent features, 20 percent shorts and one long photo essay per issue. We like sidebars—lots. Don't write long, dense copy—break it up with subheads, italics, anything. Keep your text lively. Length—2,500 words maximum; most articles run about 1500 words.

None of the above descriptions is from a real magazine, but they are all typical in tone. When editors say things like these, they are handing out clues to their mix. Writers need to figure out a magazine's mix in order to exploit it.

*Range* is a more subtle idea. This means the extremes. All magazines have things they will and will not do. The fringes of their preferences are the edges of their range. For example, a cooking magazine may occasionally do a health article; it's part of their subject range. But they will always turn down a table decorating idea; it's out of their subject range. Likewise they may do many recipes but only a few interviews; recipes are the mainstay of their genre range, but interviews are at the edge, at the extreme limit of their range.

Editors sometimes have more difficulty explaining range than they do mix. A typical sentence in editorial guidelines might be, "We're looking for fresh, new ideas." Translation: "We want ideas that are at the edges of our range." Reality: "We don't want things that go beyond that range." Why did *Sports Illustrated* run an *Audubon*-style article on the life and times of the earthworm? Why did *Audubon* run a *New Yorker*-style piece on the Army Corps of Engineers?

Both articles were definitely at the fringes for each magazine. But both make sense; a sports magazine covers fishing, and worms have a tangential connection to fishing. And the Corps of Engineers, for better or worse, affects wildlife habitat. The two articles were outside the magazines' normal ranges but not totally off the scale. The writer who knows where the edges of a magazine's range are can often make a sale. Editors really are looking for fresh ideas; such ideas are to be found at the edges of a range. If a writer wants to break in, this is where to do it, at the edge, not beyond the edge.

But how can you detect a magazine's range? Understanding a magazine's mix can be as easy as surveying titles for several issues. Understanding its range, how-ever, means subtle thinking. This is why I need charts and graphs. A magazine's range is invisible to me unless I draw it. Once I have a picture of the magazine's range, then I can develop a strategy for marketing articles to it. Here's how to do it.

## Step One: Background

First, of course, select magazines to analyze. They should be ones you think could have some interest in your topic, but try not to be too restrictive in your thinking. Slightly tangential magazines can be great targets.

One place to look for ideas is *Ulrich's International Periodicals Directory*, which lists more than 116,000 magazines—more than any other reference tool. It is organized by subject (668 categories of them). Thousands of potential target mar-kets are in SRDS (for Standard Rate & Data Service). Its *Consumer, Business* and *Newspaper* editions list every U.S. publication that takes over ten pages of national advertising a year. The *Business* volume is very important simply because it has the most magazines. For example, two magazines for the baking industry listed in this volume, *Bakery Production & Management* and *Modern Baking*, I thought might be interested in something on linzer tortes.

*Writer's Market* is an annual valuable for its sympathy to free-lancers. It has 650 magazines listed, all of which welcome inquiries from writers. The *Gale Directory* lists more than 36,000 publications by state, so it is a good source of local markets. The *Encyclopedia of Associations* can be a source of market ideas because most associations publish magazines, and they are looking for free-lancers too. The *Encyclopedia* lists over 30,000 associations.

Many specialized directories exist such as *Regional Interest Magazines of the United States*, the *National Directory of Community Newspapers*, the *Encyclopedic Directory of Ethnic Newspapers*, the *International Directory of Little Magazines and Small Presses* and *Magazines for Libraries*. Most of these will be available in any library reference department. A final source of market ideas is a large newsstand. It will never be as complete as these reference tools but is more fun to study. Also check *Folio*, the *New York Times* (Tuesdays is best) or *Magazine Week* for news of new magazines that might be looking for writers.

For analyzing the potential of the linzer torte idea I chose three magazines, *Spy, Victoria* and *McCall's*. These three seemed different enough from one another to provide a full demonstration of forms analysis, but all could be real targets for something on linzer tortes I thought: *Spy* would like the humor, *Victoria* would have a fondness for history and *McCall's*, of course, would want my recipes. I'd never analyzed any of the three before, though I'd casually read them.

After choosing magazines, I hunt for business data or trade gossip on each. This lets me assess their health. I don't want to bother sending queries or finished work to a magazine about to go bankrupt. Usually the less gossip I find, the better. Sources of magazine trade news include *NewsBank*, the *Wall Street Journal Index*, *The New York Times Index, InfoTrac, Readers' Guide* and *Business Periodicals Index*. These are all on CD-ROM (for compact disk-read only memory) in my library, so a search takes only a few minutes. I look up the names of both the magazines and the publishers. Here's what I learn from my gossip hunt:

> *Spy*, founded in 1986, is an "abrasive, New York-based magazine, often referred to as a print version of the David Letterman Show."[5] Edited by two former *Time* magazine writers, *Spy* loves to savage politicians and celebrities. The name comes from the fictional magazine in the classic movie, *Philadelphia Story*. In *Magazines for Libraries*, a reviewer said, "*Spy* has rewritten the rules for layout and content." It had been maneuvering for financing, but its circulation was strong. According to the Audit Bureau of Circulations, *Spy's* circulation in December 1990 was 136,315, a 2.7 percent increase for the year, reflecting a 10.9 percent drop in newsstand sales but a 16.3 percent increase in subscriptions. Translation: *Spy* was

healthy even with a newsstand drop because subscription sales tend to be stable over time. The editors may pride themselves on their irreverence and iconoclasm, but the numbers say (I can imagine *Spy's* editors shuddering at this) that *Spy* might be becoming an institution.

*Victoria*, another new magazine, founded in 1987, likewise seemed healthy. It was described by *Magazines for Libraries* as the "return of romance in a big way." It appeared just as the Eighties greed boom was ending and readers were hungry for some kind of escape into values, *Advertising Age* commented. Editor Nancy Lindemeyer, a former *House and Garden* editor, told the *New York Daily News*[6] that "Women are tired of being told how to manage their houses more efficiently." *Victoria* was a magazine that could celebrate mornings or penmanship or lace. Critics complained to the *Daily News* that the magazine lacked substance, that it had no information. But it must have struck a chord because it sold 80 percent of its premiere issue. It rapidly went from quarterly to bimonthly to monthly. From 55,000 subscriptions at the start, it zoomed to 805,983 as of December 1990. Its huge, meteoric rise was over (this was a jump of only 1.5 percent over December 1989), but any magazine with a circulation of over half a million is rare and noteworthy.

*McCall's* is one of the venerable "Seven Sisters" (along with titles such as *Ladies' Home Journal, Better Homes and Gardens, Good Housekeeping*). It has been a mainstay of service journalism for women since 1870. But *McCall's* has seen some hard times recently. It is last among the Seven, according to *Advertising Age*[7] and has been sold several times; currently it's owned by the New York Times Company. The new owners are trying a redesign, but as of December 1990, *McCall's* circulation had dropped 1.4 percent from 1989 and 3.9 percent from 1987. While this may not sound like a lot, with a circulation of 5,011,473, a 1 percent drop is approximately five thousand magazines. Even so, with over 5 million readers it's viable enough for any lowly free-lancer to yearn for.

## Step Two: Charts

All three magazines were healthy enough to bother with, I decided. So next I chart their forms—in minute detail. Since none of the four aspects above—subject, purpose, effect or genre—is broad enough to fully describe a magazine, my solution is simple. I look at all four. I make a sheet with four headings—subject, purpose, effect, genre. Then I read each article and try to invent descriptive words for each column. In the charts below, note how none of my words match "textbook approved" or even "Plato approved" terms. A *Spy* article on Daryl Gates is labeled "Ain't it awful" under effect and "Complex" under genre. A *McCall's* piece on raising teenagers is labeled "Trust" for subject and "Anecdotal w/experts" for genre.

"Why not," "It's easy," "Not guilty," "Evocative," "Airy," "Bizarre," "Wry" were *names* of forms on my charts. Any terms will do so long as they make sense to the one doing the chart. The object of making the chart is to use it to read closely and make decisions about the subject matter, purpose, effect and genre of each article. I like to be whimsical in my language. I'm not going to share the charts with editors, so I don't have to worry about offending them. The language you create for your charts can be as personal as you like, so long as it helps you read carefully. I usually do at least two issues per magazine. Tables 4.2 through 4.7 are the charts for two issues of *Spy, Victoria*, and *McCall's*. I included page numbers on the charts; length belongs with the genre idea, I think.

## Step Three: Design Spectra

Now comes the hard part. After charting two or three issues, allowing your language to be as free and easy as you like, look at each of the four lists for each magazine. Do patterns emerge? Here you are trying to collapse the long lists into short ones. With twenty-six articles on the *Spy* chart, thirty-two for *Victoria* and thirty-four for *McCall's*, the charts are too complex for easy use. So I try to simplify subject, purpose, effect and genre to a few ideas.

After some thought I decided *Spy* had four main subjects—culture, celebrities, lifestyle and politics. (Note they are not in that order on the graphs in Figures 4.1, 4.2 and 4.3, pages 82–84) *Victoria* looked to me like it had six subject categories— food, clothes, people, places, gardens, things. *McCall's* seemed to also have six— family, health, house, beauty, food and people. I collapsed each list in this way until I had twelve short lists, four for each magazine. (The twelve short lists appear at the bottoms of the cells in Figures 4.1, 4.2 and 4.3.)

After I think of short lists, then I try to create a spectrum for each. A spectrum is a way of illustrating relationships among concepts. It is a line on which ideas are placed next to each other so that as they progress across the spectrum, they gradually shift toward an opposite. Black becomes white; blue becomes red; left becomes right. What is actually shifting in the color spectrum is wavelength; in the black-to-white spectrum, amount of chalk on the board or light intensity is changing; in the left/right spectrum what changes is relationship to a center point. In other words, a spectrum is a measure of changing intensity of *one* idea. This is the spectrum I saw for the purposes list for *Spy*.

| Persuade | — | Analyze | — | Inform | — | Report | — | Pranks |

Do you see how persuasion and analysis are similar but pranks and analysis are dissimilar? I think the idea changing gradually over that spectrum is seriousness of intent. If I've managed to see a true spectrum, I have a picture now of *Spy's range*, its extremes, at least for the purposes aspect.

Here's the spectrum I saw for *McCall's* purposes:

| Instruct | — | Report | — | Describe | — | Narrate | — | Inspire |

**TABLE 4.2** *Spy: April 1991*

| Article | Subject | Purpose | Effect | Genre | #pp. |
|---|---|---|---|---|---|
| Great Expectations | The war | Analysis | Wry | Editorial | 2 |
| Naked City | Anything | "Observation" | Wry | Shorts | 11 |
| Party Poop | People at parties | "Observation" | Wry | Wild head; pix/captions | 3 |
| Big Man in Hollywood | David Geffen profile | Explanation | Pro/Con | BME | 7 |
| What Could We Have Been Thinking? | 90's vs. 80's | Analysis | Wry | Personal essay | 6 |
| All the People | Donald Trump's wealth | Investigation | Fact, fact, fact | Transitions w/occ. real paragraph | 9 |
| The Millionairess | Bogus princess | A prank | The gullible "they" | Catalog of letters | 7 |
| Review of Reviewers | Writers who describe themselves writing | Criticize | Caustic | BME | 2 |
| Weird Libations | A writer writes about himself writing | Mock review | Bizarre | Tell-a-story, sort of | 1 |
| Please, Please Me | Registries for singles | Persuade | Bizarre | Tell-a-story | 2 |
| Peer Review | Jury selection consulting | Inform | Mild outrage | BME | 1 |

**TABLE 4.3** *Spy*: May 1991

| Article | Subject | Purpose | Effect | Genre | #pp. |
|---|---|---|---|---|---|
| Great Expectations | Happenings | To summarize | Ironic | Editorial | 2 |
| Naked City | A collage | Innuendo | Wry | Shorts | 9 |
| Gazpacho Gestapo | Daryl Gates: Profile | Compare, describe, question | Ain't it awful | Complex, many subtopics | 8 |
| At Your Service | Memoir of Bongo | Ridicule, tell a story | Ironic | Complex, many subtopics | 6 |
| Master Phillip | P. Johnson profile | Summarize, give examples | Thoughtful, defines "influence" | Complex | 9 |
| Spy High | Celebrities in mock yearbook | Comment | Bizarre | Pix w/captions | 9 |
| The Lost Tycoons | Hollywood studio profile | Summarize, explain | Straight | Text with wild sidebars | 6 |
| Review of Reviewers | Alliteration is In | Give examples | Wry | Formal text | 2 |
| Dream House | Perelman remodels | Report | The inside scoop | Lead w/development | 1 |
| Politics | Paranoia professionals | Give details | Ironic | Formal essay | 1 |
| Press | Is Buchwald funny? | Analysis | No, he's not | Formal essay | 1 |
| Oval Office Diary | False Bush diary | Satire | Satirical | Notes | 1 |
| The Webs | Bryant Gumbel's woes | Innuendo | Reportorial | BME | 1 |
| The Industry | Hollywood & war | Interpret | Lone (biting) observer | BME | 1 |
| The Times | Mr. Moss | Report | Gossipy | BME | 1 |

**TABLE 4.4** *Victoria*: April 1991

| Article | Subject | Purpose | Effect | Genre | #pp. |
|---|---|---|---|---|---|
| Polish of Time | New furniture looking old | Example | Elegance | Pix w/text | 2 |
| Favorite Things | Things cottagy | Description | A catalog | Pix w/captions | 5 |
| Children's Corner | Anne's ruby biscuits | Explanation | Amusing, practical | Text w/recipe | 2 |
| Hidden Treasures | Source of a favorite book | Revelation | "I didn't know that" | Pix w/text & captions | 2 |
| Beauty & Fashion | Natural products | Information | Effusive catalog | Pix w/captions | 2 |
| Calling Cards | Cats on cards | Example | Cute | Pix w/captions | 1 |
| Beauty of a British Walk | Clothes for on foot | Urge to action | Soft, misty, pretty | Pix over pix w/captions | 8 |
| Magical Journey | A railroad trip | Urge to action | Elegant, exciting | Pix over pix w/captions | 10 |
| Fulfillment of a Dream | Dream home | Description | Elegance, beauty | Photo essay | 12 |
| An Idle House | Clothes & quotes | Example | Clothes as literature | Pix w/captions | 6 |
| Brimming with Curiosities | A shop | Information/description | "I want" | Pix w/captions | 3 |
| At Queen's Victoria's | Her cradles | Setting a scene | Intimate, nostalgic | Pix w/text (BME) | 7 |
| Kate Greenaway | 1840s children's author | Creating an image | Elegant, nostalgic | Photo w/text (BME) | 7 |
| English Pudding | Recipes | Urge to action | Inviting | Photos w/text | 3 |
| Chimes | A quote | To impress | Impressive | Photo w/caption | 1 |

**TABLE 4.5** *Victoria:* May 1991

| Article | Subject | Purpose | Effect | Genre | #pp. |
|---|---|---|---|---|---|
| Favorite Things | Things w/flower images | Description/example | Romantic | Pix w/captions | 4 |
| Design Studio | Lace | Description/example | Romantic | Pix w/captions | 1 |
| Beauty & Bath | Care for body | Information | Dispassionate | Intro text then pix/cap | 3 |
| Namesake | Things Victorian | Narrative/example | Matter-of-fact | Text w/pix | 2 |
| Children's Corner | Mother/daughter clothes | Example w/quotes | Elegant | Pix w/captions | 3 |
| Calling Cards | Floral cards | Example | Matter-of-fact | Pix w/captions | 1 |
| A Full Light Wind | Amy Lowell quote | Second cover | Airy | Pix w/quote | 1 |
| In a Cottage by the Bay | Light in a house | Descriptive | Matter-of-fact | Intro text then pix/cap | 6 |
| New Lines | Modern lines old house | Narrative | Nostalgic | Pix w/italic captions | 4 |
| Eloquence of Cherished Objects | Clustering collectibles | Description/example | Nostalgic | Pix w/italic captions | 4 |
| Idle Hour | The nursery | Conjecture | Remote elegance | Text w/product info | 4 |
| Stationer Winslow | Stationery | Description/example | Intimate | Text w/photos | 6 |
| Gowned for Summer | Rose-colored clothes | Description/example | Romantic | Pix on pix | 12 |
| Herb Lover's Garden | Rose-flavored foods | Narrative | Personal | Prose essay | 2 |
| Garden in the Woods | Seemingly wild garden | Intense description | Vivid, playful | Classic BME | 6 |
| Enticements for Domestic Gardener | Rare seed catalogs | Description/example | Matter-of-fact | Photos w/summary | 4 |
| On First of May | Children's tea party | Description/example | Factual | Photos | 3 |

**TABLE 4.6** *McCall's*: June 1991

| Article | Subject | Purpose | Effect | Genre | #pp. |
|---|---|---|---|---|---|
| Harrison Ford | Not so macho | Descriptive | You-are-there | Lots of quotes | 2+ |
| Over 35 Body | Menopause | Expert advice | Frank | Numbered tips/sidebars | 6+ |
| Di & Charles Tenth | Marriage assessment | Examine rumors | Let's be fair | Premise-facts-conclusion | 7+ |
| Tough Times & Kids | Share troubles w/'em | Expert advice | Let's be sensible | How-to | 4 |
| Beauty: Packing | Items for a trip | Advice (no expert) | Let's be very sensible | Numbered tips | 1 |
| Summertime Beauty | Swimsuits for big hips | Descriptive | Gently daring | Pix w/captions | 10 |
| Outdoor Cookbook | No-work barbecue | Instructive | Fantasy laden | Pix w/recipes | 10 |
| Seafood Symphony | Serious fish stew | Instructive | Let's impress | Pix w/recipes | 2 |
| Lite Eating | Fresh fruit desserts | Instructive | It's easy | Recipes | 2 |
| Vital Signs | Health news | Informative | Factual | Shorts | 2 |
| Nutrition/Fitness | Health news | Informative | Factual | Shorts | 1 |
| Wise & Wary Patient | Myths about psychologists | Narrative | Evocative | Classic w/how-to-sidebar | 2 |
| Ask Dr. Mom | Advice | Answer questions | Quick fix | Q/A | 1 |
| A Father's Story | She's hip; he's not | Narrative | Humor w/insight | Personal essay | 3 |
| Love Does Change | Nature of love | Expert opinion | Didactic | Formal | 2 |
| Pet Life | Pet news | Informative | Factual | How-to shorts | 1 |
| Reaching Out to Others | Making friends | Personal advice | Inspirational | Essay w/tips | 1 |

**TABLE 4.7** *McCall's*: July 1991

| Article | Subject | Purpose | Effect | Genre | #pp. |
|---|---|---|---|---|---|
| How to Raise a Teenager | Trust | Explain, instruct | Sympathetic | Anecdotal w/experts | 5 |
| Relax | Reducing stress | Explain, instruct | 1-2-3 | Quiz & tips | 4 |
| Billy Crystal | Profile | Describe, explain | Guy next door | Anecdotal/BME | 4 |
| Sally Field | Profile | Describe, explain | Girl next door grows up | Descriptive/BME | 6 |
| Beauty: Fresh Face | Products | Define terms | 1-2-3 | List in paragraph form | 1 |
| Wild Flowers | Floral print clothes | Illustrate | Why not stripes w/flowers | Pix w/captions | 4 |
| Easiest Makeup Guide | Summer's seven musts | Explain | It's easy | Pix w/charts | 4 |
| Pasta Fiesta | Pasta a la Mexico | Analysis | How-to | Recipes | 3 |
| Luscious Desserts | Guilt | Temptation | Luscious | Recipes | 9 |
| Lite Eating: Noodles | Not guilty | Redemption | It's easy & healthy | Recipes | 1 |
| Micro-way: Barbecue | Fast | Instruct | It's easy | Recipes | 1 |
| Bug-free Summer | Know your enemies | Annotate | Optimistic | Catalog | 3 |
| Bring a Little Summer Inside | Flower arranging | Illustrate | It's easy | Pix w/captions | 4 |
| Ask Dr. Mom | Advice | Answer questions | Quick fixes | Q/A | 1 |
| Mother's Page | Playmates' fights | Share an experience | I did it, you can too | Essay | 2 |
| Child Psychologist | Beautiful children | An expert decrees | A tad pompous | Q/A | 1 |
| Living Beautifully | Personal glimpses | Inspirational | Sweet | Essay | 1 |

Again, do you see how the items side by side are similar, but items far apart are unlike? Inspiration and narration are similar forms, but narration and instruction are radically different forms. Here, I think, the one idea changing gradually over the spectrum is emotional intensity. Inspiration is a more emotional form of writing than instruction. Once again, with the spectrum I think I have a picture of *McCall's* range of purposes.

## Step Four: Make Graphs

Don't worry if making spectra is difficult for you. It's more important to make short lists, even if forging logical relationships among items on the lists eludes you. When you have your four spectra (or at least four short lists) for each magazine, you can build graphs. I put a spectrum or list at the bottom of the chart for the horizontal axis.

The vertical axis, then, is the total number of articles from all issues read. I reread my long lists and count how many articles go into each category of the short list. There are eight political articles, ten celebrity pieces, eight culture pieces and four lifestyle ones from *Spy*'s subject list. The same articles when examined for purpose cluster into four persuasion, ten analysis, seven informative, two reportorial and two pranks. If an article seems to fit two categories I count it twice, which is why the numbers don't come out exactly. (This is analysis, not science.)

I plot the numbers on the graphs, join the lines and study the four pictures. What I should see are each magazine's expectations, its forms, both the range and the mix. (Refer to Figures 4.1 through 4.3, the sets of graphs for *Spy, Victoria* and *McCall's*.)

## Step Five: Interpretation

This charting and graphing sounds like a lot of work, and it is, though describing it probably takes longer than doing it. But the results are worth it. I am always surprised by what my charts reveal. When I read *Spy* casually, I experienced it as "just" a humor magazine, a *Mad* magazine for adults. I knew it for its pranks. In the April issue I analyzed, it ran a bogus death notice in *Variety* and asked celebrities if they remembered "poor Jack." Not one of the big names had the nerve to say they'd never heard of "Jack." I expected my analysis to reveal a magazine full of stuff like this. The charts say otherwise. Note how much *Spy* does on politics and culture. Note how much analysis there is. Note how many pieces are purely factual and how many have complex organization. It's all there on the charts.

My casual inspection as a mere consumer saw only the high jinks, but once I became a professional reader, I saw instead a magazine in the tradition of the *New Yorker* and *Harper's*, serious journalism amid comic relief.

If the editors were to read my analysis, no doubt they would shrug and say, so what? All of this is obvious to them. But it wasn't to *me*. That's the point. I saw none of this until I analyzed. Curt Anderson, one of the coeditors of the magazine, told me

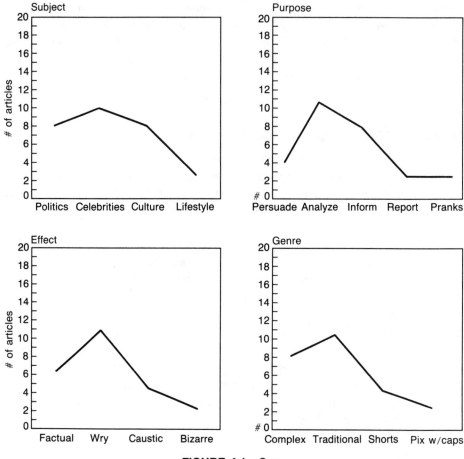

**FIGURE 4.1**  *Spy*

in an interview that one of his favorite things *Spy* had done was a sidebar to an article on a book about the Chappaquiddick cover-up. In the sidebar, theologians were asked whether Ted Kennedy was going to hell. "I loved that," Anderson said, "because we were serious and they were serious." But *I* didn't know *Spy* was serious until I had taken the time and care to see it.

If I approached *Spy* with my light linzer torte article as written now, I would just irritate the editors. My topic is too small and my style not biting enough for their goals. This is why forms analysis is so important. Casual reading is often wrong. If I'm to do anything with linzer tortes in *Spy* I need a sharp political angle. Hmm. Most raspberries are grown in former Eastern bloc countries. Could there be a link between raspberry yields and the fall of communism? I wonder if former President Nixon would be willing to discuss this theory. . . .

The *Victoria* analysis also held surprises. As a casual reader, I saw that magazine as lush, pretty, fanciful and completely divorced from reality. Children in the

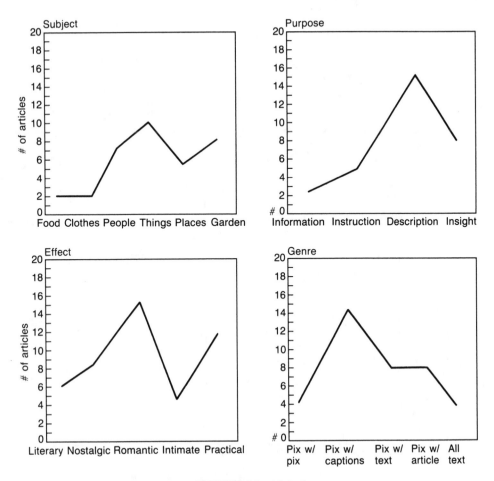

**FIGURE 4.2** *Victoria*

pictures wore white. Tea sets sat precariously on chintz-covered sofas whose fabric was clearly unprotected by chemicals. Sunlight filtered in from gardens perpetually in bloom. Windows were open but no bugs intruded. No one sweated. No one mopped floors. No one read either—the magazine seemed to be all pictures, no text. I expected the critics who complained of its lack of substance to be right.

But once again, the charts said otherwise. The critics should reread the magazine. Note in Figure 4.2 that there is a lot about people in the subject matter, that the two dominant purposes are the sophisticated, difficult ones of description and insight (my two favorite forms). While much of the effects category targeted romance or nostalgia (not my cup of tea), there were also literary pieces, which I do enjoy doing. The main surprise for me was the genre chart, which showed that there were real essays sandwiched among the photo features.

*Victoria* is not a fluff book, I was thinking; I was now sure they would be interested in something about linzer tortes, although the New York/San Francisco

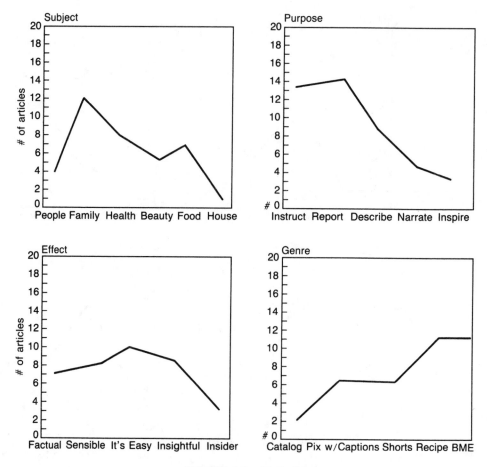

**FIGURE 4.3**   *McCall's*

focus would have to go. Unfortunately, I was too right. The editors ran a piece about "Learning to Cook with Anne of Green Gables" in one of the issues I analyzed. The article quoted Anne's struggle to master ruby biscuits. When I read the recipe, I realized ruby biscuits were my linzer tortes. I was disappointed, but at the same time I had discovered a magazine that might have room for a writer like me in their pages, if I can find a topic.

McCall's, though, was the biggest surprise of all. Truth be told, I held it in contempt—the housewife's how-to; the magazine for women who hate cooking, cleaning and dieting but do them anyway; the magazine for women whose tastes run to romance novels and the *National Enquirer.*

Once again, forms analysis proved me wrong. I discovered not a shallow gossip rag but a magazine with a wide range of subject matter; serious, complex purposes with depth and color; a variety of effects and the full range of genres in its editorial mix. In short, I found a magazine for writers—one I'd like to write for. *McCall's*, of the three magazines, was the one most likely to let me write in my natural style. I don't think the topic as written now is right for them. Again, my linzer torte piece is too small, too personal, too shallow to be useful to the readers. But I do think something about raspberries, including their history, would interest them.

When I started these analyses I only wanted three magazines that were radically different to provide models of forms analysis. I didn't think any of the three was a likely magazine for this topic. I expected that *Spy*, because of its interest in New York topics, would be the best market of the three and that *McCall's* would be the worst because of narrow, strictly controlled forms. How wrong I was. I began doing a demonstration for a textbook and instead discovered a magazine I'd really like to write for. I have work to do yet. I must flesh out my topic and send a query letter to *McCall's*. I began the chapter expecting to tell you there was no hope for this topic; I end by seriously thinking of pursuing it. Surprise is always the result of forms analysis; publishable ideas are a result as well. Charts and graphs. Just two tools in the thinking journalist's repertoire.

## NOTES

1. *Concise Oxford Dictionary of Literary Terms*, Oxford University Press, London, 1990.
2. Roger Fowler, editor, *A Dictionary of Modern Critical Terms*, Routledge & Kegan Paul, London, 1987, p. 76.
3. W. Ross Winterowd, *Composition/Rhetoric: A Synthesis*, Southern Illinois University Press, Carbondale 1986, p. 67.
4. G. P. Quackenbos, *Advanced Course of Composition and Rhetoric: A Series of Practical Lessons*, D. Appleton, New York, 1875.
5. Geracimos, Ann, "Spy, the Uppity Yuppie of News Magazines," *Washington, D.C. Times*, November 23, 1987.
6. Fulman, Ricki, "Victoria-ous" *New York Daily News*, April 10, 1989.
7. Donalson, Scott, "7th Sister McCall's Pins Hope on Redesign," *Advertising Age*, February 26, 1990, p. 31.

## FOR ADDITIONAL READING

The following texts, while not about form exclusively, do go into depth about compositional theory and are written for undergraduates. They are listed below by the aspects of form they seem to emphasize. Some are listed twice because two aspects of form seemed to guide the book's organization. This list in no way exhausts the books available. *Books in Print* lists 872 titles on "Authorship" alone. An excellent bibliography of writing texts is *The Bedford Bibliography for Teachers of Writing*, prepared by Patricia Bizzell and Bruce Herzberg (Bedford Books of St. Martin's Press, New York, 1991).

## Subject

Atwan, Robert, and William Vesterman. *Writing Day-by-Day*. Harper & Row, New York, 1987.

Dobree, Bonamy. *Modern Prose Style*. Oxford University Press, London, 1964.

Matalene, Carolyn B., editor. *Worlds of Writing*. Random House, New York, 1989.

McLeod, Susan; Bates, Stacia; Jarvis, John; and Spear, Shelley. *Writing about the World*. Harcourt Brace Jovanovich, San Diego, Calif., 1991.

Vesterman, William. *Readings for the 21st Century*. Allyn & Bacon, Needham Heights, Mass., 1991.

## Purpose

Atwan, Robert, and William Vesterman. *Writing Day-by-Day*. Harper & Row, New York, 1987.

Axelrod, Rise B., and Charles R. Cooper. *Reading Critically, Writing Well*. 2d ed. St. Martin's Press, New York, 1990.

Bond, George R., and Harry H. Crosby. *The Shape of Thought*. University Press of America, Landham, Md., 1978.

Dobree, Bonamy. *Modern Prose Style*. Oxford University Press, London, 1964.

Hall, Donald. *The Contemporary Essay*. St. Martin's Press, New York, 1989.

Kane, Thomas S., and Leonard J. Peters. *Writing Prose*. Oxford University Press, New York, 1969.

McQuade, Donald, and Robert Atwan. *Popular Writing in America*. Oxford University Press, New York, 1988.

Morris, William E. *Form and Focus 2*. Harcourt, Brace & World, New York, 1964.

Rivers, William L., and Alison R. Work. *Free-Lancer and Staff Writer*. Wadsworth Publishing Company, Belmont, Calif., 1986.

## Effect

Quackenbos, G. P. *Composition and Rhetoric*. D. Appleton, New York, 1875.

## Genre

Friedlander, Edward Jay, and John Lee. *Feature Writing for Newspapers and Magazines*, HarperCollins, New York, 1988.

Matalene, Carolyn B., editor. *Worlds of Writing*. Random House, New York, 1989.

McQuade, Donald, and Robert Atwan. *Popular Writing in America*. Oxford University Press, New York, 1988.

# Chapter

# 5

# *Structure*

Like form, structure is a central idea in nonfiction writing. Structure in this chapter means, not the codes or conventions of the last chapter, but the unique organization of single articles. As with form, much is written about what structure "should be" and little about what it "is." Structure is supposed to be unity or the coherent relationship of parts of an article to each other. But a five-minute glance at almost any magazine, from *Harper's* to *Popular Mechanics*, reveals that the liveliest parts of the magazine often get their energy from their disunity. The funniest feature in *Harper's* every month is the "Index," a list of offbeat statistics. Occasionally some numbers are cleverly juxtaposed, but the list is never structured:

Percentage of Peru's coca crop destroyed by U.S.-assisted forces last year: 1

Percentage destroyed by insects: 20

Estimated amount the national debt will increase in the time it takes to read this line: $33,000

Estimated percentage of insect species worldwide that have not yet been identified: 90

Estimated number of people per square mile during peak season in the Yosemite Valley: 3,320

Number of people per square mile in Houston: 2,986

From "Harper's Index," *Harper's*, September 1990, p. 15.

In *Popular Mechanics* a key feature each month is the "Home & Shop Journal." None of its short descriptions of new products matches the formal Beginning-Middle-End structure so beloved of textbooks:

### Eco Stripper

Woodfinisher stripping gels are biodegradable and nonflammable, have very low odor and clean up with water. They contain no methylene chloride, methanol, acetone, toluene or petroleum distillates. Their containers are recyclable plastic and can be returned to the manufacturer for recycling. A $1 refund defrays mailing costs. One gel strips oil-based and latex paints and lacquer. The other strips polyurethane, shellac, lacquer and varnish. A 32-ounce size of either costs about $9, and a 64-ounce, about $15. Both are sold at paint and hardware stores. For information, call (800) 457-7433.

From "New Products" by Roy Berendsohn, *Popular Mechanics*, August 1991, p. 59.

Anyone trying to write for either of these magazines must abandon theory and look at practice. Actually, a clear-eyed, bias-free examination of real article structures would not only challenge textbooks but shatter the way many writers have been taught to compose. "Make an outline" is the earliest advice I can remember. We were told this in grade school, told again in high school, again in college and yet again in journalism courses. It's a nice theory, but writers who practice it, I think, are doomed to be boring because they are forced to assume structure is imposed, not discovered. So forget the outline. (Haven't you always wanted someone to say that? Haven't you always known that thinking is too messy for outlining?)

Your first few drafts are better if they are explorations—a search for discoveries and happy accidents. Donald Murray, author of *A Writer Teaches Writing*,[1] calls these first attempts discovery drafts. Prewriting is another term for these experimental drafts. Play with form and focus. Structure will come later. When you prewrite, or let your mind play freely, you allow yourself opportunities to surprise yourself before committing to organization. You permit chaos. Slavishly following a preset outline would limit your ability to discover. (See Chapter 9, "Serendipity," for more ways to use prewriting.)

There does come a time, however, when you do need structure. Playing must end; discovery has happened; chaos must give way to order. But you are not free to structure an article solely as you wish. Once again, as with form, your target magazine will have some structural preferences. Not rules, preferences. Your ability—after your sojourn in chaos—to mimic those preferences will improve your odds of getting published. As with form, you will have to analyze your magazine to identify those preferences. Analyzing structure has two steps: first, identify the elements of structure. Second, observe—or map—the recurring relationships of those elements within articles in your target magazine.

## ELEMENTS

Elements are fragments, small components that should not stand alone but can be arranged and rearranged to form a whole. In chemistry, elements are the individual units of compounds, the basic building blocks of nature. (They can be broken into smaller atomic units but that means leaving chemistry for nuclear physics.) In prose, the elements or building blocks are the word; the phrase; the sentence; the paragraph; the subtopic; the beginning, or lead; the middle, or development; the ending; the focus; the refocus; the transformation; and the transition. You've known some of these terms since you were 10 years old. Some were discussed earlier in Chapter 3. But let's examine them again—briefly.

## The Word

The word is the smallest unit of writing, and the goal, as philosopher Jacques Barzun said in his classic book, *Simple and Direct*,[2] is to select "the right word." Right words, he advised, are crisp, clean, precise. But what does that mean? The right word for a 10-year-old might be completely different from that for a scientist. In *Jack and Jill*, a magazine that loves to play with the "why," many words might be needed to explain what "done" means in the expression, "bake until done." For a cooking magazine, where presumably the readers have experience, it would insult them to explain what "done" means. (What does it mean, actually? Is doneness a transfer of carbon dioxide, an expelling of water vapor, a chemical realignment of molecules, a creation of new molecules?)

A word's rightness cannot be assumed, but must be analyzed in terms of the magazine's overall concept and editorial goals. With children's magazines, help exists in tested vocabularies, which measure the grade level of individual words. In *Living Word Vocabulary*, editors Edgar Dale and Joseph O'Rourke publish 43,000 tested words.[3] For example, "abandon" can be understood by 74 percent of sixth graders, the list claims.

Once you're beyond a children's audience, though, you're on your own. What words are the right words for your audience? You could look for number of words in sentences, ratio of long words to short words and ratio of abstract to concrete for clues. These give hints to the editors' feelings about the readers' literacy levels. But counting alone doesn't measure reader vocabulary. Gluten, etude and lexeme are short words, but highly technical. Underemployed, mouthwash and granddaughter are long words but easily understood. In the end, your own common sense is the best measure of the right word. Is the magazine's vocabulary "hard" or "easy"?

## The Phrase

A phrase is a short grouping of words that cannot stand alone as a sentence. *Usually* can't stand alone. (As writer, just now I have made a stylistic decision to violate convention and put that "usually" phrase alone.) Again textbook theory abounds with uses and purposes for phrases. They can be adverbial or adjectival, prepositional or appositional, introductory or concluding (within a sentence, that is). To evaluate the use of phrases in your target publication, it's important to assess the relative number of phrases compared with sentences. Usually, the fewer clauses, as compared to complete sentences without clauses, the easier a piece is to read. Let me say that again, but without the clauses: Simple sentences are clear. A tightly edited magazine will avoid phrases, but others, either because of the complexity of the topics they cover or the freedom they give their writers, allow many more. *Assessing* clauses is one way to understand a magazine's philosophy of structure. *Killing* clauses in your own writing is one way to make it crisper. Usually.

## The Sentence

Ah yes, the sentence. So much has been written on the sentence and the role it plays in clear logical thought. . . . I've just demonstrated that it's possible to communicate an idea without a sentence. Convention holds that subject, verb and object—actor acting upon actee—is the way to convey meaning in English. What makes magazines so interesting to me, though, is how much they experiment with that convention. Consider the two examples below. Notice that certain kinds of information— numbers, statistics, frequently repeated information, summaries, how-to steps—are all easier to read in sentence fragments:

The answers to this quiz could save you gas—and money.

- For the typical automobile, the most fuel-efficient speed, in miles per hour, is: a) five-ten; b) ten-20; c) 30-40; d) above 55.
- Driving at 55 m.p.h. instead of 65 m.p.h. improves mileage by approximately what percent? (a) five; (b) 12; (c) 17; (d) 25.

From "Pump Up Your Gas Mileage" by Robert Sikorsky, *Reader's Digest* (condensed from *Parade*), November 1990, p. 137.

What are the most serious unmet needs in your state because of budget problems?

- 57% Health care
- 43% Social services
- 41% Higher education
- 41% Public works/infrastructure

26% Secondary education
24% Prisons
20% Housing
13% Law enforcement

From "Where Did All the Money Go?" *Newsweek*, July 1, 1991, p. 27.

The sentence, of course, does remain basic to nonfiction. And it remains generally true that the best sentences are as you've been taught: short ones, with subjects in front of verbs. But, as with phrases, don't assume your target magazine follows tradition. Study it. Below are several sentences. Can you tell which one came from which magazine?

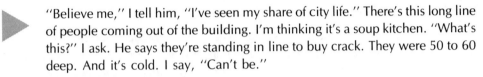

"Believe me," I tell him, "I've seen my share of city life." There's this long line of people coming out of the building. I'm thinking it's a soup kitchen. "What's this?" I ask. He says they're standing in line to buy crack. They were 50 to 60 deep. And it's cold. I say, "Can't be."

From: *Sports Illustrated* or *Esquire?*

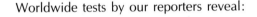

Worldwide tests by our reporters reveal:

- Major U.S. airports are wide open to intruders
- A video camera rigged as a bomb can go undetected
- Suitcases can leave on a flight unaccompanied

From *Condé Nast Traveler* or *New York Times Magazine?*

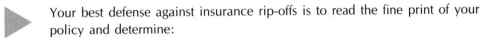

Your best defense against insurance rip-offs is to read the fine print of your policy and determine:

- What services and costs are covered by your health plan and for how long.
- If you need authorization or a second opinion for certain treatments or surgery—and if so, how far in advance.
- The out-of-pocket maximum, or the most you're expected to pay in any given year.

From *Money* or *Cosmopolitan?*

The first sentence is in a literary style such as *Esquire* uses. The second has the investigative tone of a newsmagazine, not the love-that-spa style usually associated with slick travel magazines such as the *Condé Nast Traveler*. And the last is dry, nothing like the playful italics and exclamation points style associated with *Cosmo*. And yet:

**Answers to Sentence Quiz:**
From "But Seriously, Folks . . ." by Richard Hoffer, *Sports Illustrated*, December 10, 1990, p. 72.
From "What Is This Man Doing Only Steps Away from Your Plane?" *Condé Nast Traveler*, February 1991, p. 106.
From: "Money Talk" by Elizabeth Birkelund Oberbeck, *Cosmopolitan*, December 1990, p. 62.

See why it is important to study a magazine's sentences? You can't assume anything.

## The Paragraph

In theory, the paragraph is a group of related sentences. A topic sentence announces the relationship; the remaining sentences develop that relationship. A complete idea is begun, expounded and ended within a paragraph. In theory. I remember the last time I read a paragraph that matched that description. I was younger then. It was a bright sunny day. The Mets were winning: I'm trying to say that the paragraph in theory is often ignored in practice. The truth is, paragraphs are sometimes visual units instead of thought units. Newspapers, which traditionally have narrow columns and large type, keep paragraphs to one or two sentences for looks and ease in page makeup.

In magazines, paragraphs are longer because columns are wider and type is traditionally smaller. Thus, they resemble thought units, but with the infographics explosion, this is changing. The more dynamic a magazine's typography, the more likely the paragraphs will be a function of visual use. They need to look good, not make sense. Editors have often called me asking for things like "just seven more lines" to improve the appearance of a page. Requests like this make nonsense of "the paragraph." Once again, the only way to understand the conventions of a magazine is to examine what it does. Analyze a few paragraphs at random. Do they have topic sentences and development? Or are they a string of sentences with visually placed paragraph indentations thrown in to improve the appeal of the typography? Such paragraphs make the page look better but they don't necessarily make sense if a paragraph is supposed to be a logical unit. Consider the following two examples; the first logically should be one and the second should be two. But in context the first was set in narrow columns and the second had an initial cap nine lines deep. Both looked better for being illogical:

I've found out the hard way that when it comes to essential kitchen tools, buying them cheap is false economy. Things break, or don't perform as hoped, then need to be replaced. You pay twice and more again with frustration.

What you purchase wisely will cost more—quality always does. But you acquire years of cooking pleasure with good kitchen equipment, and increase the likelihood of passing on some part of it to your children.

From "The Essential Country Kitchen" by Ken Haedrich, *Country Journal*, January/February 1991, p. 37.

At her mother's house, Anita Parks Crockett prepares for work. She serves lunch to the tourists who arrive on big boats from the Virginia and Maryland shores. Anita, like most Tangiermen, has little affection for tourists, though she appreciates their contribution to the local economy, or, more specifically, hers. "Those people just come here and gawk," she complains. "They think we live in little grass shacks. But we have water and cable." Anita pulls a striped apron over her head, ties it neatly, and bikes the quarter mile to the restaurant. In any other American town, an eighteen-year-old waitress would rather die than be caught in uniform outside of work, but affectation here is pointless. Asked what she and her friends do when they're not working, she says without humor, "Loaf."

From "A World at Bay" *Condé Nast Traveler*, March 1991, p. 140.

## The Subtopic

Just as a paragraph is supposed to be a group of related sentences, a subtopic is supposed to be a group of related paragraphs. It should add to understanding of the main idea but is not the main idea itself. Perhaps no convention of compositional theory is more violated in modern magazine journalism than this one. Magazines, in general, will be more careful about grouping related ideas together than a news-paper, but it is possible to find chaos even in magazines with the best reputations. This is from the august *New Yorker*:

[Rembert] Weakland had met the future Pope Paul VI when he was still Giovanni Battista Montini, Archbishop of Milan. In 1956, the young Benedic-tine had come to Milan to examine some original manuscripts of Ambrosian chant, which was his Columbia thesis subject. (The thesis, analyzing the origins of Ambrosian chant, which preceded the now more popular Gregorian chant and flourished with it for a time, made it as far as a first draft. The Archbishop claims that he could complete it in three months, if only he had three months to devote to it.) Montini immediately took a liking to the tall, scholarly priest–musician. In 1977, when the post of archbishop of Milwaukee—a city that Weakland barely knew, having visited it only a few times—fell vacant, Pope Paul appointed him, perhaps because of personal affection for him, which had deepened during Weakland's time as primate, or perhaps because he wanted to appease those members of the Curia who thought the American Benedictine too thorough a reformer of monastic life.

From "Profiles," *The New Yorker*, July 15, 1991, p. 48.

No, this is not incomprehensible because it is taken out of context. It is incom-prehensible because it is incomprehensible.

Subtopics tend to be crucial for opinion or analysis, but with simple reporting or straight informative pieces, a scattering of points in no particular order *can* still be understood. Consider the following short from *Bird Watcher's Digest*. It's clear, it's funny, but it's chaos:

## The Owl and the Pussycat

"And now, in the bareback competition, coming out of chute number 4, on Whiskers . . ." Why does bizarre behavior always seem to be witnessed by nonbirders? In this case it was the janitor of the Doyle Elementary School in

Chalfont, Pennsylvania. At about 6:00 P.M. on November 16, 1990, his (understandably) hysterical cat bolted through the open door of the school with an owl firmly attached to its back. The owl, identified by a local birdwatcher as a saw-whet, was removed from the cat, found to be in fine health, and, presumably none the worse for its wild ride, released. The cat, it is assumed, suffered only psychological scars.

Saw-whet owls are known to be aggressive hunters, and have been reported to tackle prey larger than themselves on occasion. An attack on a domestic cat, however, a fierce predator, probably represents the triumph of enthusiasm over judgment. The incident was detailed in the October-December issue of *Pennsylvania Birds*. No mention was made of the effect on the cat's owner.

From "Quick Takes" by Eirik Blom, *Bird Watcher's Digest*, July/August 1991, p. 10.

## The Beginning

The lead is shrouded in myth. There are writers who claim they cannot write until they've "seen the lead." Others consider it the only important element to a story. Some confidently consult lists of the "twenty-five best" types of leads. The myths remind me of golfing superstitions—does the lucky hat really improve your stroke? The lead is sometimes the last thing I write; more often than not, I chop off a lead when I revise. As for the lead's importance, it's useless unless the rest of the story delivers. A good lead, I think, has two parts: a *hook* or stylistic attention-grabber and a *focus statement*, which foreshadows or reveals the main premise of the piece. The latter has been described in depth in Chapter 3; but to repeat: a focus statement is the point in an article when the writer first reveals or foreshadows or promises the ending. It can occur anywhere but is often found at the end of the hook.

The lead should accomplish two things: make the reader want to read the story and clearly identify the topic. Beyond that, there are no *rules*. There are, however, some fascinating *solutions* to the problem of beginning, and again, studying individual magazines to see what patterns they favor is more useful than memorizing some list of twenty-five types. Leads can range from a single sentence to dozens of paragraphs, from narrative to didactic, from messy to mysterious. And the focusing statement could be a phrase, a sentence, a paragraph, a subtopic. Consider these leads from a single issue of *Esquire* (July 1991). Note the variety and the similarities. I've italicized the focus statements:

My introduction to hangovers came vicariously through a math teacher. His name was Mr. Tatum, but we called him the Prince of Darkness because at least once a week we'd file in for class and find him sitting with the lights out, the shades drawn, and a grim look on his face. Mr. Tatum spoke softly on these mornings so as not to unduly vibrate his skull. He also kept a bottle of something called nux vomica in his desk, and it was the subject of much hilarity. "Don't knock it," he said. "Someday you may need it." We liked him. Not because he'd been an all-state quarterback or because he drove a red MG and had beautiful women clinging to him wherever he went. We liked him because of his hangovers. They confirmed to us that he lived a glamorous, fast-paced private life.

*You have to remember that in those days—and I'm speaking of the early 1950s—hangovers were looked upon as an honorable, even heroic, ordeal.*

From "The Hangover" by John Berendt, *Esquire*, July 1991, p. 49.

If before long your car contains a *computer to guide you to your destination*, you'll have Rupert Murdoch to thank.

From "Can You Display the Way to San Jose?" by Phil Patton, *Esquire*, July 1991, p. 50.

My first communication from Byron De La Beckwith was a postcard from the Hamilton County jail. I had sent him a letter asking for an interview.

"You most certainly will hear from me," he wrote in his cramped, furious script, "as soon as my reply works through the bowels of SATAN. . . ." He wanted to make sure I was white, or more precisely, "a Caucasian Christian." His return address: "De La in de dungeon, 601 Walnut, 37402, CSA." The zip code is downtown Chattanooga, Tennessee. CSA is the place where Beckwith believes he lives—the Confederate States of America.

"I'm a Southern Nationalist, yes ma'am. Sho'am," he explained. "Jesus Christ and White Folks are coming back in style. . . ."

*The D.A. of Hinds County, Mississippi, says that this unreconstructed white supremacist killed civil-rights leader Medgar Evers twenty-eight years ago, that Beckwith crouched in the honeysuckle one night and fired a bullet into his back. Beckwith, seventy years old, stooped and banty, says otherwise. He has spent nearly three decades denying the murder while reveling in his sinister celebrity as the prime suspect.*

From "The Haunting of the New South" by Maryanne Vollers, *Esquire*, July 1991, p. 60.

In thick, three-ring binders with pink and yellow, blue and green pages, each Hollywood studio rates from 1,200 to 1,500 screenwriters. The alphabetical A-lists usually begin with Jim Abrahams and end with his ex-partners David and Jerry Zucker—the three writer–directors of *Airplane!*—and they always include Woody Allen. The books are forever six months out of date, with this month's hot screenwriters—Jeffrey Abrams and Richard Friedenberg—mired in the B-lists until the next revision. The ratings vary, each studio favoring writers it has worked with, but they do not vary very much. *And all the books tell the same unintentional story.*

From "Glory and Humiliation in the Screen Trade" by Aljean Harmetz, *Esquire*, July 1991, p. 79.

The first lead sets a scene but also introduces the writer to us as a strong character. The second lead is a no-nonsense, get-down-to-business type. The third again sets up the author as a presence, but this time she is a symbol of us, the rational readers, in contrast with this aberrant murderer. The last is a classic omniscient style, the author distant, all-knowing, describing an object that will represent the larger topic.

Now consider these leads from an issue of *Elle* (July 1991). Again, note the similarities and the differences.

> Irving Penn said it best: "I always felt we were selling dreams, not clothes." *Fashion photographs are dreams incarnate*, split-second tableaux stolen from a perfect world where beauty is its own reward.
>
> From "Exposure" by Sarah Ferguson, *Elle*, July 1991, p. 20.

> Sitting by the window of his hotel room outside of Ghent, Belgium, Perry Farrell, the 34-year-old surfer, artist, singer, filmmaker, and visionary who fronts *Los Angeles's premier rock band Jane's Addiction*, is musing on the differences between the United States and Europe. "It's just so gloomy here," Farrell says.
>
> From "Making Rock Matter" by Gina Arnold, *Elle*, July 1991, p. 30.

> It is perhaps little wonder that Americans have led the world in the art of biography. We adore the literal truth, which is so much stranger than our fiction. Why make anything up when you've got people like Nancy Reagan, Jim and Tammy Faye Bakker, and Ollie North to write about? *Biography and fiction have begun to merge in tantalizing ways. . . .*"
>
> From "The New Biography" by Jay Parini, *Elle*, July 1991, p. 52.

> An adventurous woman is no stranger to the androgynous allure of cross-dressing. Think of George Sand, Isabelle Eberhardt, and Katharine Hepburn. Ever since Rosalind, Shakespeare's intrepid heroine, women masquerading as men have created quite a stir and inspired everything from adoration to a criminal record. *Here we've gathered a wardrobe of men's haberdashery—*
>
> From "Suitables," *Elle*, July 1991, p. 100.

> *Open your eyes and kiss your lips goodbye—*
>
> From "Make-Up" by Janine King, *Elle*, July 1991, p. 118.

The lead styles here are, in order, The Quote, The Scene, The Unsupported Assertion, The Supported Assertion, and lastly, The Cryptic Sentence. In both magazines the leads seem astonishingly varied. But is there any pattern to them? I think in

*Esquire*, the leads tend to run long. In *Elle* they're short. It's an obvious, even silly, perception, and yet many writers never notice basic things like this.

## The Middle

The middle, the place where the subtopics and the thinking go, is seen, in theory, as an arena where the writer has total control. In *The Lively Art of Writing*, Lucille Payne says:

The big middle section of your essay—everything between the introduction and the conclusion—can be almost any length.

The number of paragraphs in it depends entirely upon how many points you want to cover and how thoroughly you want to cover them. It would be very foolish to decide in advance precisely how many paragraphs you intend to write—foolish and impossible. All sorts of influences begin working on you when you start writing. You will find yourself thinking, "I'd better use an example here . . . explain a little more clearly there . . . add this point . . . take that one out . . ." Almost the only rule you can follow is this: Write as much as you need to write in order to present your case clearly and completely and persuasively.

From *The Lively Art of Writing*, 3d ed., Follett, Chicago, 1975, p. 54.

And in *The Practical Stylist*, Sheridan Baker says almost the same thing:

The middle paragraph is the standard paragraph, the little essay in itself, with its own little beginning and little end. But it must also declare its allegiance to the paragraphs immediately before and after it. Each topic sentence must somehow hook onto the paragraph above it, must include some word or phrase to ease the reader's path: a transition. You may simply repeat a word from the sentence that ended the paragraph just above. You may bring down a thought left slightly hanging in air: "Smith's idea is different" might be a tremendously economical topic sentence with automatic transition—or an even bolder "Not at all" or "Nonsense."

From Sheridan Baker, *The Practical Stylist*, 5th ed., Harper & Row, New York, 1981, p. 26.

Both writers are giving good advice if your mission is only to argue or illustrate a topic. But the realities of professional writing add some unique problems to forging middles.

Length is one of these realities. When the editors say write 700 words about nuclear physics, they don't care that 75,000 words would only begin to explain one discovery. Seven hundred. Take it or leave it. Sometimes the difficulty of squeezing a complex topic into a one-page article keeps me up nights thinking about the compromises I've made to do it. One solution is to defy Baker's rule that paragraphs must hook together. Some magazines use subheads instead of transitions. Another technique to save space is to use abstract descriptions or vague attributions. For example:

> Naturalists advise keeping skunks away from your sheds.

Okay, that's short, but it doesn't tell you what naturalists say so or how to convince the skunks to go. Longer would be:

> Keith Marrow of the Ohio Division of Wildlife suggests three techniques for discouraging skunks. One, scatter mothballs around their dens; two, use a hose to flood the den; and three, shoot the critters. Do not attempt any of these right at dusk when the skunk is first coming out for the night.

That is clearer, but it's also thirty-one words longer—a whole inch in some editorial formats. And though longer, it doesn't give advantages and disadvantages of each strategy. Shooting requires getting close enough to see the skunk (instead of just smelling it); if you can find the den, hosing and mothballing just make the skunk mad. (I know, believe me.)

Still longer is this:

> East Coast naturalists, especially in Ohio, West Virginia and Pennsylvania, are becoming concerned over an exploding skunk population. Skunks have adapted to suburban areas, and unfortunately carry rabies along with their unsociable smell. It's only a matter of time before a pet, or even a child, contracts rabies from a skunk. Skunks are malodorously squashed by cars as often on city streets as country roads these days. Disposing of them has become a major nuisance for home owners and local governments alike. They are difficult to get rid of. Trapping is certain to bring on their unpleasant defense mechanism. Repellent techniques, such as using water or mothballs, at best, just chase them to a house next door. Poison is too hazardous to children and pets to be a viable alternative in town. "Shoot them" is the unequivocal advice of regional conservationists, none of whom seem to know how to persuade skunks to march in front of shotguns.

One hundred fifty-five words. As you can see, as the copy lengthens, the complexity of the topic emerges. Getting rid of skunks is not a simple matter. And yet, to accommodate editorial length restrictions, the article might have to make it seem easy.

## The Ending

Endings, like beginnings, are shrouded in myth. One belief about them that simply is not true is that the ending must echo the language of the beginning. Another convention breached more than honored is that the ending must tie up all loose ends. I think sometimes the fun of a piece is what it leaves untied. An ending must satisfy the reader. Beyond that, there are few traditions. There are possibilities, such as refocusing, transformation and wrap-up, but these are possibilities, not rules. Consider the endings to the *Elle* leads quoted above:

> Emulating the dream world of fashion photographs has become, writes O'Brien, "a sort of yoga that is more than skin-deep," a spiritual exercise which he calls (what else?) Voga.
>
> From "Exposure" by Sarah Ferguson, *Elle*, July 1991, p. 20.

> "My intention was never for us to just keep getting bigger and bigger, anyway. What people have to expect from me is to not expect anything, and that's what they should expect from Lollapalooza—and, really, what they should expect from life."
>
> From "Making Rock Matter" by Gina Arnold, *Elle*, July 1991, p. 35.

> I knew that if Tolstoy himself were to read my novel, he'd have shrieked: "It was not like that at all." But I felt—and I still feel—that through fiction I was able to get closer to the spirit of the man than I could ever have done by keeping to "the facts."
>
> From "The New Biography" by Jay Parini, *Elle*, July 1991, p. 56.

> But don't expect the next generation to emulate this practical fashion—a revolution of ribbons is surely not far behind.
>
> From "Suitables," *Elle*, July 1991, p. 100.

> The face to go with Mugler's space-goddess dressing is a personal interpretation—and Mugler admits to taking a "certaine liberté" in this respect—but his makeup concepts are not contradictory to those rocketing into the cosmetics mainstream.
>
> From "Make-Up" by Janine King, *Elle*, July 1991, p. 118.

As with the leads, the endings have great variety. The first is "a wry comment"; the second, "a final sage quote"; the third, "the author takes a stand." The fourth is "a reversal" in which the author disavows everything said earlier. The last is an old-fashioned "summary." But again, the question is, Does a pattern emerge? Is there anything that unites these endings into an "*Elle* style"? One thing I think they have in common is a mention of people. Maybe that's the *Elle* formula.

## Refocus

A refocusing statement, you will recall from Chapter 3, is a moment in the text in which the author either restates, develops or intensifies the promise. It's a device to up the stakes. For example, a piece on cake baking might have three refocusing statements. The first time, the writer might hint that the article has something to do with cakes. In the second refocusing statement a few paragraphs later, the writer may bluntly say that families bake cakes. Finally, the writer may assert that sharing things like baking cakes is what holds families together. At each of these refocusing moments, the reach for insight strengthens and intensifies. Refocusing is important with subtle ideas; it would be very difficult to go from premise, cake baking, to conclusion, families, without gradual refocusing.

## Transformation

Transformation in a complex essay is the moment of most intense revelation or refocusing. The writer is telling the reader finally what it all means. It usually comes near the end, but it could occur anywhere. Transformation is not needed in simpler writing, but in sophisticated writing, it's the reason we're reading. For examples, review Chapter 3, especially the section on "Sophisticated Patterns."

## Transitions

A refocusing statement is often a transition, but not all transitions are refocusing statements. Transitions are devices for switching from one element to another, and how overworked some of these are: however, on the other hand, unfortunately, another reason, of course, moreover, undoubtedly. . . . And these (in italics):

The city, *in fact*, is in the throes of an Italian boom.

From "The Japanese Are Turning Italian Too" by Lesley Downer, *Taste*, February/March 1991, p. 42.

*And then*, off to the right, up a gravel driveway, marked by a wooden sign designed not to call attention to itself, you arrive at the bay, serene and grassy smelling, hot-sunny and cool-breezy.

From "The Bird People" by Judith Levine, *New York Woman*, April 1991, p. 44.

*Now* two researchers suggest that some of the most dramatic features on Venus result not from plate tectonics, but from a process they call "blob tectonics."

From "Blob Tectonics on Venus," *Science News*, December 15, 1990, p. 382.

In all three cases you could eliminate the transition and not hurt the clarity of the sentence. Magazine writing can use transitions efficiently by being sparing or using them at key moments. Intensely compact writing often has multipurpose transitions. Newsmagazines, which have to cram much information in limited space, squeeze blood from their transitions. Consider these paragraphs from *Newsweek*; notice how many subtopics are in 126 words (transitions italicized):

 The Soviet Government has offered to pay its farmers precious hard currency in return for their grain. *But* many grain growers are hanging onto their harvest, anticipating higher, market-determined prices and using grain to barter. In the collapsing Soviet economy, food is better than money.

*Meanwhile*, officials at KGB, who have been put in charge of making sure foreign food aid isn't wasted, were panicking last week about how to clear their ports for the imminent arrival of foreign grain . . . *Meeting in Rome last week*, the European Community agreed in principle to a further aid package of $2.4 billion worth of food and medicine. *But* more than a million metric tons of various imports are already clogging Soviet ports, both unloaded and in the warehouses.

From "What Russia Really Needs" by Carroll Bogert, *Newsweek*, December 24, 1990, p. 36.

What the editors accomplish in this piece is to use transitions not only to switch from sentence to sentence or paragraph to paragraph, but to move from subtopic to subtopic and even to refocus. All with a single word. When a transition does things beyond merely introducing a paragraph, it's earning its space.

## MAPPING

After you have learned to recognize elements, the second step, mapping, can unlock a magazine's personality. Mapping is like the forms analysis we did earlier, a subjective experience. That is, the map you create is not as important as the act of mapping. A map is a "picture" of an article's structure. Theory tells us there is an ideal pattern for expository writing, but I've yet to see an article that actually matched the ideal. If it existed, the ideal structure would look like this:

    **I.** BEGINNING
        Hook
        Focus statement

**II.** MIDDLE
    **A.** Subtopic
         Transition
    **B.** Subtopic
         Transition
    **C.** Subtopic
**III.** ENDING
      Transformation
      Ending or wrap-up

I don't look for ideals. What I prefer to do is read real articles and see how they differ from this ideal. The differences tell me how the editors and their writers really think. To make perception easier, I use visual symbols instead of outlines. Abstract symbols seem to create clearer patterns for me. Figure 5.1 shows how that ideal would look in visual symbols.

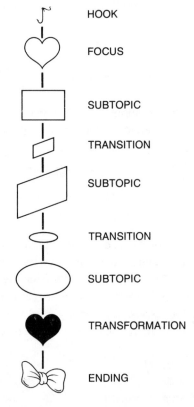

HOOK

FOCUS

SUBTOPIC

TRANSITION

SUBTOPIC

TRANSITION

SUBTOPIC

TRANSFORMATION

ENDING

**FIGURE 5.1**   The Mythical Ideal

The pattern the abstract symbols form is the map. Now let's look at this abstracting method when applied to mapping a real article I was asked to write for a lifestyle magazine. It was rejected, though.

## *The Cold*

*What good is warmth without cold to give it sweetness?*

John Steinbeck, *Travels with Charley*

HOOK

Marian, my roommate at the University of Illinois, could whistle like a Chicago cop. She didn't use fingers; she just curled back her lips and blew. One night, coming home from the library, she paused on the Quad. "Listen," she said and began bouncing her whistle off the buildings. The echoes circled their way back to us.

"I can only do that when it's cold and clear like this," she said. It was about ten below, a sharp prairie night when the sky bristled with stars. Her whistles drew a small crowd of other students: "Do that again." "Can you make them bounce the other way?" "Is that a *girl* whistling?" I decided years later that only on the prairie would people gather at ten below just to admire a whistle.

FOCUS

We were not indifferent to the cold. We shivered. Nor were we ignorant of the danger. We'd grown up on ice skates. We knew, if not clinically then intuitively, that awful things happened if we got too cold. "Too cold," first aid books were explicit, was below 90 or 92 degrees F. for vital organs. Below that, muscles would stiffen; the blood thicken; the heart weaken, slow, perhaps stop; the brain become cranky and confused until speech slurred, vision blurred or coma set in.

SUBTOPIC
The Body

None of us worried about this as we stood coaxing Marian to whistle. We were the immortal young, although the longer we dallied the more we tempted immortal laws of convection, conduction, evaporation and radiation—our own, not the universe's—to kill us.

SUBTOPIC
Convection

Convection warred upon us whenever a fresh draft of air touched us. The more air moved over us the more our fool bodies tried to heat it. This was the infamous wind chill turning uncomfortable temperatures to killers because our bodies could not quit the struggle. When Shakespeare's Henry VI railed against the "barren . . . wrathful nipping cold," it was convection that chilled him.

SUBTOPIC
Conduction

Conduction was more subtle, wrenching heat from our vulnerable hearts and brains via our feet to squander it uselessly on to the sidewalk. We'd experienced conduction many times by touching stone, earth, ice, metal or stadium seats. Metal was such a rapid conductor that our parents spent our childhoods bizarrely warning us not to lick pump handles. Conversely, air was a slow heat conductor. Moving air might have been dangerous, but still or trapped air could be warmed enough to insulate us, which is why we were swaddled in goosedown and waffle-weave underwear.

SUBTOPIC
Evaporation

SUBTOPIC
Radiation

SUBTOPIC
Clothing

Evaporation threatened us as we shivered and then perspired from the work of shaking. The intensity of heat loss as water became water vapor depended on the amount of vapor already in the air. The dryer the air, the greater the heat loss. Cold air tends to be very dry, which is why if our clothing were wet from shivering, the night would be colder still, and deadly.

Radiation was probably the main source of our danger that night. We stood simply emitting heat toward cooler objects such as the buildings the whistles echoed from. We would reverse the process later by standing near space heaters or fireplaces, but out there on the Illinois Quad, with the open, snow-quilted cornfields visible beyond the campus buildings, we blithely emitted our heart's work into the dark.

Clothing slowed the loss but didn't prevent it. Heat radiated to clothing, there to be convected, conducted or evaporated away. We wore hats, since the head was the greatest source of radiant heat loss; scarves to slow evaporation through our noses; mittens, not gloves, to reduce surface area for radiation from our hands; and large boots to permit insulating air around our feet. And yet, despite the unfashionable wisdom of our bundling, the cold was winning. We shivered.

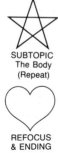

SUBTOPIC
The Body
(Repeat)

REFOCUS
& ENDING

Shivering was one of the few natural weapons we had for fighting cold, although this involuntary rattle of contractions wasn't as effective as voluntarily walking. The shivering would stop if our core temperatures dropped below 90 degrees or our supply of glucose ran out—whichever came first. None of us stayed long enough for that. In a few minutes we left, reignited by the inevitable limits of our tropical origins. But for just a moment, we had stood, defying the cold, as we would the dark, with a whistle.

Mapping, like forms analysis, is a subjective process. Another reader might draw a different version. Figure 5.2 is a simplified map for "The Cold." It says that a long hook is followed by a focus statement, then a subtopic (the body); then a group of closely related subtopics (convection, conduction, evaporation and radiation); then another subtopic (clothing); then development of an earlier subtopic (the body) and finally a refocus.

Figure 5.3 through 5.5 are maps I did of articles from three different magazines. Again, notice the wide variety. Notice how digression is drawn for the *Popular Mechanics* article. Notice, too, how a pro/con was handled in *Condé Nast Traveler* and that the map reveals an unbalanced discussion. (One subtopic is mostly pro, another mostly con.) Notice finally how a tandem focus was drawn for a *Country Journal* piece. There is nothing magical about these maps; they are just my inter-

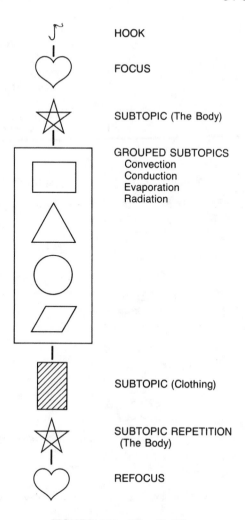

HOOK

FOCUS

SUBTOPIC (The Body)

GROUPED SUBTOPICS
Convection
Conduction
Evaporation
Radiation

SUBTOPIC (Clothing)

SUBTOPIC REPETITION
(The Body)

REFOCUS

**FIGURE 5.2**  "The Cold"

pretation of the pieces. Doing maps unlocks my thinking. The thinking is what matters; the "map" is just a piece of paper.

Although the four maps seem messy, these aren't weak articles. They only differ from the ideal, and I think the divergences give the writing vitality. Mapping is useful for seeing the subtleties of a magazine's philosophy. Doing maps of all articles in an issue or two and combining the maps with an analysis of form (see Chapter 4) and authority base (see Chapter 6) will give the writer power to adapt successfully to that magazine's style.

But mapping can have personal use too. If you apply it to your own rough drafts when you're ready to revise, you can sometimes see problems invisible otherwise.

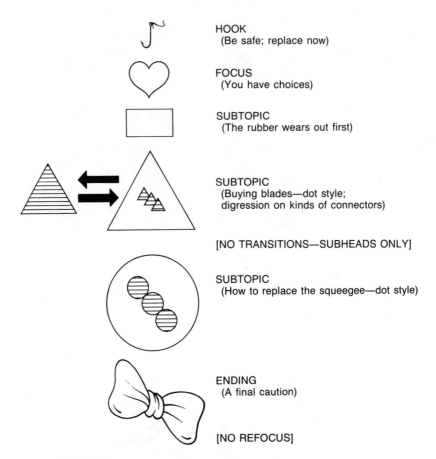

HOOK
(Be safe; replace now)

FOCUS
(You have choices)

SUBTOPIC
(The rubber wears out first)

SUBTOPIC
(Buying blades—dot style;
digression on kinds of connectors)

[NO TRANSITIONS—SUBHEADS ONLY]

SUBTOPIC
(How to replace the squeegee—dot style)

ENDING
(A final caution)

[NO REFOCUS]

**FIGURE 5.3**  *Popular Mechanics*

*"Car Care: Replacing Wiper Blades" by Don Chaikin, August 1991, p. 67.
Summary: A step-by-step guide to this safety necessity.*

Sometimes it's best to have another reader map your drafts for you. With the symbols bluntly on the page before you, it can be easier to see what needs to be changed. For example, by mapping "The Cold," I saw clearly that the hook and lead were too long, given the length of the article. I also realized that there was too little refocusing and too much factual information. The original assignment was, as the editor put it, "to describe cold as the enemy." I wrote a hypothermia piece, not a philosophical piece about cold. The map unlocked the weaknesses. Wish I'd drawn the map before I mailed the piece.

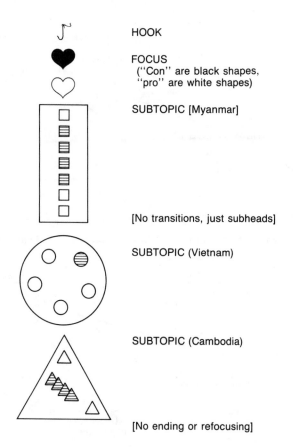

HOOK

FOCUS
("Con" are black shapes,
"pro" are white shapes)

SUBTOPIC [Myanmar]

[No transitions, just subheads]

SUBTOPIC (Vietnam)

SUBTOPIC (Cambodia)

[No ending or refocusing]

**FIGURE 5.4** *Condé Nast Traveler*

*"Safe Travel: Weighing the Risk of Asian Vacations" by Aaron Sugarman and Joseph Yogerst, March 1991, pp. 32–33.*
*Summary: Are the militarily dominated countries of Myanmar (formerly Burma), Vietnam and Cambodia safe for Americans? Pros and cons for all three.*

## NOTES

1. Donald M. Murray, *A Writer Teaches Writing*, 2nd ed., Houghton Mifflin, Boston, 1985, pp. 51–52.
2. Jacques Barzun, *Simple and Direct: A Rhetoric for Writers*, Harper & Row, New York, 1976.
3. Edgar Dale and Joseph O'Rourke, *Living Word Vocabulary*, World Book, Chicago, 1976.

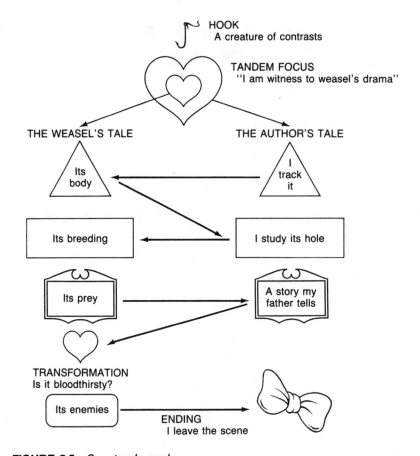

**FIGURE 5.5** *Country Journal*

*"The Least Weasel" by Tom Bates, January/February 1991, pp. 53–55.*
*Summary: straightforward zoology slipped into author's recollection of a winter day. Premise (stated only at end) is weasel's killer image comes from its need to eat more than larger animals do.*

## FOR ADDITIONAL READING

Fowler, H. W. *A Dictionary of Modern English Usage.* Revised by Sir Ernest Gowers. Oxford University Press, Oxford, 1983.

Gorden, Karen Elizabeth. *The Transitive Vampire: A Handbook of Grammar for the Innocent, the Eager, and the Doomed.* Times Books, New York, 1984.

Gorden, Karen Elizabeth. *The Well-Tempered Sentence.* Ticknor & Fields, New Haven, Conn., 1983.

Leggett, Glenn, C. David Mead, and Melinda G. Kramer. *The Prentice-Hall Handbook for Writers.* 11th ed. Prentice-Hall, Englewood Cliffs, N.J., 1991.

Kirszner, Laurie G., and Stephen R. Mandell. *The Holt Handbook.* Harcourt Brace Jovanovich, Fort Worth, Tex., 1992.

Maleska, Eugene T. *A Pleasure in Words.* Simon & Schuster, New York, 1981.

Strunk, William, Jr., and E. B. White. *The Elements of Style.* 3d ed. Macmillan, New York, 1979.

# Part III

# *Advanced Tools*

*I*n this section is one of the longest and one of the shortest chapters in the book. But difference in length is not a difference in importance. Both authority base and voice are sophisticated concepts essential to writers or editors who want to grow in skills. Authority base is language a writer uses to signal a reader that a fact has been researched. Voice is the unique characteristics of a writer's style. Mastering voice may take many years of experience. But analyzing voice means answering one question: Does a magazine permit its writers to have individual voices or must writers blend their voices into a single voice, that of the magazine? Authority base likewise may take years of experience to control, but the analysis is complicated too. What sorts of authority does a magazine expect—experts, real people, statistics, visual records? What authority bases dominate? Are departments different from features in preferred authority? The difference in length of the chapters reflects a difference in analysis, not in sophistication.

# Chapter

# 6

# *Authority Base*

With some adjustments in vocabulary, the preceding chapters on focus, form and structure might be applied to any kind of writing—fiction or nonfiction, book or article, scholarly or popular. But magazine nonfiction obviously differs from scholarly books or sci-fi novels. Facts alone do not account for the difference. Fiction, to be believable, must be factual. The James Michener novel *The Source* and the novel by Jean Auel, *The Clan of the Cave Bear*, are as noted for the accuracy of their historical detail as they are for their story lines. But they are clearly novels. What then sets nonfiction apart?

It's a given that a story must be true to be nonfiction. But equally important, the story must *sound* true too. Something in the ways words are patterned on the page must signal or cue the reader, now gently, now shrilly, that the story has not been made up. Every good writer of nonfiction learns to use these patterns or cues with grace and timing. Every editor learns to respect the virtues and hazards of these signals.

Such verbal patterns may be as simple as the phrase "they said" or as complex (and tedious) as a table of statistics with footnotes. Most cues are more subtle and less boring than these two extremes, however. Subtle or overt, they will be present whether readers are conscious of them or not. The presence of these devices makes the reader decide the story is nonfiction. A broad term for these cues is *authority base*. Authority bases are *language cues that suggest or reveal authors' information sources*.

Other terms sometimes used for authority base include *attribution, sourcing* or *sources, references* and *documentation*. These narrower terms are less useful because they emphasize the information rather than the language. For example, what is the stylistic impact of attributing information to "some people" instead of to

"Alice Jones"? Both are "attributions" but they sound quite different in text. And what are the stylistic consequences of avoiding attribution entirely, as in a recipe in a cooking magazine? There's an implied source (the test kitchen) but none actually quoted. Because there are so many language patterns, the broad term *authority base* allows us to examine all such cues and think about their strengths and weaknesses as stylistic devices as well as vehicles for information.

Language can be manipulated to signal facts in hundreds of ways. A skilled writer commands an arsenal of cues and tricks. What distinguishes modern nonfiction is not the presence of authority bases, but the variety. "Eva's Ghost" is a story I wrote for this chapter just to demonstrate authority base. I easily managed to pack twenty-six authority bases in it—although I certainly don't recommend making a practice of using this many. Fewer bases usually equals crisper prose. As you read the story, notice how the authority bases are slipped in.

But notice also when a cue is graceful or clumsy. A practical reality of writing and editing nonfiction is that authority bases must be present, but some are deadly dull and some are delightful to read. Unfortunately the easiest to read are not always the best at revealing sources. This means the writer—or editor—has to choose: readability or credibility? The dilemma of balancing the two can easily cause many a sleepless night. Is good copy good journalism? When you read the analysis of these twenty-six authority bases after the story, you will see how many tough choices there were.

## *Eva's Ghost*

1. Direct Quote

2. The Qualifier

3. Once upon a time

4. Epistemological Splash

5. Sensory Detail

6. Author's Experience

"Your house will find you," my mother said when I moved to Ohio. Nonsense, I told her and let a realtor drag me to every ugly house in the county, it seemed.

Months later, when I'd quit searching, I was on my way to a party in the country and passed a "for sale" sign. It sat beside the sort of hill geologists like to call a monadnock, a tough chunk of rock that had withstood the pressure from the Wisconsin glacier melts. The knoll stood alone surrounded by wooded valleys. Most houses in this section of Ohio, so eroded it's called Appalachian Ohio, sit in hollows or are shrouded on three sides by cliffsides. But this house sat atop its monadnock. Although it was surrounded by trees and hard to see, I caught a glimpse of an arched window as I passed. "That looks like me," I thought.

At the party I asked the hostess if she knew anything about the house. She didn't, and I forgot about it until she called three weeks later. "Were you the one asking about that house?" she began. She said the owner had been by, quite depressed, to tell her he'd had it sold until the buyer's financing fell

7. The Mind
   Reader

8. The Number

9. Generic
   Them

10. The Catalog

11. The Expert
    Has a Soul

12. The Indirect
    Quote

through. She was trying to cheer him up by finding whoever it was who'd asked about the house. She'd called half a dozen people already.

I figured if someone went to that much trouble to find me, I ought to at least look. The house, built in 1939, was a riotous meshing of nooks and crannies, cabinet built-ins, side alcoves, gables and unexpected doors. It was also a mess—inside and outside. The siding was warped and peeling on the north face, all the plaster was cracked, the basement was damp, the windows—every one—needed new putty, some of the sashes were rotted away, and the rugs were soiled and worn.

But I liked it. Most house buyers care only about size of the bathrooms, number of bedrooms, kitchen cupboard space, access to cable TV and lack of remodeling problems. I asked about none of these things. Instead my ideal home required French doors leading to an enclosed porch, hardwood floors, a view of the sunrise, a dogwood tree. I had twenty-eight such items on my list. As I walked through the house I realized all of them were present, a curved balustrade, an apple tree, lilac and peony bushes, a study downstairs, twelve-pane windows, lightning rods with blue glass globes, a hand pump in the yard, arched doorways, a fireplace, a dining room with a built-in china cupboard, a blue spruce. Only one thing was missing from my wish list—a view of water. Wherever I'd lived before I could see a stream or a pond. This place didn't have that. However, I decided as I left, one from twenty-eight is twenty-seven—not a bad score; high enough to look more carefully. I asked if I could return with a carpenter to inspect for structural faults.

"I've been in this house before," the carpenter, Royce Cooley, said. "Yes, this ceiling over the stairs—that's mine." Royce was a friend of my landlord's and of mine now too. We'd become friends when he had put up curtain rods in my rented house. He examined the back porch, which he'd built, and drawled, "I see that porch hasn't fallen."

"Not yet," I said and he laughed. I didn't know it then, but I'd slipped into Appalachian style humor, low key, gently insulting. Humor became friendship quickly in this isolated corner of the world, so I knew by now I could trust Royce to tell me the truth about the house. He said the roof, foundation and floors were sound. If fixed up, the house, already fifty years old, would outlast any of the boxy houses around it. "But, Pat, the money you put in repairs could buy you a new house," he warned.

As we stood talking in the room that would become my study I saw a bulldozer in the valley below. "What's happening?" I shrieked. "Is someone putting in a shopping mall; is that a gas station going in?"

"No, no," cooed the realtor, "That's your neighbor, Dr. Brown; he's putting in a pond."

My view of water. My house had found me.

It had belonged to a childless couple, Eva and Wilkin Allen, who'd built it as their dream house. Both had been in their forties when they moved in and they lived there until just before their deaths—Eva in 1981 at age eighty-three, Wilkin in 1987, at age ninety-five. The house had sat empty since their deaths.

**13. Literature and Documents**

When built, it had been the talk of the town. In 1938 the *Athens Messenger* under the page-wide headline, "Seven-Room Modern House Is Being Built on a Knoll," described these exotic innovations: linoleum floors in the bathroom and kitchen, built-in cupboards, asphalt roof shingles instead of tin, a built-in hot-air furnace, an indoor cistern, a coal room and, most wondrous of all, a built-in tub in the bathroom.

**14. Point-Quote**

When the house was finished, Eva and Wilkin held an open house. "Hundreds came to that open house. They parked all up and down these roads," Norm Allen, one of their nephews, told me. He said all the oak for the house had been cut from the woods behind it, although I later discovered some was salvaged too. When I tore out the bathroom to put in a new one I found old fenceposts used as studs. I liked the thrift of that.

This couple cherished their house; doorknobs were crystalline, the porch paneling was solid wood. But as they grew old, they were less and less able to care for it, which is why it came to me in poor shape. As I pruned back overgrown shrubs, repainted walls neglected for a decade, and cleaned, cleaned, cleaned, I came to know Eva and Wilkin well. Their nephews had gotten the larger furniture out before I moved in, but they'd left the small stuff, the intimate knickknacks and whatnots that reveal a life.

**15. Object/ Conjecture**

**16. Generic You**

Eva especially I thought I knew. In the basement I found a shelf of margarine tubs, all carefully sorted by size and color and packed in old bread wrappers. You know how someone thinks from a find like this. She was frugal and orderly, perhaps obsessively so, the margarine tubs said to me. She must have been a fanatic housekeeper, too, I decided when I found her feather duster wrapped in plastic and hung carefully on a hook by the basement door. It probably had not been used since she died. Yet a basket of unwound string, tangled and knotty, told me she had moments of ease when she relaxed her neatness or at least allowed Wilkin his sloppiness. I was baffled at first by two beautifully framed photographs of Forest Lawn Cemetery in the dining room; but after discovering flowerbeds in the unlikeliest of places I decided she was not obsessed with cemeteries but just enjoyed gardens. In the dining room cupboard was a cup with the seal of the Athens' Business and Professional Women's Club. In the basement were coatracks Wilkin had probably made for her. BPW was written on the rods. She must have hosted the club often, no doubt to show off her house. I decided I liked her.

**17. Trust Me**

Eva had been a bookkeeper for the Athens Lumber Co. Wilkin had been a meatcutter and an amateur carpenter. He built the garage by himself and also the chicken house. The Allens supplemented their income with the chickens.

**18. Historical Context**

Times were still hard in these years just before World War II. Wilkin was too old for that war, but he had served in World War I. I found his mildewed

American Legion cap in a cloth-lined box in a drawer. In the box with the cap was a sheet of lined paper; written in pencil were the dates the foundation was laid, the sidewalks poured, the siding put up, the plastering finished and moving-day.

In the same drawer with the cap was a box of photos. The photos told me Eva and Wilkin had been fond of dogs. They'd had five dachshunds, Gip, Beauty, Buffy, Fritz and one more whose name I couldn't read on the small grave slabs I found beyond the fence. Fritz was the first and longest lived. Buffy was the last. "Our Buffy does a fine job taking care of us and we taking care of her," Eva had written on the back of a photo dated November, 1979. "And we thought we could never love another puppy this much."

The photos also told me that Eva and Wilkin might have known Eva was very ill. Many of Eva were taken in 1980, presumably by Wilkin: Eva with her friends, with family, in the house or yard, with the dog. It was as if Wilkin were trying to hold on to her with these pictures. He was older than she by six years but would outlive her by six years. She died of inoperable cancer of the liver on

**19. Official Records**

**20. Methods Description**

Dec. 21, 1981, the death certificate said. She was buried Christmas Eve. In one of her last photos she grins impishly at the camera. I put that photo next to one taken of her when she was very young, perhaps seventeen or eighteen, in about 1915 or 1916. The grin had not changed in all those years. If the smile speaks truly she was full of gentle mischief. Perhaps the Forest Lawn photos were one of her jokes.

Eva was such a strong presence in the house that when my mother visited, we found ourselves talking about her as if she were there. We'd debate a paint color and wonder if Eva would approve. We'd ask her advice on furniture arrangements. We joked about her strictness with Wilkin, making him smoke only in the den—now my study. The den was the only room with cigarette burns in the carpet.

**21. The Expert**

**22. Results Description**

Our conversations were pretense. Neither of us thought Eva was haunting the place. Being new to the region I didn't know many Appalachian people strongly believe in psychic phenomena—ghosts, telepathy, the reading of auras. The great anthropologist, Margaret Mead, was quoted in *New Realities* in October 1978, (the same month as Wilkin's eighty-sixth birthday) that Appalachian children are gifted in psychic abilities because of their naïveté, their isolation from the modern world and their parents' strong beliefs in the supernatural. Whatever the anthropological roots, people I meet here invariably know the local haunted spots. Although they smile when telling tales, much as they smile when reading *National Enquirer* headlines, they always know the stories.

**23. Hearsay**

There's supposed to be a ghost in Wilson Hall, the second oldest building on the Ohio University campus. Near where I live is supposed to be an old railroad tunnel. Although the tunnel, railroad and tracks are gone, people claim on some nights of the year, when the moon is just so, the train still goes through. Of course, the tunnel was the site of a tragic death. All good ghost stories have a tragic death at base. I haven't gone to the tunnel myself to check it out, but there are plenty of people who say it is true. Big Foot has been seen in these woods too. In fact, so rich with ghosts is Athens County, that the local newspapers are fond of reporting—usually around Halloween—that it's the thirteenth most haunted place on earth, according to a British psychic phenomena research organization.

I didn't discover how strong these beliefs were until one day my mother and I were talking to Eva while a young woman I'd hired to help clean house was there. She became frightened. She thought the house was haunted. I had to reassure her it wasn't, astonished all the while such a conversation was needed. I never felt Eva haunted the house, but after I'd spent two years of nearly endless repairing, replastering, repainting, my mother came to visit again. "Eva seems to have let go," she commented one evening. "I think she's decided you're going to take care of the house for her. She can rest now."

I smiled, "Don't joke about ghosts down here, Mother. Too many people want to believe."

24. Reader Abuse

25. Unnamed Source

26. I'm not a Doctor but I Play One on TV.

## STRENGTHS AND WEAKNESSES

I am willing to swear in whatever court is handy that the story you have just read is true, including that the pond was being dug as I looked out the window, that somebody ranks Athens as thirteenth most haunted in the world, that Royce Cooley had been in the house before, that Eva had sorted her margarine tubs (or someone had) and that I did have lightning rods with blue globes on my wish list. All true. Every bit of it. I swear.

But the question is, without my swearing, did you believe the story as you read it? If so, it was because of the language cues I inserted. The twenty-six cues I used were devices or tools for signaling readers about the story's veracity. Yet a good editor would have been suspicious of every one of these cues and called me with lots of questions. And where one editor would accept my use of a device, another would be horrified that I'd use it. Magazines differ in which authority bases they respect or emphasize. Let's examine each of the twenty-six authority bases in depth to see the hazards—and strengths—of each.

## 1. Direct Quote   *"Your house will find you," my mother said.*

Quoting a source directly is a basic and time-honored journalistic practice. Get a person's exact words and put quote marks around them: could anyone doubt this? Nobody would make up a quote, right?

What an unsophisticated reader may fail to appreciate is that the quote records only what the person *said*, not whether what was said is actually true. It's a journalistic dodge: The president (not the author of the article) said there would be no tax hike. The mayor (not the reporter) said he did not use cocaine. The fire chief (not me! not me! not me!) said he thought the fire was suspicious. This distinction between what was said and what may be true is a troublesome one for journalists. How far can a writer go in explaining this difference to readers? To point it out might sound like editorializing—or libel. To not point it out might allow a demagogue to mislead people.

Edward Jay Epstein in his book *Between Fact and Fiction* is vehement about this weakness of the direct quote. He argues that the McCarthy era, when many innocent people lost their jobs because they were suspected of being communists, pivoted primarily on the rantings and ravings, or quotes, of Wisconsin senator Joseph McCarthy, possibly an alcoholic. McCarthy would be duly quoted in the press and peoples' lives would shatter. The arrest of Clay Shaw as a "conspirator" in the murder of John F. Kennedy in 1967 came about because New Orleans district attorney Jim Garrison seemed to be a publicity hound, Epstein argues. It took a jury less than an hour to acquit Shaw but Garrison had made headlines off poor Shaw for weeks. As Epstein commented:

A demagogue can survive only so long as the mass media take him seriously enough to print his charges and give him exposure. The relation, however, is not entirely one sided. The demagogue, free of any constraint of veracity, is always in a position to provide journalists with the kinds of exclusive stories and sensational charges which stimulate widespread interest—and circulation.

From *Between Fact and Fiction* by Edward J. Epstein, Vintage Books, New York, 1975, p. 143.

In other words, there is no law forbidding people from lying to the press, and there may even be some incentives to lie. One can be embarrassed for lying to journalists but not convicted of perjury.

Because quotes are not a guarantee of truth, many magazines limit their use, feeling they're better for supporting facts rather than *as* fact. But magazines have another reason for avoiding direct quotes: they're muddy. Rarely does a person speak as well as a writer can write. Worse, even if a quote is pithy and full of fun, it must have a full attribution identifying the source. Since many magazines have policies against one-source articles, an attribution is needed every time someone is quoted. Nothing is as muddy as an attribution. Consider these examples:

English conductor Sir Thomas Beecham, an energetic defender of the idea of classical music as a democratic institution, remarked, "Composers should write tunes that chauffeurs and errand boys can whistle."

From "Hum-dingers: Catchy Tunes, Memorable Melodies Making Beautiful Music Again" by Steve Metcalf, *Hartford Courant*, reprinted in the *Columbus Dispatch*, Sunday August 26, 1990, p. F-1.

Identifying Beecham as a conductor and giving his key idea force the author to write an attribution that's eight words longer than the quote. Being a canny writer, Metcalf had the sense to bury this, the first attribution of the story, six paragraphs into the article.

"Price is also important to older consumers," says Judith Langer, president of Langer Associates in New York City. Her qualitative research indicates that many older customers are more cautious about spending money than their youthful counterparts: "They realize their high earning years are coming to an end."

From "What Is Good Service" by Patricia Brause, *American Demographics*, July 1990, pp. 36–39.

Here Brause broke the attribution into two sentences to smooth out the sound of the necessary details.

Aaron Schickler, for instance, who is best known for his portrait of former first lady Jacqueline Kennedy, eschews the portrait painter label, noting, "I don't conceive of portrait painting as giving me a separate identity. I am an artist."

From "The Life of a Portrait Painter" by Daniel Grant, *American Artist*, July 1990, p. 27.

This cram-a-fact style, using a value judgment to identify the source, rather than the "name, rank and serial number" approach of news, is one way magazine writers get around the boredom of attributions. A newspaper might have said "Manhattan studio artist" but a magazine goes for the glitter. Jackie-O. Yes.

"We went through a year and a half of hell basically," says co-lead guitarist Greg Steele, a sentiment that's echoed by vocalist Taime Downe, "We went through hard problems, hard times, a lot more pressure than we had with the first album."

From "Faster Pussycat Rebounds after a Painful Year" by Toby Goldstein, *Circus*, July 31, 1990, p. 61.

In this quote the author, Toby Goldstein, seems to think one way to alleviate the sound of direct quotes is to jam them together and damn the torpedoes, full speed ahead. Most magazines disguise their attributions by stringing them out a paragraph or two before or after the quote—anything to avoid that "quote comma he said" tone that characterizes newspaper features.

With attributions ugly and quotes suspect, some magazines have policies against "talking head" pieces. Yet if magazines insist on many sources but won't permit too many attributions, what's a writer to do? I solve the problem of attributing a direct quote in my story simply by not identifying my mother (except as "my mother").

However, this means an independent reader, or more likely, a magazine's fact checker, can't verify whether the quote is accurate. They don't have enough information to find her. Who is she? When did she say this? And where?

This is the central issue with most authority bases. How much should the writer reveal to the reader? Reveal too little and credibility (or authority) suffers. Reveal too much and readability (or, if you prefer, the crystalline beauty of the prose) suffers. A common practice when writers truncate attributions for the sake of style is for the author to give the editor the background details for fact checking. When drafting this piece I felt if I had a sentence at the beginning polluted with full attribution (name, address, title, time and place of utterance), no one would read on to the second sentence. The price I—and you—pay for my decision is that now you have to trust that my editors checked with Mom. (She said I got it "mostly right.")

## 2. The Qualifier ... *it seemed.*

Stuck in the second sentence of my opening paragraph are the two innocent words: "it seemed." They're necessary because the sentence is technically untrue, an exaggeration. I couldn't possibly have visited every house in the county, nor could they all have been ugly. It only felt that way to me, and how I felt is the "fact" of this sentence. The qualifier is reassuring you, the reader, that I know I'm reporting feelings, not a reality.

Qualifiers are very important in keeping nonfiction sounding like nonfiction, and I use a lot of them in this piece: *perhaps, may, probably, maybe*—words like that are meant to limit what is said in the sentence, to let you and me collaborate in recognizing that such sentences are stylistic devices. The qualifier is necessary so other facts in the article remain credible. Actually, I think the irony in the sentence is so clear I don't need a qualifier, but in the examples below, the qualifier is important for both clarity and style:

> How this brand of wolf hunting can be condoned and encouraged by Alaska officials becomes *slightly more understandable* if you consider the prejudices of many Alaskans toward wolves and the way the state game board operates. (Italics mine.)
>
> From "How to Kill A Wolf" by George Laycock, *Audubon*, November 1990, p. 48.

Note how Laycock avoids stating a bald opinion while not quite avoiding opinion either. The author of the letter excerpted here is doing something similar but with different intent:

> I have been wondering what piece of worldly advice I as a dean *might have* to offer that *could be* of assistance to you in this transitional period in your lives. It *occurred to me* at the conclusion of one of our recent seminars that the

following counsel *might perhaps* enhance your career prospects; *at least* it should prove helpful in getting you through the lengthy interviews that often precede employment offers. When you are preparing to attend a meeting that might last for two hours or more, you should reserve a little bit of time right before the meeting to go to the bathroom. (Italics mine.)

From "Go With The Flow," an excerpt of a letter by James Carey, Dean of St. John's College in Santa Fe, New Mexico, sent to all seniors, reprinted in *Harper's*, July 1990, p. 23.

The qualifier can be an important tool in humor; in the example above it's a way of twisting something that might be taken literally into the intended irony.

## 3. Once upon a Time   *Months later . . .*

The third sentence of the story sets events in time and action. It's later; I'm on my way to a party. You don't know how much later or where the party is because, as with the attribution in the opening sentence, I decided too much detail would hurt readability. But though this isn't as detailed as an airline itinerary, it does draw on the storyteller's tradition that stories happen in time and over time. This sense of unfolding action might be considered more style than authority, but I think it does create believability. Time is an anchor to reality we're all familiar with.

## 4. The Epistemological Splash   *. . . geologists like to call a monadnock . . .*

Bluntly, this windy description of monadnocks and Wisconsin glacier ice melts is pompous; it should be revised out. But I included it in this demonstration of authority base because I find the technique so often in magazine writing. An Epistemological Splash (such a pompous technique requires a pompous name) is the attempt to extend the reach of an article (or the author) by throwing in small chunks of book learning. Perhaps that's all these splashes do, add status. But if they impress or intrigue the reader, they can improve a piece. These short splashes come in many varieties. Mine here might be called the Geological Splash. In a how-to piece on making a bark canoe from *Country Journal*, the second paragraph, extolling the virtues of wood over aluminum, ends with the following sentences:

Wood, even if it is not shaped into a boat at all, still floats. It is a boat even if you don't make a boat of it. The first canoe was probably a log with a man astride it. The next step was to hollow the log out and sit inside it. That way you could keep your feet dry and carry some cargo besides.

From "The Wooden Canoe" by Robert Kemper, *Country Journal*, June 1988, p. 59.

That version might be called (literally) the History Splash. An extravagant and delightful use of an Epistemological Splash is in an essay by Vicki Hearne, "Consider the Pit Bull." In arguing for the virtues of this much-maligned breed, she has so many Philosophical Splashes she could start a pond. She quotes Ralph Waldo Emerson, the deconstructionist and philosopher Jacques Derrida, Kirkegaard and Nietzsche, Stanley Duval's *The Claim of Reason*, C. S. Lewis plus Chaucer and James Thurber, if you can imagine such a combination. Here is her handling of Derrida:

> A word about names. The French philosopher Jacques Derrida once remarked in a lecture about memory and mourning that we never know—that we die without being quite sure—what our proper names are. This is not always obvious to us, except in the case of some newlyweds. We do not generally feel puzzled or at a loss for an answer when someone asks, "What's your name?" The uncertainty Derrida spoke of is obvious, though, when we turn to the pit bull. There are a number of breeds that are related to the pit bull and often confused with it.
>
> From "Consider the Pit Bull" by Vicki Hearne, reprinted in *Contemporary Essays* edited by Donald Hall, St. Martin's Press, New York, 1989, p. 241.

In all these examples the epistemology was technically irrelevant information, stuck in to gain respect in the reader's eyes. I've rarely had an editor challenge such splashes, so they and readers must like the technique. Or do they? I ask you, Did I get away with it? Or did your eyes glaze over as you thought "Ugh. Geology"?

## 5. Sensory Detail    *. . . an arched window . . .*

This description of the house and the additional descriptions two paragraphs later ("riotous meshing of nooks and crannies . . . siding warped and peeling") seem innocent enough. But description has long been a controversial technique in modern journalism. Can an observer, who is also reporter and writer, be trusted with facts based on physical senses—seeing, hearing, touch, smell, taste? In most news reporting and even some magazine reporting pure description would be considered suspect because it could be subjective, dependent on one person's perceptions and thus limited. Any police officer knows how prone to error an eyewitness description is, and so do editors. And yet, some of the most evocative and provocative writing of the past half-century has been just this, one person taking a look at something and describing it sensually.

Despite the hazards, I sometimes think sensory detail is taking over magazine writing. To find examples I picked up three magazines, opened each at random and found their pages bursting with visions:

> The [soy]beans assume a protean range of shapes, sizes and colors. The seeds of some varieties are as small and round as a BB; others are as large as your thumbnail and shaped like kidney beans. Colors range from ebony to pearl;

some are zebra striped or appear to have the yin/yang symbol molded into them in brown and white.

From "Miracle Bean" by Craig Canine, *Harrowsmith Country Life*, July/August 1990, p. 67.

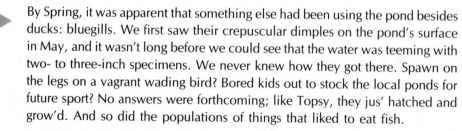

By Spring, it was apparent that something else had been using the pond besides ducks: bluegills. We first saw their crepuscular dimples on the pond's surface in May, and it wasn't long before we could see that the water was teeming with two- to three-inch specimens. We never knew how they got there. Spawn on the legs on a vagrant wading bird? Bored kids out to stock the local ponds for future sport? No answers were forthcoming; like Topsy, they jus' hatched and grow'd. And so did the populations of things that liked to eat fish.

From "A Pond Is Born" by Glen Martin, *Audubon*, July 1990, p. 64.

The cloudless dawn sky towers, intensifying a feeling of unbounded space. The mountains that rim this valley, streaked with ocherous beiges and paprika reds, appear barren, but they are full of plants and animals that merely elude the eye. A pocket mouse the size of a walnut. A desert tortoise asleep in its burrow. Evening-snow, a wispy stemmed plant that remains invisible against the ground until its white flowers open suddenly at nightfall . . .

From "California Desert: A Worldly Wilderness" by Barry Lopez, *National Geographic*, January 1987, p. 51.

Some grumpy critics might argue that yin/yang beans, crepuscular dimples and ocherous beiges are purple prose. But that's a matter of taste, a value judgment, and separate from the serious journalistic concerns about potential bias that comes with description. The doubts cautious editors have about description are valid. Can one person's perceptions be reliable? Well, *I* think I got mine right, and since I now live in the house, I've had opportunities to look again. However, experience has taught me that if I want to use description accurately, a second look is vital to my research. I've known this ever since I wrote a piece about windmills. I happened to have owned a windmill at that time. It had stood outside my study window for seven years, but the day I sat down to describe it, I discovered to my embarrassment I needed to get up, go outside and look before I found the words. This sobered me. Do all reporters look twice before writing?

### 6. Author's Experience   *I asked the hostess . . .*

The first two sentences of this paragraph go further than sensory information of the reporter. Action is described. The author is involved in an experience. But the same question has to be asked: Is one person's experience a valid authority base? Can it be trusted? Some editors are reluctant to use authors' experiences because these are even harder to check than sensory observation. In theory, observed details might be checked by sending a staff editor to the scene to confirm the reporter's description, although the tight economic realities of most publications make this unlikely. But all the money in the world won't bring back time. No fact checker, no matter how tenacious, could recreate the events the writer experienced.

I am the only person who knows if this account is true and I'm hardly a disinterested party. I want to tell a good story; I want to entertain. Could I be embellishing? These are important questions, and a conscientious editor thinks about them. In my story a fact checker might find the hostess and ask her if I got the incident right, but in most cases people have dispersed, weather has changed, life has gone on and there's only the reporter's word that the event happened at all. Are author experiences nonfiction? Tough question in this business. Some magazines refuse to publish any pieces based only on personal experience (that no-single-source policy again). But others thrive on them and consider them the stuff of literature. Where one might refuse authors as sources, another would see them as gateways to the human condition. Consider this lead to an article on mental retardation:

> I went dancing one night last September with a glad crowd of nearly a thousand merrymakers at one of the Red Lion hotels in Portland, Oregon. The dance was the climactic event of the Labor Day weekend convention, following a formal dinner and a day of workshops and lost hotel registrations. The conventioneers were members of an organization called People First, and almost all of them were mentally retarded. The band wore Hawaiian shirts and played loud Sixties music, and I stood to one side clutching a glass but already punch drunk with the day's events.
>
> From "Neither Morons nor Imbeciles nor Idiots" by Sallie Tisdale, *Harper's*, June, 1990, p. 47.

The author's being at the dance adds a subtle but key element to this story. She hints that she has felt ambivalent toward the retarded but that the time she has spent with them has freed her. An account without this ambivalence would have been just another report on the mentally handicapped. With the author's involvement, the article forces us to look at ourselves and our own prejudices toward such people. Author experiences may be hard to fact check, but they may also be the only way to get at deeper truths.

## 7. The Mind Reader   *She was trying to cheer him up . . .*

If ever there were a controversial technique, it's this one. Consider what this sentence says. The hostess was trying to cheer up the owner. How can we know what her motives were? How can we know what was in her mind? I don't write, "She told me she was trying to cheer him up." I simply assert, as if this were a novel, that she was trying to cheer him up. I have entered that woman's mind. Is this a legitimate nonfiction authority base? A rougher question (please forgive my asking): Did you notice the sentence? Were you suspicious; did the technique bother you as you read it?

It bothers a lot of editors. The literary term for this is third-person point of view; it is describing a person's motives, thoughts or unseen actions as if they could be known rather than conjectured. It's omniscient. That, some editors say, crosses the line into fiction. A famous case of the use of mind reading was a story by Tom Wolfe in 1962 for *New York* magazine called "Tycoon of Teen." It was a profile of Phil Spector, at the time a 23-year-old rock and roll producer who became rich by picking hits. He succeeded, wags joked, because he actually liked the music. The story opens inside Spector's mind:

> All these raindrops are high or something. They don't roll down the window, they come straight back, toward the tail, wobbling, like all those Mr. Cool snow heads walking on mattresses. The plane is taxiing out toward the runway to take off, and this stupid infarcted water bobbles sideways across the window. Phil Spector, twenty-three years old, the rock and roll magnate, producer of Philles' records, America's first teen-age tycoon, watches . . . this watery pathology . . . . It is *sick. Fatal.*
>
> From *The Kandy-Kolored Tangerine-Flake Streamline Baby* by Tom Wolfe, Farrar, Straus & Giroux, New York, 1965, p. 47.

Spector was imagining a future plane crash and it so frightened him he insisted the plane turn around and taxi back to let him and his buddies off. The plane then flew safely on to Los Angeles. The incident made the New York papers. Tom Wolfe's description didn't say "Phil Spector said he imagined." The language was present tense. Wolfe wrote it as if it were happening right then.

Wolfe reports in his book *The New Journalism* that one of the news magazines approached Phil Spector and asked if Wolfe's version were true. Spector said it was *exactly* true. About the highest praise anyone can pay a reporter is to say he got it exactly right. Impressed, the reporter went to Tom Wolfe and asked how he'd done that, gotten inside Spector's head. Wolfe said it was easy, he'd asked Spector what he'd thought. All Wolfe had done, and what was so controversial, was drop the authority cues. He'd dropped the "he said" or "he said he thought." This is still radical to do in nonfiction.

In my case I surmised the hostess's motives. I didn't ask her. She said the owner was depressed. She said she had called a lot of people. I then deduced that she was trying to cheer him up. That sentence is unadulterated speculation, but I don't tell you that. Have I crossed the line into fiction? You judge. I think the sentence is within bounds. But I also know editors who would pull it out.

## 8. The Number    *... built in 1939 ...*

Numbers were once a mainstay of journalistic prose, but now, here I am, four paragraphs into the story, and this is the first hard fact of this kind. Magazines are finding ways other than sentences and paragraphs to present "data." Sidebars, graphs, lists, infographics are the rage, and at many publications, writers no longer have to contort themselves to get deadly-to-read numbers woven into sentences.

But examine this number closely. Like the direct quote, it can be misleading. There's nothing in that simple phrase that tells how *I* know the house was built in 1939. To unsophisticated readers just the presence of a number is so believable they do not notice it is not attributed. Just for the record, the sellers told me, the deed told me and a sheet of manila paper I found with Wilkin's cap told me. Three sources is the same number Woodward and Bernstein had to have before their editor would let them print a Watergate story. Three sources seemed safe.

## 9. Generic *Them*    *Most house buyers ...*

Is it possible for any one author to know what most house buyers or most people know about anything? This is a slippery but common technique in magazine writing. Vague generic *people* phrases like *some people, many people, most housewives, few students*, or worse, *some psychiatrists, many sociologists, some doctors* are suspicious because they imply the author is citing formal research but reveal nothing about the studies. Who collected the data on those house buyers or sociologists or housewives? Or is the phrase just based on the author's commonsense supposition that most people ought to think or do such-and-such?

When used as transitions to introduce a specific description of research, these generic phrases do no harm and, in fact, are efficient transitions, as in this article on tomboys:

> No one's sure but *by some estimates* 10 percent of girls Carolyn's age and 3 percent of boys consistently act in ways that fit part of the behavior for the opposite sex. Why are girls more likely to act like boys than the other way around? For one thing, says Heino Meyer-Bahlburg, a clinical psychologist at Columbia University . . . (Italics mine.)

From "Daughter John" by Bonnie Blodgett, *In Health*, July/August 1990, p. 26.

Another harmless use of generic *thems* is linking them with qualifiers (e.g., my use of "some grumpy critics might argue . . ." on p. 122). This clearly signals the reader that the author is commenting, not reporting. But when such generic phrases stand alone they're dangerous. Whenever I see such a phrase bells go off in my mind. I immediately suspect the author is trying to mask sloppy research or slide through a tough transition without any real facts. The summer I wrote "Eva's Ghost" I happened to have attended an editorial meeting with the staff of *Professional Builder* magazine. One of the things we talked about was what house buyers like. I learned developers can improve sales by having their homes fully decorated. Few home-buyers are willing to do the remodeling I was.

So I was right in drawing a contrast between me and "most homebuyers," but wrong in the details. It's not the number of bedrooms but the presence of wallpaper that distinguishes me from them. I wrote my "most homebuyers" sentence before I attended the meeting and remember thinking as I listened how hard it is to generalize accurately about people. I thought about revising the sentence to make it more accurate, but then decided to let it stand as an illustration of why the generic *them* is risky. Normally, I would never let such a sentence stand alone; it's too easy to be wrong, or as I am here, half-wrong, which may be worse.

But I can see why some editors like the generic *them*. It just took me eighty-nine words to explain how I know what I know about house buyers. Compare that with the three words I actually used in the story. Space is tight in magazines and efficiency counts. Even my sloppy use of the generic *them* could be defended by an editor as just a transition, not crucial to the story and so not required to be precisely accurate. I don't buy that argument. It would have been easy to add a qualifier (Other homebuyers might . . . but I . . .) or to insert an attribution (The editors of *Professional Builder* say . . .). So I feel guilty letting a generic phrase stand alone— even in a demonstration.

## 10. The Catalog   . . . *hardwood floors, a view of the sunrise* . . .

A catalog is a list and here mine is playful, lyrical perhaps. But usually in magazine writing, catalogs are dry matters of fact. A catalog is putting directory information in paragraph form: names and addresses of restaurants; the ten best health spas in town; where the bargain hunters' antique shops are; where to buy wildflower seeds. As a result, catalogs are most commonly seen in service or state and city magazines. I'm of the opinion that readers would be better served if lists were indeed put in list form. They would be easier to read. In more and more magazines editors are doing just this. Sometimes writers are able to work with a catalog and still produce engaging prose. But most catalogs seem to fall into patterns like this:

For a taste of Western fare and hospitality, dine and bunk at the historic Rough Rider Hotel, a favorite also of Teddy Roosevelt. A stuffed buffalo greets you in the lobby. Waitresses in red calico dresses serve buffalo-burger lunches and prime-rib dinners in the red-velvet-curtained dining room. Other Medora accommodations: Badlands Motel, Medora Motel, and a 300-site camp-ground.

From "Planning Your Frontier Tour," *Midwest Living*, June 1990, p. 68.

## 11. The Expert Has a Soul   *I've been in this house before . . .*

For better or worse, we live in a culture where expertise is highly regarded. What the doctor or professor or administrator says gets attention in our culture and our media. The reasons for this are no doubt complex. Perhaps it's the tradition of the scientific method or the high status of education. It would take an expert to explain the power of the expert, but that power is pervasive. Experts, that is, people with formal credentials (and not just personal experience), are always part of any developing news story. Mideast scholars and economists are much in demand in recent years.

The credentials are the key. Training, whether it's a Ph.D. in anthropology or apprenticeship to a carpenter, defines an expert for media. News features almost always require an expert, and magazines, even those that are shy of "talking heads," want the power of their authority in articles too. You might say an authority is the ultimate authority base. Sometimes, the more routine or trivial the topic, the more the editors insist on an expert as authority. Note how *Cosmopolitan* and *National Enquirer* use experts to give their articles some weight:

> Indeed, resisting an emotional shakedown is often as easy as recognizing that we *are* being victimized. We'll start, then, by introducing you to some of the most common practitioners of the blackmailer's art. . . . *According to Penelope Russianoff, a clinical psychologist* in private practice in New York City, and author of *Why Do I Think I'm Nothing without a Man?*, "Men can sense—often without being aware of it—that women blame themselves for everything." (Italics for emphasis mine.)
>
> From "Emotional Blackmail: How Others Manipulate You with Their Displeasure" by Carol Hoidra, *Cosmopolitan*, August 1990, p. 188.

> Don't let sarcastic people get you down. You can cope with their caustic, taunting remarks by following these tips from *Dr. Virginia Topper, founder of Sarcastics Anonymous.* . . . (Italics mine.)
>
> From "How to Cope with Sarcasm" by Robert M. Schwartz, *National Enquirer*, January 9, 1990, p. 25.

But expertise often makes for tedious prose. True experts know the complexity of their subject matter and so will go on and on and on and on explaining every parameter and paradox. They don't mean to be boring; they just can't simplify things; they know too much. Jonathan Weiner, in his book *The Next One Hundred Years*, which tries to explain the data (and confusion) about the global warming issue, comments on this exchange between Senator Tim Wirth of Colorado and two scientists during a hearing:

> Senator Wirth: So, you would say that the heat wave and drought [of 1988] are related to the greenhouse effect. Is that right?

Dr. [James] Hansen [of NASA]: Yes. If you look over a time period of, say, 10 years, the number of droughts you get in that period, it appears that will be larger because of the greenhouse effect. But whether you get a drought in a particular year depends upon the weather patterns that exist at the beginning of the season, and that is a noisy phenomenon which is basically unpredictable. So, I can't tell you whether next year is going to have a drought or not. All that we are trying to say is that the probability is somewhat larger than it was a few decades ago.

Not good enough. The senator did not want "on the one hand, on the other hand." (They have a saying in Washington: "I'd like to meet a one-handed scientist.")

Sen. Wirth: Dr. [Michael] Oppenheimer [of the Environmental Defense Fund], do you want to take a shot? Any of the others of you want to answer the question? I think it is a perfectly logical question to ask, isn't it? . . . Are we having the drought because of the greenhouse effect?

From *The Next One Hundred Years: Shaping the Fate of Our Living Earth* by Jonathan Weiner, Bantam, New York, 1990, p. 96.

In this exchange, Senator Wirth is deeply annoyed by the scientists' refusal to give a firm answer. The senator's frustration is the same faced by any writer or editor who tries to present complex information in clear readable copy.

By the way, Dr. Oppenheimer, with a great many words, said "maybe." The result of all this equivocating is rough sledding for a reader. No serious editor would try to compromise the expert and oversimplify the topic. Instead, what some do is to try to bring the copy to life by adding short biographical or narrative inserts about the expert. These can be quite lively, as in this article, which debunks dream theory by quoting the work of psychiatrist and neuroscientist Allan Hobson:

Hobson's voice grows loud and indignant. "That was the best I could do. It's the best that my mind could do under the circumstances [of dreaming]." He pauses for breath and adds a soupcon of incredulity to the mix, his voice now almost a squeak.

From "What Dreams Are (Really) Made Of" by Edward Dolnick, *Atlantic*, July 1990, p. 42.

These microprofiles give a human dimension to the expert and make the technical information more digestible. That's the strength of the technique; the weakness is that these brief biographies usually have little relevance to the topic.

In my story I quoted two experts: anthropologist Margaret Mead and carpenter Royce Cooley. Since Mead is dead and I never met her and since I do know Royce Cooley, he was the expert I chose to flesh out and give a soul. But I'm troubled by the intrusiveness of the two paragraphs. Yes, they make Royce come alive, but showing Royce joshing about the back porch of some other house is at best irrelevant to the story and at worst confusing. I would prefer to edit the whole thing out and instead just say, "The *carpenter* said the roof was sound . . . "

## 12. The Indirect Quote    *He said the roof . . . was sound.*

I don't quote Royce's exact words. I paraphrase what he said. The indirect quote, like the direct quote, has the weakness of being limited to what a person says rather than what may be true in fact. It also loses the credibility of the quote marks. But its strength over the direct quote is that the language often is clearer than the source's. An indirect quote is simpler to read.

From a reporting perspective, though, it is much easier for a source to deny. With a direct quote, the mayor's or county commissioner's only option, if reception to the statement goes poorly, is to claim that his or her words have been taken out of context. With indirect quotes, sources can more easily deny having said them. Even if the subject matter isn't controversial, editors and writers like the indirect quote because of its readability. For example, note the mixing of direct quotes, numbers and indirect quotes below to create a compelling dramatic "scene" in this description of the 1960 execution of Caryl Chessman (indirect quotes are in italics):

On the Morning of May 2, the State Supreme Court convened at 8 A.M., two hours before Chessman's ninth scheduled execution, to hear an appeal from Chessman's lawyers based on the *Argosy* "evidence." At 9:15, *a clerk told* the waiting lawyers that the court had denied the writ by a vote of four to three. The lawyers raced to the Federal Courthouse, where a judge was ready to hear another last-minute plea. Reporters on the steps delayed the lawyers for a minute. A slow elevator took more time. It was after 10 A.M. when Judge Louis E. Goodman looked up from the papers handed to him and said, "I will grant you at least a 30-minute stay while I study this." *He asked his secretary* to phone the prison; she dialed a wrong number. When the judge finally got through, *an assistant warden told him* that the cyanide pellets had already dropped into the acid; the execution was too far along to stop. Caryl Chessman was declared dead at 10:12 A.M.

From "A Matter of Life or Death" by Dick Adler, *Memories*, February/March 1990, p. 72.

## 13. Literature and Documents    *In 1938, the* **Athens Messenger** . . .

Quoting other print media in an article is more common to magazine journalism than with newspapers, partly because of the differences in timeliness of the stories. News stories are breaking now, which means even if reporters have time to get to the library, they probably won't find anything. But magazine topics and deadlines unfold more slowly, allowing time for library research. Some magazine journalists (and their editors) consider library resources a major component of their research efforts (see Chapters 9 and 10). However, others think quoting another article in a new article is not original research. The criterion for using print resources is, Does the new article use the quoted material only for background or tangents? If the quoted article and the new article are almost identical, it's better not to use it. A piece on gorillas for *National Geographic* had better not quote a similar article from two years ago in *Smithsonian*. However, a story for *Ohio* magazine on moving an adolescent gorilla from the Columbus Zoo to an Idaho zoo could probably quote either *Smithsonian* or *National Geographic* with impunity because both articles would be "just background" to the new story.

Etiquette for quoting documents does demand fuller attributions than quotes. The same editors who permit quoting "some people" or "a bystander" or "my mother" without further identification probably won't accept an attribution to "an article last year" or "something I once read." Having written that sentence though, I picked up a collection of articles I'd assembled for a class, opened it at random (this at-random phenomenon has begun to frighten me) and found the following sentence:

> *I once read* about an experiment that determined what cats dream—and researchers believe they do experience something closely resembling human dreaming. When cats go to sleep—or when we go to sleep, for that matter—the muscles below the neck are more or less paralyzed. Oh, we can roll over and twitch and scratch, but that's about it. (Italics mine.)
>
> From "Are Cats Smart? Yes, at Being Cats" by Penny Ward Moser, *Discover*, May 1987, p. 80.

Despite that example, it is still rare for editors to let writers get away with this "I once read" gambit.

In the story about my house, I used two print sources, the *New Realities* article by Margaret Mead and the description of the *Athens Messenger* article. Both are hedged. The *Athens Messenger* attribution refers to "a 1938 article." The only way you could check up on me would be to do what I didn't bother to do, sit down with the whole year and try to find it. What I had was a photocopy of the article Norm Allen had given me. He had bent the headline back just enough so that I could read only the year, not the day on my copy. I wrestled with my conscience for about half a day: Was I going to go to the library and read the microfiche for all of 1938 just so I could give one silly date? The answer was no, not unless my editors made me.

As for the *New Realities* reference, the article was mentioned in a newspaper article. I tried to check it, but our library did not subscribe. I entered an interlibrary request giving the information I had, date and magazine only. After two-and-one-half months, the request was returned—ten libraries could not find it. An alert editor would notice that the attribution was incomplete and challenge my use of it. Did you?

Stylistically, there's another weakness to literary quotes similar to that of the direct quote; they're cumbersome. To do them right, the date, name of the publication, title and author need to be included. Scholarly writing solves that problem with footnotes, but few consumer or trade magazines use footnotes. Yet because the document quote adds so much credibility, editors will tolerate the intrusion as long as the source isn't just a lift from a recent (or rival) magazine. Ugly though the attribution is, it can add a powerful, if sometimes inflated, authority.

## 14. Point/Quote   *. . . held an open house. "Hundreds came . . .*

This is a variation on the direct quote that is perhaps too common in magazine writing. The point/quote (or quote/point) is seen when an author summarizes a quote and then follows it with the quote (or vice versa). Here I write that Eva and Wilkin held an open house and then follow with Norm saying that they held an open house. The wording shifts slightly but it's repetition, pure and simple. Consider the repetition in these examples:

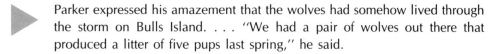

> Parker expressed his amazement that the wolves had somehow lived through the storm on Bulls Island. . . . "We had a pair of wolves out there that produced a litter of five pups last spring," he said.
>
> From "Matchsticks" by Frank Graham, Jr., *Audubon*, January 1990, p. 49.

> Car phones were an imperative, not a luxury, in the fast-lane lives of Ruth and Tom Touhill. "We didn't need them just for business," explains Ruth, "but to stay in touch with each other."
>
> From "Field of Dreams: Making Country Living a Reality" by Candace Ord Manroe, *Better Homes and Gardens*, August 1990, p. 80.

I don't know why this is such a popular technique. It always seems like a space waster to me. If I revise Eva's story I will cut either the point or the quote. Once is clear enough, in my opinion. Yet the form is popular; obviously editors like it. Their defense, I imagine, is that repetition increases clarity. Who's right here? Who cares? The problem for a writer is to deduce what an individual editor likes. When I write for a magazine that likes point/quote, I write point/quote style.

## 15. Object/Conjecture   *. . . margarine tubs . . . frugal . . .*

To use this subtle authority base, the author takes a concrete fact and speculates as to its meaning. Technically the speculation departs from nonfiction but the fact anchors it in reality. Here I take evidence, such as margarine tubs, and draw conclusions about Eva's personality. Note the pattern. Fact, observation, then a fact, then an observation. I don't group all the facts, then all the conjecture, but alternate.

This bombardment of facts makes the speculations sound factlike. Qualifiers ("must have been a fanatic housekeeper") help ease the speculative tone as well.

## 16. Generic *You*  *You know how someone thinks . . .*

This is the one and only time in this article I address you, the reader. I'll edit the sentence out if I revise this, because here it's a voice or style change and thus sloppy writing. But though inappropriate here, the generic *you* is important in magazine writing and even dominates some publications. Its advantages are that it's intimate, friendly, personal and—er—authoritative: "You should eat fiber daily and exercise at least three times a week." Could you argue with a sentence that confident? That's a secret weakness of the generic *you* form; its seeming intimacy can be a powerful substitute for actual persuasion and facts. Another hazard is that if the content is not matched to audience, the intimacy will backfire. Imagine how readers of *Lear's* or *Harper's* would react to "You don't want to anger your hubby, do you?"

In skillful hands, the generic *you* can be wonderful, full of humor and grace. Consider this example from *Science News*, a magazine that usually is no-nonsense, fully attributed and devoted to the most conservative of authority bases. Yet in a cover story, the editors let a writer cut loose:

For *Salmonella* bacteria hiding in spoiled foods and contaminated water, the search for a home in a human host resembles an adventure scripted for Indiana Jones. First there's the flood of human salivary enzymes and the enameled molars that nearly grind you to death. Then having tumbled into a bath of stomach acids, biliary detergents and pancreatic enzymes, after squeezing between cell walls and wandering blindly through interstitial labyrinths—just when you think you're home free in the bloodstream where nutrients flow like nectar—a behemoth white blood cell, the macrophage, lumbers over and engulfs you.

All is quiet for several minutes in this ominous, intracellular air pocket; then spigots open from every direction, spraying you with powerful acids, hydrogen peroxide and protein-degrading enzymes.

Surely the film ends here.

But no. You are *Salmonella* Jones. . . .

From "Making the Most of MIPs" by Rick Weiss, *Science News*, June 23, 1990, p. 394.

More typical of the generic *you* is the following:

Sheer is the operative word this season, in everything from skin care to makeup colors borrowed from a tropical seascape. Corals. Pinks. Melons. Some bright. Some light. All guaranteed to take you out of the shade and into the summer spotlight.

From "Sheer Beauty," *Lear's*, June 1990, p. 48.

## 17. Trust Me    *Eva had been a bookkeeper . . .*

Notice the assertions here. I just tell you Eva's been a bookkeeper and Wilkin's been a meatcutter. I don't reveal how I know these things. Instead, I assume that by this time in the story either you trust me or you don't so I won't slow down the prose with a lot of space-wasting source notes. Either you believe I've checked these facts against a couple of sources or you don't. Take it or leave it, I'm saying. This is a style most common in advice or recipe writing: "Take two cups flour, one teaspoon baking powder . . ." Imperative voice or pure assertion is an authority base that assumes the reader doesn't need to know which home economist or sociologist or close relative provided the information. Who says the following works?

 Cut the center panel strips (A) to the size listed in the Bill of Materials plus 2" in length. Now, crosscut a 1¼"-long spacer (B) from one end of each center strip. Then, trim each center strip (A) to a 16¾" finished length. And finally cut the side strips (C, D) to size.

From "Talk of the Town at Sundown: Low Voltage Lighting," *Wood*, June 1989, p. 50.

No one says these directions will work; you're just expected to trust the magazine.

The trust-me style has the advantage of being efficient. It takes very few words to give a command or make an assertion. Magazines, particularly service magazines, which are trying to squeeze six-dozen recipes, forty sweaters, and eighty-two recommended resorts or childcare practices into a single issue, depend on the trust-me style. Any other base would take too much space. The weakness of the trust me is, if it's wrong, the readers are angry with the magazine, not the writer or source.

My sources for saying Eva kept house while Wilkin cut meat? Dave Allen told me about Eva being a bookkeeper. Later I went over to the lumber company to ask if they remembered her and they did, with enthusiasm. She was a wonderful woman, the owner told me. It was Norm who told me about Wilkin being a meatcutter and Dave who told me about his building the garage. As for the chickens, I found pictures of Wilkin standing in the middle of huge flocks of chickens. The chicken house still stands behind the garage and I now use it for a tool shed, although I want to have chickens in it someday myself.

## 18. Historical Context    *Times were hard . . .*

Unlike the Epistemological Splash earlier, sometimes tangents, especially historical facts, are essential for understanding the story. They are not merely stuck in; they are integral to development. They add context. Compare the sentence here, which places the Allens in time, with the earlier geological musings. The geology was a digression; the history is development. The distinction is subtle but significant. Compare the following excerpt from a profile of Simon and Garfunkel with the way Vicki Hearne quoted Derrida earlier.

At the time Columbia Records released Simon and Garfunkel's "Bridge over Troubled Water" in early 1970, *Billboard*'s Top 40 chart was dominated by rock and roll. "Bridge," a melancholy gospel–ballad featuring tenor Art Garfunkel and written by partner Paul Simon, was a stirring melody all right, but the pair thought it was too pretty and too much of a ballad to make it as a hit single. Despite the skepticism, Simon's spiritual song of comfort struck a responsive chord with Americans weary of the war in Vietnam. By April 1970, the tune had topped the charts for six weeks running. . . .

From "Bridging Troubled Waters" by Susan Elliott, *Memories*, April/May 1990, p. 86.

It is impossible to understand the impact of the song without knowing what the record charts or the war feelings were like in 1970. It is possible to know there is confusion over the naming of pit bulls without quoting Derrida.

## 19. Official Records    . . . *the death certificate said.*

I found the death certificate at the health department. I went there after searching for Eva and Wilkin's marriage or birth records at probate court. I could find neither. Official records are another classic mainstay of journalistic authority and may be the most credible of all sources. Since it is one of the duties of government to keep accurate records, there is little possibility of disbelief. A quote might be denied, but a court record is harder to tamper with and more easily checked. Yet, even with all the majesty of government behind this base, there are hazards to veracity. Although we found Eva's death certificate, Wilkin's was missing. The clerks and I went through all the books for the 1980s and never found it.

But Eva's death certificate did list her place of burial, West Union Cemetery. The caretaker had no map of the stones. Instead he had memorized each grave location. He pointed without hesitation to where their stone was. "Near the Hoopers," he said. "She was a Hooper, you know." On the stone was Wilkin's date of death and one more fact no one had told me. Wilkin was his middle name; John had been his first name. So despite all my conversations with friends and relatives, all my search for official documents, the key fact of his life, his name, was dependent on the memory of a cemetery caretaker. That bizarre reality—that the fact of facts, a name— could be dependent on luck made me feel strange as I stood by the graves. These people had become real to me, but that stone, small, flat against the ground, changed my experience of them. Nothing, no document or quote, was quite so authoritative as that stone. And it was one authority base I could never quite describe in text. There are limits to authority—or words. I went back to the health department asking them to look for a John Allen deceased in 1987. Nothing. He must have died in a nursing home outside the county, they said. One of these days I've got to ask Norm about that.

## 20. Methods Description   *I put that photo next to one . . .*

Journalists rarely describe their research methods in their prose. Scientists always describe their methods. This, and not the turgidity of the prose, may be the chief difference between so-called academic writing and journalism. How the journalist got the data is considered too boring to tell. The seventy-five phone calls to get that one interview, the six days in the library, the hours spent sitting in a hall waiting for a source to honor a promise of "just five minutes"—none of that gets in the final story. It's boring to do, so it must be boring to read about too.

Yet knowing how information was gathered may be crucial for understanding it. Consider the oat bran uproar in recent years. Some scientific studies said oat bran was significant in reducing colon cancer and food companies immediately launched oat sales campaigns of unparalleled glee. Even a candy advertised it had oat bran in it. Then new studies said oat bran was not so significant. The food companies quieted down (or switched to touting wheat bran) but the public was left confused. The research had differed in ages, sex, health and genetic makeups of people studied. In short, the *methods* were different so the *results* were different too. Knowing only results without knowing methods makes data meaningless.

The science essayist Stephen Jay Gould is especially critical of modern journalism for ignoring methods in favor of results. He writes:

> Science, in its most fundamental definition, is a fruitful mode of inquiry, not a list of enticing conclusions. The conclusions are the consequence, not the essence. My greatest unhappiness with most popular presentations of science concerns their failure to separate fascinating claims from the methods that scientists use to establish the facts of nature. Journalists, and the public, thrive on controversial and stunning statements. But science is, basically, a way of knowing—in P. B. Medawar's apt words, "the art of the soluble." If the growing corps of popular science writers would focus on *how* scientists develop and defend those fascinating claims, they would make their greatest possible contribution to public understanding.

From "Sex, Drugs, Disasters and the Extinction of Dinosaurs" by Stephen Jay Gould, *Discover*, 1984, reprinted in Donald Hall's *The Contemporary Essay*, 2d. ed., St. Martin's Press, New York, 1989, p. 222.

People would be less confused about our world, Gould is saying, if descriptions of research techniques were always part of the story. Some magazines, especially science magazines, do include methods as a matter of course:

> Every spring, thousands of volunteers drive along predetermined census routes, usually rural roads. Each counter makes fifty stops at half-mile intervals and listens for singing males. . . .

From "Mystery of the Missing Migrants" by Chris Wille, *Audubon*, May 1990, p. 83.

*Science News* so religiously describes methods in its articles that every report has a methods paragraph:

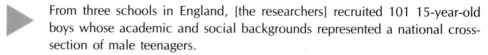

From three schools in England, [the researchers] recruited 101 15-year-old boys whose academic and social backgrounds represented a national cross-section of male teenagers.

From "Biological Clues Linked to Criminal Record" by R. Bower, *Science News*, November 10, 1990, p. 293.

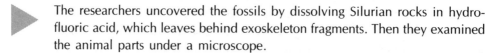

The researchers uncovered the fossils by dissolving Silurian rocks in hydrofluoric acid, which leaves behind exoskeleton fragments. Then they examined the animal parts under a microscope.

From "Fossils Push Back Origin of Land Animals" by R. J. Monastersky, *Science News*, November 10, 1990, p. 292.

The researchers blasted the seedlings with tiny tungsten pellets coated with multiple copies of the antibiotic-resistance genes.

From "Green Genes Blasted into Chloroplasts" by R. Weiss, *Science News*, November 10, 1990, p. 295.

None of these excerpts from *Science News* gives the full text of the methods descriptions actually in the articles, and yet these brief samples, I think, illustrate why editors of general interest magazines avoid them. They get dull in a hurry. I am a long-time *Science News* devotee and will admit that even I skip over the methods paragraphs to get to the results. I want to know what was learned, not how many petri dishes were washed. I agree with Gould that knowing research methods would end a lot of confusion, but I sympathize too with the long-suffering reader. My solution in my own story is to hint at my methods—a phrase here, a clause there. I say I put the photos side by side but do not mention I also got out a magnifying glass and asked others to look at the photos for additional opinions. Why bore you with all that?

## 21. The Expert   *The great anthropologist . . .*

I said most of what I had to say about the expert in The Expert Has a Soul (number 11, p. 127). But one further thought: notice that phrase "the great anthropologist." I added it because one risk with experts is that readers often have not heard of them. The attribution or identifying clause must include some kind of description so readers might understand Margaret Mead's significance. She was famous in her day, but she died in 1978. Younger readers might not know of her work. She began her studies of adolescence in Samoa; her 1928 book, *Coming of Age in Samoa*, started lively debates about adolescence around the world. Her work has deeply influenced the American popular notion that adolescence is a culture, a distinct period between childhood and adulthood. None of this could be packed into the attribution—not without turning it into an Anthropological Splash.

## 22. Results Description   *Appalachian children are gifted . . .*

To reiterate: how little is known when only the results of research are described. This single sentence describing attitudes toward psychic behavior in the Appalachians is too skimpy for a reader to evaluate. Even if the paragraph that contains it weren't already in trouble for being a second-hand reference, it still should arouse the suspicions of an editor. What is the definition of "psychic" for this research? How were the children observed: at home? at school? at their psychic activity? How were the observations recorded: by field notes? questionnaire? tape recorder? Who was interviewed for the research: children only? parents only? teachers? Who actually did the research: graduate students? elementary school teachers? or one lone field worker? Answers to these questions would significantly change the value and credibility of the data.

## 23. Hearsay   *There's supposed to be a ghost . . .*

Much of the information in the story so far could technically be called hearsay. I heard from Dave Allen that Wilkin built the garage. I heard from Norm Allen that Eva and Wilkin held an open house. But that's not the same as this. The ghost stories are repeated third-hand. Norm and Dave actually remember their stories. But these ghost stories are repeated by people telling stories people told to them that other people told to them. They are two and three and four times removed from the original source, if there ever was an original source. And that is what distinguishes hearsay. Is it nonfiction? Well, no, obviously not; at least in this case I don't think any of the stories are true. But is it legitimate to use hearsay in nonfiction? Well, that's another question. And as with other authority bases, the answer may depend on what the editor of the magazine thinks.

I made a special effort with my use of hearsay to be sure the stories were in an ironic frame so that readers would know I don't believe them. I didn't want to throw doubt on the rest of the story. I am sure there are people in my audience who not only believe in ghosts, but may have had encounters with them, but I have not met any ghosts so, for the moment, don't believe in them either. I thought it was important that this be clear to readers. So the ironic sentences, "All good ghost stories have a tragic death at base" or "I haven't gone to the tunnel myself to check it out," are like the phrase "it seemed" in the first paragraph—signals to you the reader to watch out, just kidding. Big Foot? Honest, just kidding.

## 24. Reader Abuse   *. . . psychic phenomena research organization*

I would have skipped this authority base entirely if there weren't so much of it in all journalism: " . . . according to a British psychic phenomena research organization." What kind of fact is that? How can you check it?

Actually there's more to this base than I put in the text. In order to research this part of the story I went to the Special Collections at the Ohio University library. Over the years, many of my students have solemnly assured me that Athens County, Ohio, was the thirteenth most haunted place in the world. Where were they getting such a fact? I asked the collection's secretary, Karen Jones.

She laughed and asked if I wanted to look at the "spook file." This file, officially named "Folklore & Legends—Southeast Ohio" had twenty-two articles in it, some about the railroad tunnel, some about Wilson Hall; but three of the stories, and only three, quoted a study that had ranked Athens County. Each article quoted a different source. An October 26, 1969, piece in the *Athens Messenger* attributed the study to the British Metaphysical Society. An October 31, 1978, story in the Ohio University *Post* quoted a British Society for Psychical Research as its source. And an October 30, 1980, *Athens News* story quoted the British Psychic Institute. This last story then went on to quote a psychic in Columbus who said the survey was silly because "half the earth is haunted."

None of the three stories mentioned when the study had been done, the title of the study or what criteria defined "haunted." I checked both the *Encyclopedia of Associations: International Edition* and *The World of Learning: Fortieth Edition.* There was no organization listed under any of the three names, nor was there any association under United Kingdom, London, metaphysical, psychic, or parapsychology. There was a Turkish psychic institute with seventy members and an American psychic institute. While this does not conclusively prove there is no British psychic institute, it suggests there is not, enough of a suggestion for me to decide that this fact, a fact that launches dozens of term papers at Ohio University each year, is suspect. Yet students trust it implicitly. It was printed in a newspaper so it must be true, right? I don't know which upsets me more, media that abuse readers by using such thinly grounded authority bases or readers who lack the analytical skills to notice when they're being thus abused.

## 25. The Unnamed Source   *. . . a young woman I'd hired . . .*

So far, there have been several unnamed sources in the article—my mother, the clerks at the health department—but this time the avoidance of a name has the intention implied by an unnamed source. That is, I've not used the woman's name because I didn't want to embarrass her. There are many reasons for protecting a source—to avoid invasion of privacy or libel, to protect the source from retribution from his or her enemies or to allow the source to say things not yet safe to say for the record. For example, "a high government official" means someone who works for the president or a cabinet member. When diplomacy requires official silence, unnamed speakers may be the only vehicle for public dialog. Editors are nervous enough about use of unnamed sources by government officials, but when stories are about ordinary people, their concern deepens. Could the reporter who uses unnamed sources or, a variation, changes the names of sources, be making the story up? One infamous instance of a reporter who did this is Janet Cooke, who wrote a Pulitzer Prize winning story about "Jimmy," an 8-year-old heroin addict, for the *Washington Post*. Social workers frantically tried to find the boy; when they couldn't, editors got suspicious. Finally Cooke admitted she had made the story up; the *Post* returned the Pulitzer. Editors don't like anonymous sources.

Yet without anonymous sources, some stories about the social problems of our time could not be written. An AIDS mother, a homeless man, a rapist—these people would not tell their stories without identity protection. So once again, individual magazines set their own policies. Some refuse to use articles with unnamed sources. Others insist that such stories be shown to sources prior to publication. Other magazines just use routine fact-checking procedures (call the sources, explain they will not be named, but could they verify such-and-such). Still other magazines trust the writer, although not completely. At the bottom of almost every magazine contract I've signed is a clause something like this:

> Your signature below as author or agent for the author warrants ownership, originality and authorship by the author, and that exercise of the rights granted will violate no copyright or other proprietary right whatsoever and will not defame nor violate the privacy of any person.
>
> From standard contract form, *Esquire* magazine.

Despite such clauses, most magazines I've worked with have a lawyer examine my article if unnamed sources are being used.

## 26. I'm Not a Doctor but I Play One on TV  . . . *she commented one evening.*

Perhaps the name I gave this authority base too blatantly (or flippantly) reveals my opinion of it. It comes from a television commercial of a few years ago in which an actor stood before a coughing family and earnestly explained that he wasn't a doctor but an actor. Then he proceeded to give medical advice anyway. Every time Princess Di, Liz Taylor, Madonna, Jackie O. or Elvis graces a magazine cover, this authority base is at work. Whenever Angela Lansbury answers aspirin questions, it's at work again. A shorter term for it might be *transference*. Whenever a person's expertise or talent in one area is assumed to give that person authority in another, transference is taking place. It's either a perversion or a logical extension of the expert authority base. Whatever, it's pervasive, especially in magazine journalism and advertising.

Celebrities advise us on child care, health, social causes, fashion, election candidates, sneakers, breakfast cereals, cars and underwear. They also tell us how to live full, meaningful lives; but their only expertise in all these arenas is their celebrityhood.

While my mother is not quite as famous as Jane Fonda, she is something of a local celebrity, but however famous she may be, she's no expert on parapsychological phenomena. I quote her as if she were. By no stretch of editorial principles is this logical, but transference is so popular I think editors expect it. The magazine that can resist the appeal of a celebrity may not exist in this culture. Ask ten celebrities how they put on makeup. Ask ten celebrities how they arrange furniture. Ask ten celebrities how they invest money. The article will be read. My mother doesn't know anything about ghosts; nevertheless she had an opinion on the state of Eva's ghost. I listen to her because she's my mom, but as a reader, writer and person of critical intelligence (everyone says so, especially Mom), I should be embarrassed to base text on transference. It is weak reasoning. It is also strong economics. I saw a cookbook by NFL stars a few years back. Football players. Maybe they were good amateur cooks, but their expertise was football. Yet, if the book had been titled *Ten Big, Strong Guys Cook* (the quarterback does the dishes), would the book have sold?

## WRITERS AND AUTHORITY BASE

The foregoing discussion of twenty-six authority bases doesn't begin to exhaust the possibilities. For example, the story "Eva's Ghost" didn't use the generic *we*, an authority base that, much like the generic *you*, uses first-person plural to create intimacy with the reader. How many authority bases are there? Editors and writers seem endlessly inventive. A recent foray into one magazine yielded a Double Generic *Them:* "Some say farmers began . . . "A student of mine found this attribution: "As my friend Elizabeth Taylor says, . . ." She named that one Pal Privilege.

With so much diversity, a complete list of authority bases is impossible. It would be out of date daily. Don't bother to memorize my twenty-six. Restricting yourself to just those would limit your creativity. Instead learn to notice what language cues are actually used as you read. Don't rely on what someone else, such as a textbook author, professor or even editor, says are used.

Even editor? Yes. Editors sometimes unintentionally give misleading guidance to writers. For an assignment on resorts, an editor told me she wanted strong, active, descriptive language. "A sense of place," she said. It was a new magazine so I couldn't read it for myself. My idea of descriptive language is concrete detail, so I wrote about the blueness of the lakes, the kaleidoscopic tones of the sunsets and the plant and animal life to be found and where to find it. I even wrote about a sighting of wild turkeys. It took several hundred words. The editors calmly killed all this deathless prose. They revised the whole thing to a single sentence that began "This jewel-like resort . . ." End of description.

The rest of the now very short article gave address, rates, season and activities at the resort. Why didn't they tell me they wanted a catalog instead of sensory detail?

Perhaps they truly believed that the abstract phrase "jewel-like" was description. At any rate, we clearly had a communications gap. Without a sample magazine to read, I couldn't figure out what they really wanted. With editors, I've learned, it's important not to do what they *say*, but to do what they *do*.

This means a key skill for a writer is reading editors' work. What authority cues do they like? Which ones do they avoid? Are they consistent? A technique that sharpens my reading skills is to try to name authority cues. Do as my student did with her Pal Privilege. Create your own names for cues when you notice them. A student discovered an Epistemological Splash in one of her magazines; she didn't know my name for it so she called it Perhaps You've Heard. Another student named the Mind Reader The Voice of God. The names aren't important; the naming is. The act of naming helps you concentrate as you read. Concentration is important because it's easy to read over authority cues. For example, although I didn't use a generic *we* in the story, I did use one at the beginning of the "Strengths and Weaknesses" section. ("Let's examine each . . .") You read right over it didn't you? Ordinary readers don't need to notice such cues consciously; it's enough to feel them unconsciously. But professional editors and writers must notice these cues. Naming helps you find them.

Unfortunately, simply naming authority cues is a chaotic technique for observation. It makes it easy to miss something major. A second trick for noticing authority cues is to search for patterns. Are any authority bases dominant in the magazine? Does the magazine use some more than others? Are some always present or always absent? Does every article have an expert? What sorts of expert? Do articles use "just folks," and if so, how—as supporting detail or as major authorities? Do individual articles have a few authority bases or many? Does the magazine seem to let the writer choose appropriate authority bases, or does it impose its own ideas on the writers? Does the magazine seem to have clear policies for or against controversial authority bases such as the Unnamed Source or the Mind Reader?

When you have determined the patterns of authority bases a magazine uses, you know three things—what to emphasize in your query letter, what to emphasize in your research and what to emphasize in your article. If the magazine doesn't use experts, why waste precious research time (and money) scouring the country for them or brag that you have them in a query? If the magazine insists on "real people" don't give them experts or personal experiences. Knowledge of authority bases makes your work efficient. Your research should be thorough, but not foolish. Why waste time cultivating a source who won't allow you to use his or her name, when the magazine never uses unnamed sources? Analyzing authority bases saves time, money and rejection for a writer.

## EDITORS AND AUTHORITY BASE

For writers, just noticing authority base cues could be enough to understand a magazine's philosophy. For editors, noticing cues may be the beginning of some soul searching. Do the authority bases restrict writers' styles too much? Are there too many for the magazine to have a strong identity? Are authority bases that "sound good" being emphasized at the expense of credibility? Or, the reverse, has "credibility" and its accompanying dense attributions made the magazine unreadable? Are instructions to writers clear?

Some magazines do a thorough job of spelling out what authority bases they want used. *Savvy*, for example, used to say in its writers' guidelines:

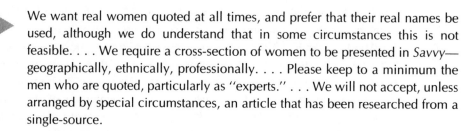

We want real women quoted at all times, and prefer that their real names be used, although we do understand that in some circumstances this is not feasible. . . . We require a cross-section of women to be presented in *Savvy*— geographically, ethnically, professionally. . . . Please keep to a minimum the men who are quoted, particularly as "experts." . . . We will not accept, unless arranged by special circumstances, an article that has been researched from a single-source.

From "Writers' Guidelines," *Savvy* magazine, November 1984.

**Harvard Business Review** is nowhere near as explicit as *Savvy*, but it, too, has some strong ideas of how writers should handle authority:

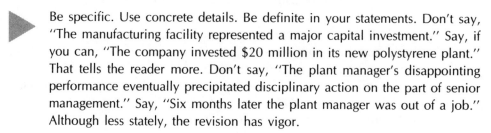

Be specific. Use concrete details. Be definite in your statements. Don't say, "The manufacturing facility represented a major capital investment." Say, if you can, "The company invested $20 million in its new polystyrene plant." That tells the reader more. Don't say, "The plant manager's disappointing performance eventually precipitated disciplinary action on the part of senior management." Say, "Six months later the plant manager was out of a job." Although less stately, the revision has vigor.

From "Writing an Article for Harvard Business Review," Boston, January 1984.

But other magazines, perhaps the majority, delight in being mysterious. *Rolling Stone*'s writers' guidelines consist of three sentences on a postcard:

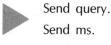

Send query.
Send ms.
Send SASE.

An SASE is a self-addressed, stamped envelope. Anyone who has read *Rolling Stone* even casually knows it has a highly complex style and so an equally complex pattern of authority bases as well. The only way to understand that magazine would be to toss away the postcard and study its authority cues. But when magazines have complex authority cues—and most sophisticated ones do—putting the burden of analysis entirely on the writer is asking the writer to fail. Better written writers' guidelines, ones that spell out preferences for authority cues, would improve writer performance.

Editors face a deeper challenge than writers with authority bases. Writers need only match the standards of the magazine. Editors must set those standards. Too often, cornered by space limitations, deadlines and a sense that readers are too fickle to be trusted with a complex sentence, editors choose weaker authority bases. Such choices can easily result in distortions of topics, unreasonable confusion for writers and condescension to readers.

# Chapter

# 7

# *Voice*

Some years ago I was walking near a river when I saw cars stalled on a road ahead. I thought, an accident, but as I got closer saw instead that ducks had strayed into the road and stopped traffic. I walked over and waved papers I was carrying to try to herd the ducks back to the water. The birds were terrified and difficult to keep together. People in the cars whistled and applauded or laughed words of encouragement to me, but no one got out of a car to help. Perhaps this didn't occur to them. Eventually, with much flapping and hopping about, I got the ducks to the river and traffic resumed.

I'm thinking of the incident now because I see in it parallels to writing. The cars were like readers: interested, involved but unable to actually interact with me or the ducks. The ducks were the facts, to be organized and controlled, and I, the duck herder, was the writer whose antics—or *voice*—made the ducks a flock. Voice or style, however, is an elusive concept. It's thought to come from the writer's true character, to be a part of his or her genuine identity. A writer can't hide, young writers are warned.

And yet my waving papers at ducks was definitely out of character for me. I'm reserved, shy even. But the ducks needed help. So I hopped. Maybe *voice* is doing whatever needs to be done to get the ducks to the water. *Persona* is the literary term for this distinction between a writer's voice and real-life identity, the person you are when you're not writing. Persona is the identity or voice you create, unconsciously, when you write. It is natural; it is your voice but not actually you.

None of this explains voice, however. I do know things it is not. Voice is not fancy language or something a writer puts on. It is how a writer writes when not thinking about writing. The elements of voice are words and syntax, grammar and diction; but though these create voice, they do not explain it. Syntax consists of the bits and pieces, single ducks strayed from a river. The whole is mystery. Writer after writer has paid homage to the mystery. William Zinsser, in his classic *On Writing Well*, argues that voice is inevitable:

> Style is organic to the person doing the writing, as much a part of him as his hair, or, if he is bald, his lack of it. Trying to add style is like adding a toupee. At first glance the formerly bald man looks young and even handsome. But at second glance—and with a toupee there is always a second glance—he doesn't look quite right. The problem is not that he doesn't look well groomed; he does, and we can only admire the wigmaker's almost perfect skill. The point is that he doesn't look like himself. This is the problem of the writer who sets out deliberately to garnish his prose. You lose whatever it is that makes you unique.[1]

E. B. White, in *The Elements of Style*, becomes lyrical in his effort to explain "nondetachable, unfilterable" style:

> There is no satisfactory explanation of style, no infallible guide to good writing, no assurance that a person who thinks clearly will be able to write clearly, no key that unlocks the door, no inflexible rule by which the young writer may shape his course. He will often find himself steering by stars that are disturbingly in motion.[2]

All very noble, but if you are a young writer trying to develop your skills, being told to steer by the moving stars isn't of much practical value. Neither is the advice "be yourself." Nor does either match common sense. Any athlete knows that talent cannot be realized without training; training always has method. There must be a way to develop voice. All nonfiction writers noted for their voices—E. B. White, John McPhee, Joan Didion, Tom Wolfe, Lewis Thomas, Edward Hoagland, Maxine Hong Kingston, Annie Dillard, Stephen Jay Gould, Garrison Keillor and many, many more (see Appendix 7.1)—had to grow into their skills. Even if the goal is to become yourself, how do you train?

I think you start by ripping everything out of your work. Everything. Every stray adjective or gratuitous adverb or phrase or clause—all chatter—must go, until all that is left is the bare bones of thought and story. Then what remains is the beginning of voice. By this theory, a voice emerges not during writing, but through revision and tightening. A piece should be written again and again until what remains is what the writer meant to say. Commitment to revision then, its tedium and time, is the beginning of true voice; but only the beginning.

## THE ART OF FACT

What comes after the beginning? Perhaps E. B. White is right; it may be easier to write of moving stars than of voice. But not to attempt to describe voice is begging the issue. Thinkers who dismiss voice as mystery cast young writers to the whirling stars. If voice is constructed of language, can it be described by language? Perhaps by carefully examining the work of a single writer who does have a strong voice, clues will emerge. John McPhee is such a writer.

In an interview with the *New York Times*, McPhee said the idea for one of his books, *The Control of Nature*, occurred by chance. His daughter so loved the works of novelist Walker Percy that he promised to take her to Percy country in Louisiana. While there, canoeing on the Atchafalaya River, he heard about the Army Corps of Engineers' attempt to keep the Mississippi from jumping over to that river. "It struck me as a fairly sizeable symbol," he told the *Times*.[3] Are symbols voice?

McPhee is one of my favorite writers. Always perceptive, he is never intrusive; exhaustive in detail, he never gets boring—at least not to me, although a critic once said his 149-page book on oranges was "more oranges than we need." "Not even John McPhee," the critic went on, "can remove the pulp from this one."[4] I liked *Oranges*.

In each of McPhee's twenty-plus books, he has selected a mundane topic and tried to penetrate its essence. He's written on geology, Alaska, physics and canoes. He's also written book-length profiles of a basketball player, an art museum director, a tennis pro and a school headmaster. (A list of the titles of McPhee's books through 1990 appears in Appendix 7.2.) Like all good journalists, he's a generalist, but his writing has excited people who usually don't give a second thought to journalism. Literary critics pay homage to John McPhee.

One such critic, Kathy Smith, has written:

> John McPhee has earned a reputation for poised writing, in two senses of the word. His polished and confident style balances deftly on the verge. The respect bestowed on him by colleagues and journalism professors nationwide can be attributed to this poise, which has been described for the most part in a New Critical vocabulary more generally applied to fiction: The McPhee style consists of well-crafted sentences, fresh and spirited metaphors, consistency of mood and tight organizational control, strong narrative voice and an uncanny form/content justification, an organic unity that reaffirms the aesthetic value of parts fitting the whole.[5]

Consistency of mood? Uncanny form/content justification? Is she talking about voice? I think this sort of enthusiasm embarrasses even McPhee. I'm not sure I'm willing to gush like this, but I will admit I admire the way he blends information, language and quirky personal observation into smooth prose. Consider this passage from *The Control of Nature*, describing the dam structures holding the Mississippi away from the Atchafalaya:

> The Old River Control Auxiliary Structure is a rank of seven towers, each buff with a white crown. They are vertical on the upstream side, and they slope toward the Atchafalaya. Therefore, they resemble flying buttresses facing the Mississippi. The towers are separated by six arciform gates, convex to the Mississippi, and hinged in trunnion blocks secured with steel

to carom the force of the river into the core of the structure. Lifted by cables, these tainter gates, as they are called, are about as light and graceful as anything could be that has a composite weight of twenty-six hundred tons. Each of them is sixty-two feet wide. They are the strongest the Corps has ever designed and built. A work of engineering such as a Maillart bridge or a bridge by Christian Menn can outdo some other works of art, because it is not only a gift to the imagination but also structural in the matrix of the world. The auxiliary structure at Old River contains too many working components to be classed with such a bridge, but in grandeur and in profile it would not shame a pharaoh.[6]

Note that, as befits a good piece of journalism, this has the numbers: sixty-two feet, twenty-six hundred tons. But it also has soaring metaphors: matrix, gifts of imagination, shame a pharaoh. Is metaphor voice?

Or consider this passage a few pages later, when the engineers who maintain this wonder of the world catch their boat on a sandbar. McPhee has fun with the irony that some of the boldest technicians in the world can't steer a boat. This is his description:

They behave as if it were absolutely routine to be aiming downstream in mid-current at zero knots. In a sense, that is true, for this is not some minor navigational challenge, like shooting rapids in an aircraft carrier. This is the Atchafalaya River. A poker player might get out of an analogous situation by reaching toward a sleeve. A basketball player would reverse pivot— shielding the ball, whirling the body in a complete circle to leave the defender flat as a sandbar. John Dugger seems to be both. He has cut the engines, and now—looking interested, and nothing else—he lets the current take the stern and swing it wide. The big boat spins, reverse pivots, comes off the bar, and leaves it behind.[7]

Here again analogy releases the meaning of the scene. The comparison to game dilemmas recreates the human scale, but that line, "shooting rapids in an aircraft carrier," attempts to contain the engineers' audacity. This kind of image-laden writing is rich with voice.

For subtleties like these, McPhee has been praised for his "artistic vision," a phrase not often given to journalists. Critic Barbara Lounsberry writes:

[His prose] is rooted in Emerson and Thoreau and composed of circles and levels, the one and the many, the representative man or woman and levels of achievement.[8]

The one and the many? Sounds positively religious. Another critic, Ronald Weber, argues in *The Literature of Fact* that there's a difference between using art forms to extend journalism and using facts to make art. Using artistic devices, such as dialog, scene setting and plotting, as McPhee does, to enhance journalism would not be art. But when facts are woven to create insights, as McPhee also does, then journalism reaches a dimension thought to be unavailable to it. Art.[9] Naturally with such achievement, the critics are interested in figuring out how he does it.

An essay by Jack Roundy, "Formal Devices in the Prose of John McPhee," argues that McPhee's use of planning and structure, which seek to develop a theme, plus his use of metaphor, are McPhee's secrets for overcoming "the liability of information."

Interesting that literary critics consider facts a hazard to good writing.

McPhee's structure, Roundy continues, is a reordering of reality. He never traces a story as it happens but loops backward and forward in time to create a theme.[10]

Kathy Smith sees more to McPhee than metaphors and theme. Unlike Roundy, she sees facts as essential to McPhee's voice rather than its appendage. She is awed by his ability to maintain "the integrity of journalism and the art of his writing." She comments, "It is important that McPhee retain the label nonfiction so the subject of his narrative can produce the power."[11] McPhee has to be a journalist or he wouldn't be an artist, she is saying.

Barbara Lounsberry thinks McPhee's secret is to create circles and levels. In her essay "John McPhee's Levels of the Earth," she traces a fascination with the circle in McPhee's writing that seems to border on mystic. The circle throughout world philosophy represents harmony or eternity; and McPhee, whether the circle is a basketball hoop or a bear encircling a camp, seems to be reaching for this. Levels, too, are another philosophical notion describing metaphysical consciousness, whether they are levels of earth or of archdruids. "McPhee's gradient way of seeing is that of a landscape painter. His descriptions frequently capture foreground terrains and then ascend in levels,"[12] she writes.

All this carrying on over journalism?

Are all these critics, who extravagantly praise McPhee's writing, describing his voice? Is voice adeptness with metaphor and symbol and metaphysics? Is it skill with scenes, dialog, plotting and tight organizational control as they say above?

I don't think so. I keep seeing McPhee in his canoe on the Atchafalaya and the coincidence of it. The *Times* account went on to explain how McPhee heard about debris basins in Los Angeles while researching the Atchafalaya River control project. Then when he went to California to see those, he met a geologist who told him about Iceland's effort to control lava flows on one of that country's islands. These three stories became his book, *The Control of Nature*. Despite all the enthusiasm of the critics, I don't see an artist at work here. I see a journalist chasing a story. He has voice, yes. But the "spirited metaphors," "well-crafted sentences" and "organic unity" don't explain the story. There is more to voice than technique. But what?

## THE ART OF PERCEPTION

A writer, I said in Chapter 1, is a person who makes connections. What the writer gives us, the service performed, is to link ideas and objects not obviously connected, for example, corn with yearning, raspberries with culture differences, house hunting with ghosts, cold with mystery. A friend of mine who owned a shoe store in Tennessee once had a customer come in wearing two right shoes. She fretted about this odd thing for days.

"Did you ask the woman about it?" I said.

"Oh, no," she said, "I couldn't. It wouldn't be right. What if she were too poor for a pair of shoes, or retarded?"

I thought how Southern that was, to be agitated about something but too polite to ask, and I imagined how the same incident would be handled around the country. I told another friend my thoughts: "In New York, the store owner would have said, 'Hey, lady, d'juh know you're wearing two right shoes?' In California, she would have said, 'Cool shoes, Babe,' and in the Midwest, 'Pardon me, but is your left foot bothering you today?'" My friend tilted his head and said, "That's why you're a writer; because you see things like that." Connections.

Another time I was Christmas shopping with my mother; we went into an accessories store that had a display of intricately folded scarves in front. The table was too beautiful to disturb, and I said so to the shopkeeper. "I wouldn't have minded if you had. I love to fold," she said.

"I do, too," I replied, and the two of us began to excitedly exchange folding tips—towels in thirds, T-shirts at the shoulders, the turtleneck inside—my mother watched the two of us with utter disbelief. Two crazy folding nuts on one planet?

"I've never been able to fold fitted sheets," the shop owner confessed sadly.

I knew how, and I told her how long ago I was struggling with a fitted sheet in a laundromat, when a woman came over, took my sheet away and without a word folded it for me. Now, years later, in that fancy accessory store, I passed on the secret to the shopkeeper by folding an imaginary sheet for her on her counter.

Later my mother asked to be shown the secret too, though she quickly added she didn't want to know everything about folding. She didn't intend to become a crazed folder; she just wanted to fold sheets. It was then I tried to tell her what folding meant to me—that it kept things from wrinkling or taking up space, but most important that a cupboard was like the soul, hidden, so it ought to be beautiful. Again the tilt of the head. "Oh," was all she said, but again I knew I'd made another connection. A writer's connection.

When I teach, I tell students the first day of class about this idea of the writer as connector, but then I give them their first assignment, an awful one. I've many versions of it, but my favorite is to send them to draw. The scene must be public and familiar, I tell them. They're not to sit alone in their rooms. Then with the drawings as notes, they're to write a description of the scene.

The description is just a smoke screen. I'm really interested in the drawings and ask for them at the beginning of next class. They groan. "You're not going to collect these?" they say. I brandish a roll of masking tape, threatening not only to collect them, but to display them on the blackboard. They howl with horror at that.

"Why," I say, "what's so awful?"

"They're no good," the students say. "They're ugly." "I can't draw."

"So what?"

Then I ask them if people came up to them while they were drawing; usually this happened. How did they react, I ask. By slamming shut their notebooks, they say.

I rebuke them for that, telling them how they've prevented others from participating in their experience forever. Who knows what might have happened if, instead of protecting their egos, they had let other people talk to them.

This is when I finally tell them the truth. That idea about writer as connector is true, but it's just the feel-good idea. A better definition—one that comes closer to unlocking the mystery of voice—is that the writer is a professional fool.

What distinguishes a writer from everybody else is that a writer is fool enough to share the connections he or she sees. To be a writer is to be foolish, to be willing to wave papers at ducks. As writer, your real job is to put aside self-awareness, self-consciousness and self-protectiveness long enough to risk telling others what you see.

All people are capable of connections. One doesn't have to be a writer to be intrigued by two right shoes. Any child can see linkages like these. But few people are brave enough to voice them. Dormant in most people is the silly person who lets them speak up. Young children are free of fear, which is why they say insightful things. And writers, if not free of fear, at least act as if they are. I am a writer not because I see culture in raspberries, yearning in corn or souls in cupboards. I am a writer because I am fool enough to say so.

Craft is important, but it's not voice. The structural subtleties, the play with metaphors that McPhee's critics see are really there, but those are not his voice. His voice is encased in moments like the one when he was canoeing on a river and saw a link between dams on the Mississipi and the works of the pharaohs. It's what he thought, not how he said it, that makes his writing unique.

The word *voice* originally comes from a Latin root meaning sound. Thus the link with language is only incidental in that language has sound. But it is the sound—giving voice to the thought—that matters. What do I know about my own voice? That it emerges only after revision. That I am both conscious of it through revision and unconscious of it when writing. That revision, a component of voice, is engagement with language, word by word, sentence by sentence, paragraph by paragraph; but revision alone is not voice. That I can change my voice somewhat to suit a market, but I'm happiest when I'm free of market restraints. Yet that those same market restraints are doors to publication. This paradox has been painful sometimes.

Most important, though, I know voice is not language but perception. Culture and experience shape my perceptions, but so do deliberate searches for insight. Jacques Barzun once wrote, "The very ethics of writing [is that] the reader's part of the effort must never become a strain."[13] Perhaps this is voice too—a genuine love of sharing with readers one's deliberate and accidental perceptions, no matter how foolish. Now there's a mystery for you.

To train voice, then, the writer needs to practice revision and observing. Paeans to mysteries are fine, but the writers who swallow pride and let the world see what they see, have voice. "My observations are too obvious," you maintain. To you, yes, or you wouldn't have seen them. But not to others. Until you risk sharing your foolish perceptions, you do not have voice. You must remember, however, you're observing the world, not yourself. You are a vehicle, a medium, a fool whose antics make connections and nothing more. The duck herder hopping about is not the topic and never was. Ducks are the topic.

## NOTES

1. William Zinsser, *On Writing Well*, Harper & Row, New York, 1985, p. 20.
2. William Strunk, Jr., and E. B. White, *The Elements of Style*, Macmillan, New York, 1979, p. 66.
3. Philip Shabecoff, "Defying Nature May Be the Only Choice," *New York Times*, August 6, 1989, Section 7, p. 22.
4. *New York Times Book Review*, February 26, 1967, p. 45.
5. Kathy Smith, "John McPhee Balances the Act," in *Literary Journalism in the Twentieth Century*, edited by Norman Sims, Oxford University Press, New York, 1990, p. 206.
6. John McPhee, *The Control of Nature*, Farrar, Straus & Giroux, New York, 1989, p. 52.
7. Ibid., p. 56.
8. Barbara Lounsberry, *The Art of Fact*, Greenwood Press, New York, 1990, p. 66.
9. Summarized from Ronald Weber, *The Literature of Fact: Literary Nonfiction in American Writing*, Ohio University Press, Athens, 1980.
10. Jack Roundy, "Formal Devices in the Prose of John McPhee," in *Literary Nonfiction: Theory, Criticism, Pedagogy*, Chris Anderson, editor, Southern Illinois University Press, Carbondale, 1989, pp. 70–92.
11. Smith, "John McPhee Balances the Act," p. 226.
12. Lounsberry, *The Art of Fact*, p. 95.
13. Jacques Barzun, *Simple and Direct*, Harper & Row, New York, 1975, p. 7.

# Appendix 7.1

# *Selected Nonfiction Authors*

Many nonfiction authors have been recognized for their strong voices. Below are a few, with their major titles. All titles were in print as of this writing.

Abbey, Edward. *Desert Solitaire: A Season in the Wilderness*. Simon & Schuster, New York, 1985.

Didion, Joan. *Slouching Towards Bethlehem*. Farrar, Straus & Giroux, New York, 1990.

———. *White Album*. Farrar, Straus & Giroux, New York, 1990.

Dillard, Annie. *Pilgrim at Tinker Creek*. Harper & Row, New York, 1988.

———. *Teaching a Stone to Talk: Expeditions and Encounters*. Harper & Row, New York, 1988.

Ehrlich, Gretel. *The Solace of Open Spaces*. Viking Penguin, New York, 1986.

Gould, Stephen Jay. *The Panda's Thumb*. W.W. Norton, New York, 1992.

Greene, Bob. *American Beat*. Viking Penguin, New York, 1984.

Hoagland, Edward. *Heart's Desire: The Best of Edward Hoagland*. Summit Books, New York, 1988.

Janovy, John Jr. *Keith County Journal*. St. Martin's Press, New York, 1980.

Keillor, Garrison. *Happy to Be Here*. Viking Penguin, New York, 1985.

Kidder, Tracy. *House*. Avon Books, New York, 1990.

Kingston, Maxine Hong. *Woman Warrior: Memoirs of a Girlhood*. Random House, New York, 1980.

Least Heat Moon, William. *Blue Highways: A Journey into America*. Houghton Mifflin, Boston, 1991.

Lopez, Barry. *Of Wolves and Men*. Macmillan, New York, 1979.

Orwell, George. *A Collection of Essays*. Harcourt Brace Jovanovich, San Diego, 1984.

Schell, Jonathan. *The Fate of the Earth*. Avon Books, New York, 1982.

Steinbeck, John. *Travels with Charley*. Viking Penguin, New York, 1980.

Theroux, Paul. *Riding the Iron Rooster: By Train through China*. Ivy Books, New York, 1989.

Thomas, Lewis. *The Lives of a Cell*. Bantam Books, New York, 1984.

Trillin, Calvin. *Travels with Alice*. Avon, New York, 1990.

Walker, Alice. *In Search of Our Mothers' Gardens*. Harcourt Brace Jovanovich, San Diego, 1984.

White, William, editor. *By-Line: Ernest Hemingway*. Macmillan, New York, 1981.

Wolfe, Tom. *The Kandy-Kolored Tangerine-Flake Streamline Baby*. Farrar, Straus & Giroux, New York, 1987.

———. *The Right Stuff*. Bantam Books, New York, 1983.

# Appendix 7.2

# *Works by John McPhee*

In reverse date order. All published by Farrar, Straus & Giroux, New York, unless otherwise noted. If I could assign only one title, it would be *Coming into the Country*, first published in 1977 but reissued in 1991.

*Looking for a Ship*, 1990

*The Control of Nature*, 1989

*Outcroppings*, Smith Gibbs, 1988

*Heirs of General Practice*, 1986

*Rising from the Plains*, 1986

*Table of Contents*, 1985

*La Place de la Concorde Suisse*, 1984

*In Suspect Terrain*, 1983

*Riding the Boom Extension*, Metacom Press, 1983

With Galen Rowell, *Alaska: Images of the Country*, Sierra Club Books, 1981

*Basin & Range*, 1981

*Giving Good Weight*, 1979

*A Sense of Where You Are*, 1978

*Coming into the Country*, 1977

*The John McPhee Reader*, 1976

*Pieces of the Frame*, 1975

*The Survival of the Bark Canoe*, 1975

*The Curve of Binding Energy*, 1974

*The Deltoid Pumpkin Seed*, 1973

*Encounters with the Archdruid*, 1971

*The Crofter & the Laird*, 1970

*Levels of the Game*, 1969

*A Roomful of Hovings and Other Profiles*, 1969

*The Pine Barrens*, 1968

*Oranges*, 1967

*The Headmaster*, 1966

# Appendix 7.3

# *Theoretical Works*

There is usually no time in a writing or editing class to allow in-depth study of single authors, but this can be an excellent honors, extra credit or grad student project. I recommend the following to students as a starting point for their research. These books could be used as the foundation for a graduate seminar in "literary nonfiction" as well.

Anderson, Chris. *Style as Argument: Contemporary American Nonfiction*. Southern Illinois University Press, Carbondale, 1987.

Anderson, Chris, editor. *Literary Nonfiction: Theory, Criticism, Pedagogy*. Southern Illinois University Press, Carbondale, 1989.

Fishkin, Shelley Fisher. *From Fact to Fiction: Journalism & Imaginative Writing in America*. Johns Hopkins University Press, Baltimore, 1985.

Hellman, John. *Fables of Fact: The New Journalism as New Fiction*. University of Illinois Press, Urbana, 1981.

Lounsberry, Barbara. *The Art of Fact*. Greenwood Press, New York, 1990.

Sims, Norman, editor. *The Literary Journalists*. Ballantine Books, New York, 1984.

————. *Literary Journalism in the Twentieth Century*. Oxford University Press, New York, 1990

Weber, Ronald. *The Literature of Fact: Literary Nonfiction in American Writing*. Ohio University Press, Athens, 1980.

Wolfe, Tom. *The New Journalism*. Harper & Row, New York, 1973.

# Part IV

# *Beyond Analysis*

$S$o far, the guiding assumption of this book has been that if you can analyze something, you can imitate it. But there are some writing and editing skills which, although they rest on a foundation of analysis, are best mastered by practice. These are called process skills. In this section are grouped four such skills, even though, in the case of tightening, it may be the last skill used in preparing a manuscript, or as with serendipity it may be the first skill used, the one that launches the whole process of writing an article. The other two process skills covered in these chapters are research and the editor/writer collaboration. This last gives a few tips on writing query letters.

# Chapter

## 8

# *Tightening*

Tightening is an editing process, whether it is done as self-editing by a writer or as manuscript preparation by a staff editor. Tightening is the fervent belief that eliminating words will improve a draft. Some writers tighten as they write; others prefer to get their thoughts out before they start killing them.

I used to tighten as I worked, stopping after almost every paragraph to "polish." But then I had a terrible auto accident and afterward a long convalescence. My mother came to stay with me during it because I was pretty helpless for a while. At the time I'd had several articles researched and ready to write, but I was too injured to type. She suggested I dictate to her and she'd type. She thought it would be good mental therapy—convalescence is boring work. She was right, but it meant that for the first time in my career I couldn't tighten as I wrote. And I discovered I do both better if I separate them. Write—and finish writing—first. Tighten second. Now that I am fully recovered, I've stuck to the new pattern; write first, tighten separately.

I would like to see a neurological scan of the brain during tightening. I feel as if I am using a different region of the cortex. When I write, I'm trying to find my thoughts, my meaning, my ideas (right brain?). I'm trying to get my ducks in a row. But when I tighten, I'm out for the kill (left brain?). I want to get rid of as many words as possible by concentrating on language, not meaning. Since that accident, I am convinced that tightening and writing are two different processes. To do both at once was like getting dressed while I sewed the garment. My work is better now that I've finally learned the differences between tightening and writing.

When tightening I do not think "Now I will hit adjectives; now I will challenge phrases." I just tighten. But afterward I can describe what I did. For each of the sixteen examples below, remember I tightened first, then analyzed. There was no pattern to my thinking other than an attempt to shorten the text. Each was a different problem with its own solution. In fact, as you examine the examples, you will notice sometimes I did opposite things; combined sentences or broke them up; inserted introductory clauses or killed those clauses. It was no trouble to find examples for this exercise. I opened magazines at random. Not once did I fail to find a paragraph that could use tightening. In each analysis I comment only on one or two tactics used. But some paragraphs required a dozen techniques, so also study the boldface phrases of the originals and compare with my versions. The boldface words were ones I changed or deleted. The secret to tightening is not just recognizing an adverb, but hearing its clumsiness.

## EXAMPLES OF TIGHTENING

**1**

### Tightened: 56 words

The trial made Falcone a national hero. But his accomplishments faded as many of those convictions were overturned or sentences shortened. Today only 50 are still behind bars. Meanwhile, his popularity bred professional jealousy. Passed over in 1990 for chief prosecutor in Palermo, he later moved to Rome for a senior post at the Justice Ministry.

### Original: 76 words

The trial **turned** Falcone **into** a national hero. But **much of what he** accomplished **there has been undone**. Many of those convicted **have since managed to have their** sentences shortened or their **convictions** overturned. Today only 50 are still behind bars. Meanwhile, **Falcone's** popularity bred professional jealousy. In 1990 **he was** passed over for the job of chief prosecutor in Palermo. Last year he moved to Rome **to take a** senior post at the Justice Ministry.

From "The Grip of the Octopus," *Newsweek*, June 8, 1992, p. 36.

### Analysis

*Simplify Predicates.* Notice the phrases "has been undone" and "managed to have." When tightening, I hunt for overloaded predicates and try to substitute a single verb, "faded" for "has been undone" here. I was especially pleased to get one auxiliary verb, "were," to serve two verbs, "overturned" and "shortened," in that sentence.

2

### Tightened: 48 words

In a March poll, climate researchers disagree substantially over global warming. At the same time, they fear delaying action on the issue. Social scientists at the State University of New York, Albany, selected the 118 scientists in the poll through a computer network serving oceanic and atmospheric sciences.

### Original: 81 words

A poll **of scientists involved in** climate research **reveals substantial** disagreement over **predictions on** global warming. At the same time, the **researchers do not advocate** delaying action on the issue. **Conducted by** social scientists at the State University of New York at Albany, the poll, **released in** March, **queried** 118 scientists, **almost all of whom had participated in some activity related to climate change research. The pollsters** selected **respondents** through a computer-based network **that primarily** serves oceanic and atmospheric scientists.

From "Climate Change: A Diversity of Views," *Science News*, May 30, 1992, p. 365.

### Analysis

*Use Pronouns.* If a pronoun can be substituted for a noun phrase and still be clear, it almost always improves a text. But antecedents have to make sense. I made sure when I used "they" for "climate researchers" that only one group of scientists in the preceding sentence could be "them."

3

### Tightened: 130 words

Diane Sawyer and I talked extensively over three years ago, when Arledge, the master of the medium, wooed her from CBS with his dream of a newsmagazine showcase for her. This time she seemed more confident. She invited me to her cozy New York penthouse duplex recently redecorated by Kitty Hawks. She greeted me at the elevator. Her getup, jeans, a yellow sweater with a badly stretched V neck, and flats, was the sort a college girl wears around the dorm, or Elaine May would don if she were doing a send-up of a bluestocking. These days, Sawyer takes no chances with the glamour rap. She was bitten for that after Annie Leibovitz photographed her for this magazine in 1987. Now she strives for high-mindedness at all times.

## Original: 170 words

**This was not the first time I had interviewed** Diane Sawyer. **We had** talked extensively more than three years before, when Arledge, the master of the medium, **had won** her **away** from CBS with his **mesmerizing** dream of **creating a revolutionary** newsmagazine **as a** showcase for her. This time **around**, she seemed **far** more confident. She invited me to her **New York pied-à-terre**—a cozy penthouse duplex **in an East Side hotel—which Mike Nichols** recently **had redone by the** decorator Kitty Hawks. **Sawyer** greeted me at the elevator, **dressed in** jeans, a yellow sweater with a badly stretched V neck, and flats—**the kind of** getup you might **expect** a college girl to wear around the dorm, or Elaine May to don if she were doing a send-up of a bluestocking. These days, Sawyer takes no chances with the glamour rap. She was bitten for that **when she posed** for Annie Leibovitz for this magazine in 1987. Now she strives for high-mindedness at all times.

From "True Grit" by Edward Klein, *Vanity Fair,* June 1982, p. 143.

## Analysis

*Eliminate Adjectives and Adverbs.* My rule with modifiers is they have to add information or I kill them. What's the difference between a mesmerizing dream and a dream? When is a dream not revolutionary? Both—out.

*Stop Wheezing.* To my knowledge, wheezing has never been officially recognized as a grammatical concept. But you can hear it. "Not the first time I have interviewed . . ." Come on, stop talking about yourself and tell us about Diane. "New York pied à terre . . . East side hotel . . . Mike Nichols hiring Kitty Hawks . . ." If I read this story correctly, it's supposed to be about Diane Sawyer. If this other stuff comes out, the story moves along more quickly.

**4**

## Tightened: 101 words

By the seventh night, after more than 400 films, we had covered almost half the sky. I guided on yet another star. My mind wandered. At 12, when I was already in love with the sky, my father told me at dinner of a novel he had read when he was young, *Cole of Spyglass Mountain* (1923). It was about a young man observing Mars from his small homemade observatory. The novel ended when Cole found evidence one night of life on Mars—and instantly became a celebrity. "If you ever find that book," Dad said, "I'd like to read it again."

## Original: 126 words

**Now it's late on our** seventh night **of observing. We have taken** more than 400 films, cover**ing** almost half the sky. As I guide on yet another star, my **lazy** mind **starts to** wander **to a childhood memory of a conversation at the family dinner table. At age** 12 I **had already fallen** in love with the sky, **and** my father **was telling me** of a novel he had read when he was a young**ster.** Called *Cole of Spyglass Mountain* (1923), **it was** about a young man observing Mars from his small homemade observatory. The novel ended **one night** when Cole found evidence of life on Mars—and instantly became a celebrity. "If you ever find that book," Dad said, "I'd like to read it again."

From "A Sky Watchman Discovers Comets and Immortality" by David H. Levy, *Smithsonian,* June 1992, p. 82.

## Analysis

*Place Modifiers Carefully.* When clauses, phrases, adjectives or adverbs do contain information, I look for other more efficient places to put them when I tighten. The whole half-sentence about talking at dinner becomes a simple prepositional phrase when moved down. By turning subordinate ideas into clauses to modify the main idea, "photographing the sky," I make the opening clearer and shorter. As for "one night," moving it doesn't eliminate words but does eliminate confusion. I am certain the novel didn't end one night.

**5**

## Tightened: 66 words

Twenty years ago, there were fewer "hyphenates" (writer-director, actor-director) in Hollywood. True, John Huston, Billy Wilder and Sam Peckinpah all started as writers. Charlie Chaplin, Elia Kazan and Sydney Pollack began as actors. But studios compete so hotly for scripts and talent today, agents can make tough demands. The director's job can sometimes depend on who controls the material, or "holds the script hostage."

## Original: 86 words

**Such crossover rarely happened** twenty years ago, **when** there were fewer "hyphenates" (writer-director, actor-director) in Hollywood. True, John Huston, Billy Wilder, and Sam Peckinpah all started **in the business** as writers, and Charlie Chaplin, Elia Kazan and Sydney Pollack began as actors. But **there is such hot competition among the** studios for scripts and talent today **that** agents can make tougher demands **than ever.** The director's job can sometimes **be**

**leveraged according to** who controls the material, **otherwise known as** "holding the script hostage."

From "Persons with Experience Need Not Apply" by Sean Mitchell, *Premiere*, June, 1992, p. 42.

### Analysis

*Reword Prepositional Phrases.* By making "studios" the subject of the sentence instead of the object of "among," I can get rid of "there is" and substitute a vigorous verb. I see such gambits when I look at all prepositional phrases with suspicion. Sometimes prepositions can be eliminated outright without harming the meaning, as "in the business."

**6**

### Tightened: 80 words

Earth-hugging Taliesin, the quintessence of Frank Lloyd Wright's architectural vision, was also his Wisconsin home, school and working farm. The building, without dominant front or back, shoots low walls well into the landscape. They root equally in all directions like a tree seeking nourishment. For Wright, the structure of a house began with the ground, which already had form; the architect was like a water dowser, his pencil a divining rod sensing the land as it designed the house.

### Original: 85 words

Earth-hugging Taliesin was the Wisconsin home, school and working farm of Frank Lloyd Wright, **and is the** quintessence of his architectural vision. The building **has no** dominant front or back **but** shoots low walls well into the landscape, root**ing** equally in all directions like a tree seeking nourishment. For Wright, the structure of a house begins with the ground, which already has form: The architect **is really like** a water dowser, his pencil a divining rod **that** senses the land **actually** designing the house.

From: "Architecture's Genius, America's Hero" by Joseph Giovannini, *House Beautiful*, June 1992, p. 34.

### Analysis

*Suspect All Clauses.* Sometimes clauses are very efficient, sneaking sentence-caliber information into few words. But much of the time they're tiresome. When tightening, I check first to be sure my clauses vary in placement, from beginning, to end, to midsentence. In this paragraph, I both inserted and killed clauses. "The quintessence . . ." I subordinated to modify Taliesin but elevated "rooting equally . . ." to full sentence status. Both strategies improved clarity, although only a few words were eliminated.

7

## Tightened: 68 words

Once you have nice stacks of roughed-out parts, plane one face and one edge of each. This creates working surfaces for what follows. I usually stack parts by function—all the door rails or drawer fronts or boards for carcase sides together. Then I group these by the thickness of the rough-sawn boards. One or more shop carts are handy for wheeling parts to each machine.

## Original: 90 words

Once you have nice stacks of roughed-out parts, **things begin to move more smoothly. The** next **task is to** plane one face and one edge of each **part,** creating working surfaces **from which all subsequent operations are gauged. I** usually stack parts **according to** function—all the door rails **together,** drawer fronts together, boards for carcase sides **and so on—then** group these by the thickness of the rough-sawn boards. One or more shop carts are **very** handy for wheeling **stacks of** parts **from one** machine **to another.**

From "Thinking Like A Craftsman" by Roger Holmes, *The Woodworker's Journal,* May/June 1992, p. 34.

## Analysis

*Kill Repetition.* Of all my tightening tricks, this is the most important; of all my tightening tricks, this is the most important. Sometimes repetition adds flavor or voice and is worth saving, but often it is noise and needs to be killed. In this example, most of the repetition is straightforward. I eliminated repetition of "part" and "together." But I also tried to simplify repeating ideas. "From one machine to another" now is "each machine."

8

## Tightened: 126 words

There was no revolution in East Germany. People talk about one, and a painter, Barbel Bohley, an activist in the East German peace movement, is sometimes referred to as its mother. But the Wall came down because East Germany was coming apart. The fall had little to do with Prenzlauer Berg poets or political prisoners, or even chanting crowds marching in Leipzig, Dresden and Berlin. East Germany fell because industry, agriculture and the state were bankrupt. There was no money, and no way, short of massacre, to stop East Germans from leaving. East Germany had become too expensive and embarrassing for Mikhail Gorbachev's *perestroika.* He was happy to give it up in exchange for twenty-one billion dollars from Helmut Kohl, who wanted East Germany himself.

## Original: 176 words

There was **never a** revolution in East Germany. People talk about **"the revolution,"** and a painter **by the name of** Barbel Bohley, **who was** active in the East German peace movement, is sometimes referred to as **the** "mother **of the revolution,"** but the Wall came down **in East Germany** because East Germany was **literally** coming apart—and it had **very** little to do with **the** Prenzlauer Berg poets, or **with the thousands of** political prisoners, or even **with the** crowds that marched in Leipzig and Dresden and Berlin chanting, **"We are the people!"** East Germany fell because the state **was bankrupt,** industry **was bankrupt,** agriculture **was** bankrupt, **and** there was no money, and **thus there was** no way short of **a** massacre to stop East Germans from leaving. **There was no way because** East Germany had **got to be too** expensive and too embarrassing for Mikhail Gorbachev's **new** perestroika **East, and Gorbachev** was happy to give up—which he did in exchange for twenty-one billion dollars from Helmut Kohl, who wanted East Germany **for** himself.

From "Letter from Europe," *The New Yorker*, May 25, 1992, pp. 42–43.

## Analysis

*Kill Repetition.* If simply looking for duplicate words were all that were needed, eliminating repetition would be easy. But usually subtle language handling is needed to simplify a repetitious sentence. In this example, "revolution," "East Germany" and "bankrupt" are repeated over and over. But the paragraph is about revolution, East Germany and bankruptcy. To eliminate the repetition would be to kill the sense of the paragraph. To solve the problem, I created several subordinate clauses. I linked ideas before key words; industry, agriculture and state now modify bankrupt rather than shape separate clauses. But the main thing I did was go after other weaknesses. I killed adverbs, simplified predicates, eliminated prepositional phrases and dropped adjectives. This had the effect of speeding up the prose, making the repetition less onerous even though much is still there.

9

## Tightened: 83 words

Preventing founder is critical. Don't turn ponies, draft horses, or even light work horses from barn feed to unrestricted lush grass pasture. Avoid sudden feeding changes. Reduce grain intake on heavily worked horses or those laid up for a day without exercise. Don't give a hot horse grain. Give only small amounts of water until it is cooled out. For first aid, think cold. Either stand the horse in cold water or wrap its feet with soaked burlap bags. Get veterinary help immediately.

## Original: 105 words

Preventing **"grass founder," or any form of** founder, is critical. Don't turn ponies, draft horses, or even light horses **with draft-type characteristics** from barn feed to unrestricted lush grass pasture. Avoid sudden changes **in** feeding, **and** reduce grain intake on **horses** heavily worked **and** laid up for a day without exercise. Don't give a hot horse grain, **and only** give your horse small amounts of water **at a time** until it is cooled out. For first aid, think cold. Either stand the horse in cold water or wrap its feet with burlap bags **soaked in cold water. Be sure to** get veterinary help immediately.

From "Keeping Pastures Safe" by John J. Mettler, Jr., D.V.M., *Mother Earth News*, April/May 1992, p. 44.

## Analysis

*Kill Repetition.* This is another subtle repetition problem with no easy solution. The topic is feeding hot horses safely, so heat, horses and feed are going to appear in every sentence. My solution in this one was to turn almost every sentence into a command. It may be repetitious but at least now it's brisk.

**10**

## Tightened: 89 words

Enid Haupt sees herself as a serendipitous benefactress, saving gardens as if anyone in her right mind would do the same. Of restoring the New York Botanical Garden's Victorian "crystal palace," she won't tell about the endless meetings she attended. Rather she'll say she sold her emeralds, diamonds, and sapphires for the $10 million restoration and let it go at that. Yet, she is a serious gardener. A conversation about orchids can last for hours. And she has a keen sense for knowing when a botanical treasure is threatened.

## Original: 142 words

**Should one attribute a divinely inspired role to her,** Enid Haupt **will dismiss that idea with an airy gesture. She** prefers to present herself as a serendipitous benefactress, saving gardens as if anyone in her right mind would do the same **thing. Ask her what was involved in** restoring the New York Botanical Garden's **crown jewel,** its Victorian "crystal palace" **conservatory,** and she won't tell **you** about the meetings **she attended**. Rather she'll say she sold her emeralds, diamonds, and sapphires **to pay** for the $10 million restoration and let it go at that. Yet **Enid** is a serious gardener (**if you get her talking** about orchids, **the** conversation can last for hours). And she has a keen sense for knowing when a botanical treasure is threatened, **when community funding has been exhausted and garden directors are at their wits' end.**

From " A Star in Our Crown: Enid A. Haupt Garden Maker," *Victoria*, July 1992, p. 80.

## Analysis

*Throw Manuscript off Cliff.* Actually sometimes I've done this. My thinking remains so cluttered, I trash my first draft and start over. I think this would have been the merciful thing to do here. Note in this paragraph the distinction between editing and tightening. Tightening is maintaining the meaning but polishing the prose. Editing is discovering gaps in logic or information and demanding an accounting from the writer. The last sentence contains too many ideas for a single paragraph. To kill it is editing. If I were actually editing this, I would demand the writer rework the piece and have separate subtopics, one on working with plants and another for working with people. The same goes for contrasting Haupt as a gardener and as benefactor. Those are separate topics. I cannot see using them in the same paragraph, let alone the same sentence, as this writer has done. I should point out, though, I often discover my own logic gaps only in the tightening phase. Tightening overlaps with the problem of editing for sense or meaning.

**11**

## Tightened: 100 words

The world's more than 25,000 species of food fish and shellfish, from cod, snapper, and shrimp, to snook, ulua, and zander, are attractive nutritionally because many are low in fat, especially compared to other protein sources. Orange roughy, grouper, haddock, sole, cod, pollock, and mahi mahi contain less than 10% of their calories as fat. These low-fat fish are tender, flaky and pale in color. But some fish is as high in fat as meat and poultry. Bluefish, swordfish, mackerel, sockeye salmon, herring, chinook salmon, pompano and rainbow trout range (in order) from 30% to 53% calories from fat.

## Original: 141 words

**There are** more than 25,000 species of fish and shellfish **in the world, all grouped together as** seafood—from **favorites such as** cod, snapper, and shrimp, to **the more unusual,** such as snook, ulua, and zander. Nutritionally, **what attracts many people to seafood is that some of it is extremely** low in fat, especially **when** compared with other protein sources. Orange roughy, grouper, haddock, sole, cod, pollock, and mahi mahi **are all fish in which** less than 10% of the calories **come from** fat. These lower-fat fish are tender, flaky, and pale in color. But **not all fish fit that profile.** Some fish is **pretty** high in fat—**in fact, not so different from** meat and poultry. Bluefish, swordfish, mackerel, sockeye salmon, herring, chinook salmon, pompano, and rainbow trout range (in **that** order) from 30% to 53% calories from fat.

From "A Fish Story" by Janis Harsla and Evie Hansen, *Walking*, May/June 1992, p. 24.

## Analysis

*Be Kind to Facts*. This is another example of editing. Reading the paragraph for sense reveals that the main point "nutritional value of fish" was buried. In order to make that the point of the sentence, I also, happily, eliminated fifteen words. This way of tightening, finding the main point and emphasizing it, is easier for me than thinking about clauses, phrases or adjectives.

**12**

## Tightened: 67 words

Ecribellate spiders coat their dry webs with a moist glue, the better to detain flies, but how do they avoid getting moist on their own foulards? That is, how do they avoid the stuff? The answer, according to arachnologists Edward Tillinghast of the University of New Hampshire and Fitz Vollrath of Oxford University, is simple. The spiders tiptoe around it because the glue is in spheroidal globs.

## Original: 80 words

Ecribellate spiders coat the dry **silk of their** webs with a moist glue, the better to detain flies. **Which raises an interesting question:** How does the **spider** avoid getting moist on its own foulard? That is, how does it **manage not to step in** the stuff? The answer, according to arachnologists Edward Tillinghast of the University of New Hampshire and Fritz Vollrath of Oxford University, is **commonsensical. Ecribellate** spiders **simply** tiptoe around **the glue, which they deposit in** spheroidal globs.

From "Breakthroughs in Science Technology and Medicine," *Discover*, June 1992, p. 11.

## Analysis

*Tiptoe*. In this example, I use most strategies mentioned already, eliminating adverbs and adjectives, substituting simple active verbs for complex predicates and so on. I especially tried to get rid of the chatter. "Raise an interesting question''? Forget it. Just ask the question. But I left that awful pun. Maybe I'm wrong; maybe it's chatter too. But then maybe it's voice. Is this the real writer? No, on second thought, it's such a bad pun I should have killed it. But, the point here, there is such a thing as overtightening. It's important not to tighten all the flavor out of a piece.

**13**

### Tightened: 77 words

My father didn't like the arts. He wished the June Taylor Dancers wouldn't keep breaking in on Jackie Gleason. I don't think anybody on either side of my family liked the arts until my generation. They all liked church. So it did not seem outlandish to me when a prospective juror in the Mapplethorpe obscenity trial in Cincinnati last year said he'd never been to a museum and couldn't relate to art or to people who did.

### Original: 128 words

My father didn't like the arts. He wished the June Taylor Dancers wouldn't keep breaking in on Jackie Gleason, **and he didn't like *Hamlet*. I know because our family went to a performance of *Hamlet* once. . . . Of course, I agreed with him about the June Taylor Dancers. And T. S. Eliot had reservations about *Hamlet*. But T. S. Eliot liked *some* things about *Hamlet*, whereas my father didn't. In fact,** I don't think anybody on either side of my family liked the arts until my generation. They all liked church. So, it did not seem outlandish to me when a prospective juror in the Mapplethorpe obscenity trial in Cincinnati last year said he'd never been to a museum and couldn't relate to art or to people who did.

From "Your Art's Showing" by Roy Blount, Jr., *Spy*, June 1992, p. 72.

### Analysis

*Kill Irrelevancies.* As with the Diane Sawyer profile, here I killed details that seem to belabor the point or be off focus. An argument can be made that my version is clearer and to the point and yet the part I killed had subtleties about his father, so did I improve the piece or ruin it? Did I tighten or damage the voice? Is this overtightening?

**14**

### Tightened: 11 words

We're mad and we're not going to take it any more.

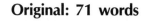

## Original: 71 words

When in the course of human events, it becomes necessary for one people to dissolve the political bands which have connected them with another, and to assume among the powers of the earth, the separate and equal station to which the Laws of Nature and of Nature's God entitle them, a decent respect to the opinions of mankind requires that they should declare the causes which impel them to the separation.

From The Declaration of Independence.

## Analysis

My version is shorter. My version definitely has cultural validity. My version would never be respected. We are looking at prose from two different eras, but the differences are as much explained by their times as by their words.

**15**

## Tightened: 4 words

Okay, guys, let's go.

## Original: 61 words

Once more unto the breach, dear friends, once more;/ Or close the wall up with our English dead./ In peace there's nothing so becomes a man/ As modest stillness and humility;/ But when the blast of war blows in our ears,/ Then imitate the action of the tiger;/ Stiffen the sinews, summon up the blood,/ Disguise fair nature with hard-favoured rage.

From Shakespeare's *Henry V* [III.i.1]

## Analysis

There's an even greater time distance between the two versions, but in this case, time alone doesn't explain the differences. Here genre has an impact. One is poetry and a speech in a play; the other, a comment in a football huddle. (Football huddles are a legitimate literary form.)

**16**

## Tightened: 10 words

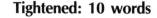

Wild flowers don't work, but they're better dressed than royalty.

## Original: 36 words

Consider the lilies of the field, how they grow; they toil not, neither do they spin; And yet I say unto you, that even Solomon in all his glory was not arrayed like one of these. Matthew 6:28.

Yes, my version is shorter, but in no way does it equal the beauty of the original. I don't claim that *any* of the tightened paragraphs above are better than the originals— only that they are tighter. Beauty, personality or voice can be realized in wordy versions—as these last three examples unequivocally show. Efficiency of prose is only part of strong writing. Tightening is a good practice for a writer but is not itself writing. Don't destroy musical elements in writing by emphasizing tightness. "Consider the lilies of the field" is inefficient, but magic.

The reverse is equally true, however. Writers who fall in love with their words are probably not musicians but mudskippers. They tend to have too many words and too little content. How do you tell when wordiness is beauty? Ear. It is clear to my ear that "Once more unto the breach" can't be improved by tightening, but the story about ecribellate spiders can. I just hear it, and how easy it is to hear when someone else's prose is muddy. But I can't always hear my own turgidity. Time and again, an editor has marked excess words on my copy, words I would have easily caught on someone else's. My students suffer the same deafness. They quickly master the art of killing words in others' copy but are unable to find the same flaws in their own.

One trick that works for me is to read a short segment of copy out loud. Then look away and *tell* someone else what the paragraph just said. Almost always the spoken version is brisker, clearer, sharper (and shorter) than the written one. Quickly jot down the spoken version, before you forget it. This technique forces you to zero in on the key ideas of the segment, much as was done in the shellfish example above. Superfluous details drop out.

Reading your copy aloud is a good technique for training ear, whether or not you use the second, look-away, step. I also read aloud stories by other writers just to learn from them, and I sometimes read to my students, even if we all have the article in front of us. I think it helps improve ear for all of us, or at the very least it takes us all back to the read-me-a-story period of our lives. All writing should have a language-out-loud quality, and tightening is one tool for achieving it.

## TIGHTENING TRICKS

- Break up sentences (one idea per sentence).
- Combine sentences (let one subject serve three verbs).
- Drop the introductory clauses.
- Ruthlessly kill prepositional phrases.
- Ruthlessly kill adjectival and adverbial clauses.

- Ruthlessly kill repetition (such as "ruthlessly kill").
- Eliminate adverbs.
- Eliminate adjectives.
- Substitute pronouns for nouns.
- Avoid conjunctions.
- Use simple predicates (without the has's, have's, will's, etc.)
- Use simple past tense.
- Use simple subjects.
- Use simple subject/verb construction.
- Truncate attributions.
- Avoid assertions.
- Place background details carefully (especially appositions).
- Use real paragraphs (topic sentence with development).

# Chapter

# 9

# *Serendipity*

Much has been said so far about analysis. Sizing up an audience for its demographic and psychographic qualities; examining your competition by studying the focuses of other articles on a topic; studying a target magazine's forms, structures, authority bases and voice restrictions—all have been suggested as tools for editing or shaping an approach to an editor. But little has been said about coming up with article ideas in the first place. Where do you find ideas? How do editors and writers think of topics?

Bluntly, I don't know. You are unique. You will in time invent your own strategies for being creative and unlocking your imagination, but it will be an utterly private process. Even so, perhaps another person's technique for thinking of ideas will help you create yours. The technique is "serendipity."

Serendipity means "happy accident." It is a deliberate effort to set up conditions that force encounters with tangents, stray ideas, off-beat connections, anything that might take me out of my narrow experiences and push me into looking at things in a new way. Intentional luck is the goal of serendipity. My serendipity has three steps: remembering, talking and free play.

## REMEMBERING

Whenever I need to find an idea, I set aside time to just sit, to let memories, no matter how trivial, float into my mind. Then I jot down notes about the memories. "The Corn," "The Linzer Torte," "The Cold" and "Eva's Ghost" all started this way with just scraps of notes as I tried to grab onto passing memories. A memory will never be the final article. It's too personal, too small. But it can be a launching point in the hunt for a new article.

For example, this memory wandered into my mind one afternoon:

## Lists (fragment)

I am embarrassed to admit it now, but I used to keep a four-foot list of things to do in my kitchen. The paper was from the waste end of a printer's stationery run so it was of high quality. Inspired by the paper's beauty, I made my entries with a calligraphy pen. The list contained everything:

- patch cracks in basement walls
- prune the dying pear tree
- train the dog
- start an asparagus bed
- paint the shed
- fix the kitchen faucet
- build a work bench
- make a new suit
- buy fireplace tools
- take shoulder pads out of winter coat
- go fishing

But where I saw beauty in my list, friends saw an intimidating burden. "Thank God you put fishing on the list," said one. My family studied the list and worried. I was doing too much. I would crack under the strain. So many friends seemed to think I was heading for a breakdown, I began to believe them and tore up the list.

Within a month I was making lists again, first on scraps of paper; then the scraps became backs of Far Side cartoons. Then the cartoons began to be sorted by categories—upstairs, downstairs, basement, outdoors, garden— which was outside but not part of outdoors—and shed—which was outside by the garden but was neither outdoors nor garden. It all made sense to me. When the categories "soon" and "today" joined the mix, I knew I had a sickness.

## TALKING

After jotting down a memory, I study the notes. If they look promising, I'll risk testing the idea by talking with friends. Most of my friends have gotten used to this. They know I am not actively researching a story at this point. I'm just thinking out loud with their help. This is how the conversations with friends and students went when I asked them about their to-do lists.

## *(fragment)*

My graphics arts students who kept lists, without exception, put dingbats or dots before each item. Molly was unique in that she drew intricately curved arrows before each item. Lisa would dot her items, like other graphic artists, but her pattern was to faithfully dot things on a scrap every morning, and then lose the slip before leaving the house. Nonvisual people had, appropriately enough, nonvisual idiosyncracies. Tracey, for example, had memorized the layout of her grocery store and would arrange her shopping list by aisle. Her life would lurch into crisis whenever the store had a marketing vision and moved things. Rich, when I asked him if he kept a list, hauled out a Radio Shack pocket computer which tallied his daily duties, complete with names and phone numbers. His eyes glowed insanely as he punched the buttons, reveling in his opportunity to make a high tech complexity of something most people do on the backs of junk mail. Charles, too, kept his lists on computer and would call them up by modem.

Lists were sometimes a source of conflict for couples. I talked to Phyllis and Joe the day before they left on a trip. It used to be, Joe said, that four weeks before a trip Phyllis would make a list, a horrible list, of everything: "clean the garage," "stain the shutters," "achieve world peace." He hated that list because she believed everything on it really had to be done, when all anybody needed before a trip was to "get money."

"Wait a minute," Phyllis said, "Here we are the day before a trip and no list." It was clear she wanted one; it was even clearer he knew it. Did I detect unresolved anger here, or was this no-list-before-a-trip deep growth for them? Interestingly, both Phyllis and Joe kept personal lists. Phyllis liked hers on lined paper with a Kliban cat at top. Joe preferred making his lists after he did things. Whenever he felt overwhelmed, he listed things he'd done recently just so he could tell himself, "Hey, I'm not doing so bad."

The occasional list users, like Joe and Phyllis, were most common in my conversations. But there were also list deniers. Mike said he never did one because he felt it confined his creative energies. Patrick said he made his lists only in his head, in a tone that implied only a total idiot would need to write anything down to remember it. Another Mike told me firmly no, he did not use lists, again with that of-course-not tone, but when I probed, he admitted he does put daily goals on a 3 × 5 card. He's a friend so I didn't ask him what the difference was between a list and a 3 × 5 card. My brother, Tim, was also a hostile list denier. "There's always now," he said. "Who needs a list for now?" Then he added. "I figure no task is so big, so complex it can't be ignored for six months."

Most deniers were like my brother, firm in their sense of moral superiority over us list makers. But another Tim said he admired his wife's lists and then described himself as "listless." By now, I had been attacked by enough list deniers that I was beginning to feel defensive. "So you think it's foolish to keep lists," I said. "No," he said, "I'm just lazy." I could have hugged him.

Most fun for me, of course, were the list fanatics, and I found a few. Always when discussing this sensitive topic, they began with an apology. How did the nonlisters persuade us list makers to be ashamed? Belinda, after her apology, said lists were very important for her. She wrote them on a slip and then put the slip in her back pocket. That way, she said, the stress was outside herself, literally behind her. Also she said, lists are "something to hope for—how I want the world to be, rather than how it is." I am still thinking about that; was that why I needed lists, to chronicle my dreams?

Ann too began with an apology, not sure she could trust me on this intimate topic. "I put things on a list I've already done just so I can cross them off," she began. I did that too, I reassured her. She began to relax. "And the first item on my list is always 'make a list' just so I have something to cross off when I'm done." I did that too, I said. She knew now she had a kindred spirit in me and began to tell me everything. "I make subcategories, not just 'grade,' but 'read papers,' 'write comments,' 'record' or not just 'clean house,' but 'clean kitchen,' 'clean dining room' and so on," she said.

Ever since I was a girl everyone in my family—mother, sisters, aunts, cousins—had always subdivided laundry into three categories on our lists: wash, dry and PCA (for Put Clothes Away). One day I was sorting laundry and I thought—"Sort, that's a step. It should be SORT, wash, dry, PCA." I called my mother. She called my sisters, cousins and aunts, and soon I could feel waves of gratitude swelling toward me from all over the country. Sort. Wash. Dry. PCA. Ann's eyes opened wide when I told her this; she had never thought to subdivide laundry before, let alone divide it four ways. She moved to North Dakota last fall and has taken the good news to the people there.

## FREE PLAY

At this point I'm ready for a major decision. Is this fuzzy idea worth the effort of trying to generate a real topic idea? With lists, I'm thinking, yes, for two reasons. First, with hardly any effort at all, I had a rich collection of detail from my conversations. Second, and more important, was the surprising intensity of peoples' interest in this topic. It may be trivial, but for some reason, people loved talking about lists. So I was now determined to play with the idea in earnest.

I always do my free playing in the library. It is very important to understand that library serendipity is NOT research. It is play. It is a search for happy accidents. I want to discover if there is anything to this topic beyond things obvious. So far, everything I had might be cute, but anybody on earth could get anecdotes like the above. If I'm to create a fresh angle, I have to reach beyond the simple topic "list" and find something to say about people. People are always the real topic. What do lists have to reveal about *us*?

For a library serendipity, I usually start with encyclopedias. When I did a serendipity for "The Linzer Torte," I didn't find anything in the *Encyclopedia Americana* on linzer tortes, but I did find an entry on "Linz." That was the first time I was aware there might be some Austro-Hungarian rivalry over this cookie. But the encyclopedia strategy didn't work for lists; there was zilch. So I went to the library computer catalog, keyed in a subject search for the word "list." Up came 1,563 entries, but almost all the titles were lists of books. This was useless. I wanted "to-do" lists. There is such a thing as being too tangential.

Next, I keyed in a title search, asking the computer to find books that used the word "list" in their titles. There were 1,712, and these were a lot more fun. Among them:

- a list method of psychotherapy
- an index to 92,000 molecular formulas including lists of compound names and references to published infrared spectra
- a list of historical statistics of Australia
- a list of the Sumerian kings of Babylon
- a selected list of useful publications for Ohio
- a list of customs records of Britain from 1697
- a list of English dialogs of the dead
- a list of monumental brasses on the continent of Europe

This last one was published by the Monumental Brass Society, and I began to wonder how many organizations are there whose sole purpose of being is to make a list of something? Who did the hiking around Europe to find the monumental brasses? Who decided when a brass wasn't brassy enough to be monumental? I'd give anything to have sat around the conference table listening when the organization tried to decide which cherubs in which town were worthy of their list. Was my serendipity done? Should I do an article just on silly lists?

I probably could, but I kept playing anyway. After all, I was having such a good time. I next looked at *Reader's Guide* and *Business Periodicals Index* and found only six articles. That was good news. Maybe I really did have a marketable topic going here. Two of the articles were about managing computer data bases, so were irrelevant. Three were predictable advice pieces on how to do a to-do list. That was the last thing I wanted to do in any article I'd write. But one of the articles, in *Prevention*, really caught my attention: "List Writing, an Emotional Disorder?" The article referred to a *New England Journal of Medicine* report, which I tracked down. It cited a study of 900 patients that concluded the majority of list writers were emotionally stable. "Most notes seemed to be written . . . because of no lurking Freudian distemper, but because patients and family simply want to get things straight," the researcher wrote. Well, that was a relief.

I briefly checked into business books about time management, but I wasn't interested in going in this direction. Whatever I would do with the topic, it wouldn't be one of those awful advice pieces that hold up standards of perfection to the hopelessly doomed. I moved my serendipity over to the literature shelves, hoping to find less perfection and more humor.

I checked concordances for Shakespeare and Emily Dickinson. A concordance is an index to words that appear in an author's work. Dickinson used "list" only seven times in all her poems, but one of the poems, "Of All The Souls That Stand Create," had the line "Behold the atom," which seemed to me a wonderful description of a list. A list is a way of looking at something very small. I thought about this for some time. It's very difficult for most people to notice little things. This was just a glimmer of an idea at this point, but I held on to it. I can't explain why. I just felt it. This idea that lists are for small things seemed important.

In a concordance for Shakespeare, the word "list" appeared sixty-three times, and he used it in more than one way. Sometimes he meant it to listen. "What man is this/Stand close and list him" (*Antony and Cleopatra*). Sometimes he meant it as a catalog. "Elves, list your names" (*Merry Wives of Windsor*). Sometimes he meant desire or want. "She may make, unmake, do as she lists" (*Othello*). And last, he used it to mean a border, a confinement. "I cannot be confined within the weak list of a country's fashion" (*Henry V*).

All Shakespeare's usages, when I checked the *Oxford English Dictionary* (OED) next, had long and well-traveled histories. The word *list* comes originally from the Old Norse *hylst* for hear or ear. The earliest record of this word in English is about A.D. 550 and meant *listen*. From there, the word moved into Latin to become *lista* meaning border. I always thought it was the other way around, that Latin words moved into English. I had no idea that English words affected Latin. From Latin, the word moved into Old French, to become *hem*, or what today would be selvage for cloth. The OED didn't explain the change directly but did hint that perhaps measuring a speaker by listening and measuring a cloth by its edges may be the linguistic bridge as the word jumped back and forth over the Rubicon.

*List* to mean *border* returned to English and first appeared in writing in the Magna Carta. I was baffled as to why the Magna Carta would care about cloth selvages and checked it. The OED referred to paragraph twenty-five, but that was wrong. (Yes, the OED made a mistake.) This forced me to read the whole Magna Carta to find the quote. I'd never done this before. It is wonderful, brimming with passion and anger.

> No widow shall be forced to marry unless she wills.

> No sheriff or bailiff of ours, or any other shall take horses and carts of any free man for carrying, except by the will of the free man.

How lively the writing, how intense the desire for fairness and justice contained in its short paragraphs. I found my reference to lists in paragraph thirty-five.

> There shall be one measure of wine throughout our whole realm, and one measure of beer, and one measure of corn, to wit, the London quarter, and one breadth of dyed cloth, and russet and haberget cloth, to wit, two ells within the lists, and of weights, it shall be as of measures.

This was a paragraph setting standards of weights and measures. All governments do this today, but was this the earliest time in England that weights and measures had been codified? I filed that away for a future women's topic ("A History of the Measuring Cup"?). I also found myself thinking how crucial it is in all research and all thinking to check originals. The Magna Carta was a far livelier document than history courses had led me to believe. Besides it isn't every day you find an error in the OED.

The usage of lists to mean catalog or register was first used by Shakespeare in *Hamlet*, and this is the main meaning of the word today. Shakespeare's use of the word *list* to mean *want* may be actually an accident of dialect. Another word from Old Norse, *lysta*, meaning pleasure, in Welsh became *lust* and was pronounced in rural areas *list*, and implied not only *lust*, but *like* or *please* or *care* or *want*. Stratford-on-Avon is near enough to the Welsh border that Shakespeare may have had a bit of a Welsh twang.

This tidbit made me remember Belinda's idea of a list as the world as she *wants* it, and at that moment, the stray facts and incoherent melange of data came together into an idea. A list is a border or frame, a limited portrait of reality, I thought; and yet it holds forth potential reality—desires and hopes. Its parts heighten the whole. This is what art does. Art is a frame for viewing the world intensely. On the one hand, art is a fragment of reality—a way to behold the atom. But on the other hand, it's an extension of reality. It gives us a heightened experience, a dream—as do lists. Perhaps a list is not a dry catalog of tasks but an art form for perceiving the very precious small things of life. If so, the list maker is an artist.

I used this idea as the focus for a speech a few months after this serendipity. The speech began by my taking listeners through the stories pretty much as you've read them. Then I shared with the audience my serendipity, in more detail than I have given you here. Then I argued that lists were an art form, though it took quite a few poems and definitions of art to finish the argument. People laughed in the right places. After the speech, a man came up and told me he liked it because there were many layers of meaning. Almost immediately thereafter, another came up and asked had I ever considered stand-up comedy. I guess that means the speech worked.

I do not know exactly how I saw this connection between art and lists. I just did as I stood there reading the *Oxford English Dictionary*. That's how serendipity works. If my audience found the idea interesting, I suppose that's all that matters. I do know that when I need to find connections like these—and since they're the foundation of my writing, I always need them—the serendipity technique works. If I probe memory, talk to friends and play in the library, wonderful things happen. They will be accidents, but accidents most deliberate.

# Chapter

# 10

# *Evidence*

*Research is when you're puttering around without a clue to what's what.*

—fortune cookie message

## GETTING STARTED: DO NOTHING

When analysis is done; when you understand a magazine's audience and the forms, structures and authority bases it prefers; when you know the topic and focus; when the query letter is written; when the editor has said yes; when the contract is signed; when breakfast is eaten; when coffee is drunk; when you're dressed, down to your socks, it can't be avoided any longer: research.

The beginning writer makes two mistakes about research, though usually not both at once. One is to delay too long, to put off research until three or four days before the article is due. The hazards of that are obvious and not worth discussing here. The other mistake is more subtle and just as serious. This is to begin too *soon*. Even with your socks on, there is much to do before picking up a phone or going to the library. And the first thing to do is—nothing.

Inactivity can make the people who depend on your income nervous, but it is the way to begin. Research begins in your own mind. It is a creative, not mechanical process. The researcher who ignores this reality wastes time. Yet it is hard to persuade students to wait and think before plunging in. Just as I was beginning this chapter, one of our seniors, Tracey Modic, asked to do an honors project with me. I suggested she help me write this research techniques chapter. She agreed and added she had specific questions for us to explore:

how to find leads—"creative hunting," we called it

how to check facts, especially quotes

how much research a story needs, or how to know when it's done

how to design a research project, including budgeting time, setting goals and planning

But her biggest question was, How to begin? We talked first about the difference between shaping a topic and researching one. In shaping, or serendipity (see Chapter 9), explore tangents. In researching, though, ignore tangents and get the job done. Efficiency counts in research. But the process is no less creative. To demonstrate, we selected four topics:

milk

peonies

hair care products

sleeping in public

I'm sure neither of us could tell you today why we picked these topics, but they seemed to be "typical magazine ideas." Milk would be first, to let me see how Tracey researched at present. I mentioned I'd heard a news report linking milk consumption and ovarian cancer. Tracey returned a few days later with the following observations. (Notes are typed verbatim; items in brackets, usually on left, are Tracey's thoughts):

## Milk

*Original topic*: link between ovarian cancer and milk sugar. Start w/encyclopedia entry on milk—get background info about topic (*Academic American Encyclopedia*, 1990, vol. 13, p. 423):

[Who says it's so nutritious?]

- Milk is "highly nutritious" substance widely consumed in its natural form and in dairy products.
- Contains casein, lactose, calcium, phosphorus, salts, vitamins A, D.
- *Lactose*—Major source of energy—sweetener (carbohydrate)—about 5% of milk.

[This substance I know to be implicated in ovarian cancer link.]

- *Lactase*—enzyme that splits lactose so it can be digested.

[These are some of the foods linked to o.c.]

[Why different from U.S. to Europe?]

[Apparently the o.c. study is too recent to be included in an encyclopedia]

- Part of lactose is broken down in fermented milk products (yogurt, sour cream, etc.)
- In Europe milk is ultrapasteurized and stored in small, transparent plastic pouches.
- See also "Nutrition, Human" entry. Vol. 14, pp. 304–307.)
- Importance of "milk group" in diet.
- Milk very low in iron, ascorbic acid.
- Low in niacin.
- Very high in calcium, phosphorus.
- High in vitamin A.
- Deficiency in vitamin A can result in xerophthalmia (eye disease).

[Next, to periodicals. At this point, I see one of three article focuses as possibility:

1. "Milk and You," nutritional analysis for women's magazine.
2. Update on link between lactase and ovarian cancer (also for women's magazine, but maybe for a health one).
3. Business piece about regulations/FDA control of industry vs. freer industry in Europe.]

*NewsBank* subject head "Milk" is cross-referenced to "food, milk." Here were the following subject heads:

1. Bovine growth hormone
2. Cholesterol-free
3. Consumption
4. Licensing, laws, regulations
5. Low-cholesterol
6. New products
7. Reduced fat
8. Studies and reports

Subjects "cholesterol-free," "new products" and "reduced fat" all reveal articles dealing w/milk industry effort to improve its health profile. But nothing on ovarian cancer. *NewsBank* subject heads "ovarian cancer" and "cancer, ovarian" list nothing related to milk. Now I start to think that topic #2 might work.

I move to *Medline Express*. Combining key words "milk," "ovarian" and "cancer" yields 29 entries. Four entries in *American Journal of Epidemiology* and one in *Cancer* are about the link between dairy products and ovarian cancer. But no popular magazines are listed.

Place to look for popular magazines is *Readers' Guide*; subject head "ovarian cancer" yields sixteen entries including these two:

1. "Pour on the Protection" (low-fat milk may reduce risk of ovarian cancer), *Prevention*, June 1991, pp. 11–12.
2. "Dairy Sugar Linked to Ovarian Cancer," *Science News* by Kathy Fackelmann, July 22, 1989, p. 52.

I concluded that two popular magazines have already beaten me to my topic. But I find the same two entries under "milk"—and no new ones—so my broader idea for a nutritional profile-style piece might work.

## Freewriting

Some of Tracey's strategies here were excellent. Starting with an overview article from an encyclopedia, using the "see also's" in periodical indexes as clues for sorting the "just interesting" from the "truly relevant" and taking notes on her notes—all were good moves. But the final result of her research was that she discovered the article she wanted to write had already been written.

There are several reasons this happened. One is just bad luck. But some explanation for the dead end rests with her approach. First, she began too narrowly, researching "milk" rather than "nutrition." Just because the *topic* is milk doesn't mean research is limited to milk. Second, she was looking for focus instead of choosing a focus beforehand, perhaps by using the serendipity technique of Chapter 9. But her biggest mistake was to begin her research without a do-nothing phase. She plunged immediately into research.

A kinder term for doing nothing is *freewriting*. This is deliberately spending time thinking about the topic before trying to research it. I prefer to write while I think, looking for patterns to emerge, and I use four steps. I start by trying to list *What I know*, facts I'm sure of, although I often discover later I was wrong. Perhaps this step should be called *What I think I know*. Then I list *What I don't know*, trying to think of questions. After that, I write for a few minutes about *What I think readers want*. This forces me to consider how I am like and unlike readers so I can avoid wasting time on research I'd like but readers wouldn't. The last step is to analyze my freewriting. I try to write down what assumptions I may have made in the first three steps.

If Tracey had spent a few minutes freewriting, perhaps when she examined her assumptions she would have realized a story that's been on the news has to have been done already, so she would have to reach beyond a simple informative piece.

This knowledge would have saved much library time. Freewriting usually takes no more than half an hour, but it saves me days in the library. It's a method popularly taught in freshman English composition courses now, but I can attest it works for professional writers too. And I set out to prove this to Tracey when we tackled the second topic, peonies.

I have one scrawny peony bush in my yard. Tracey had vaguely heard of the flower but couldn't remember what it looked like. "I'm not into gardening," she said. This, of course, made us both qualified and eager to write about it. Following the four-step process, we wrote silently for a few minutes. Below are Tracey's freewriting notes, followed by mine:

# Peonies

## [Tracey's Notes]

*What I Know*: Round flower, pink or red.

*What I Don't Know*: Good description—color, size. Biology (genus, species, etc.) Climate. Soil. Annual or perennial? Can be grown indoors?

*What Readers Want*: What flowers are complementary (can be grown in same soil and look good together)? How to care for them. Pesticides. Plant foods. Can they be brought indoors?

*Assumptions*: Readers are home owners interested in landscaping their backyards w/peonies and other flowers. I'm assuming they have no interest in history, myths, stories about their flowers.

## [My Notes]

*What I Know*: Peonies come from China. The flowers are three to four inches in diameter. A perennial. Blooms in May or June. Leaves are big and pointed. Grows in poor soil. Has to have sun. Don't prune during the growing season.

*What I Don't Know*: Should I feed it? Should I cut off dead flowers? How do I plant and propagate it? How did it get here from China? Is it the same as the lotus? (I think so, not sure.) Does it have any diseases or pests? (How to control them.) What varieties does it come in? How many colors are there? Where can you buy them?

*What I Think Readers Want*: Reassurance that it takes time to establish peony plants and that they're easy to care for. They want their questions answered in an easy-to-read format. They want a bit of trivia. They want planting information: size, light, blooming, etc.

*Assumptions*: That the readers are home owners. They already have some gardening experience. They want more than just how-to's.

When Tracey and I compared these lists, what interested me was she assumed botanical issues were important and I assumed history and lore were. We both could be wrong in our assumptions, but at least they gave us three directions to explore: the how-to's, the history and the biology.

## Resistance

With the peony demonstration, I felt sure Tracey knew how to begin a research project. Teachers are always foolishly persuading themselves that all is clear. Freewriting worked, didn't it? We had searched our minds, made sense of what we already knew, imagined what we didn't know, imagined the readers and then analyzed the thinking. Before going to the library, we thought and then talked about our thinking. As a result, our time in the library was already organized around three subtopics. How could Tracey resist the power of the technique? I sent her out to do the third topic, hair care products, confident that the first thing she'd show me later were her freewriting notes. We agreed to work separately this time and meet in two weeks. I was very curious how her actual research would differ from mine.

She called me a few days later. Two weeks was too long, she said. She was stuck *now*. When we met, she pulled out her notes and began her tale of woe. Just in *Readers' Guide*, there were 653 articles on hair styling, 183 on hair care, 70 on hair care products and so many other subtopics on the hair care industry, from acquisitions and mergers to chemistry, that she didn't know what to do. She didn't even know what to look at.

I asked Tracey if she had done the freewriting exercise before going to the library. As I asked the question, it dawned on her why she got in trouble so quickly; but something occurred to me too. Tracey was a sharp student. I couldn't dismiss her ignoring my advice as lack of understanding. Something else was at work here. Why had she visited the library instead of visiting her mind?

I was realizing that the creative demands of research are stressful. We talked about this a while. It was hard, Tracey admitted, when you know you're ignorant on a topic, to believe in the contents of your own mind. It's easier to believe that someone else has the answer. It's also hard for a beginner to accept that there's no such thing as "the answer." All research can do is uncover splinters and fragments. A writer has to assemble those fragments into an article. But always there is the hope—the corrupting hope perhaps—of finding whole boards, complete realities, solid answers. There are no answers, only versions, from which the writer assembles *today's* version.

Libraries, with their neat shelves, carefully punctuated indexes and swift computer data bases reinforce the illusion that finding answers, rather than building a search, is possible. Librarians, too, with their ready knowledge of reference materials, also reinforce the illusion that the researcher is supposed to find the answer rather than construct a search. Tracey so strongly needed the security that answers existed out there that she spent much time hunting for them. I don't blame *her* for the time she wasted. I blame a culture that values goals over process and destinations over a journey. To research, one has to permit confusion. This is difficult. At least Tracey was now convinced. Her fourth try, sleeping in public, went in imaginative directions, as you'll see in the case study at the end of this chapter.

## AFTER THE BEGINNING

With the freewriting done, it's now that your magazine analyses become crucial. Those charts of forms and lists of authority bases, together with the freewriting, help set limits on what to do next. The freewriting should have shown what can be done with the topic and focus. The magazine analysis should have shown what to do with the *audience*. You will have uncovered key words and broad concepts to use in the actual research. For example, I discovered with the freewriting for peonies that "perennials" and "plants—history" would be important in my research. And my earlier study of the *McCall's* audience, focuses, forms, structures and especially authority bases told me what to do for the magazine. When put together, there may be conflicts between topic and magazine. The peonies *topic* might logically be best researched by digging into horticultural journals, but the *magazine* may want people, people, people, meaning I need to find peony growers. Early in the research is the time to resolve these apparent conflicts. If I know the magazine's needs well enough and also understand the topic's potential, I have the essential information for efficient research.

Efficiency is modern society's polite term for not doing anything unless you have to. You're paid only for the article, not for the research. If you spend hours and hours ferreting out science journals when you need only one or two, because the magazine would never cover so much technical jargon, then you've wasted your time. I like to give myself an imaginary salary. When I research, every minute of my time is worth three dollars (adjusted for inflation, of course). If I spend it on research that will never be used, I'm wasting money; if I spend it on more research than I'm being paid for the article, I may be cutting my own throat. But on the other hand, if I get too efficient—the rude term is *stingy*—I won't have enough material to write a good article.

Most advice to beginners recommends getting more research than needed. Some advice books are even specific, saying you need ten times more information than you'll use. I agree in part with these sentiments. It is important to have more research than needed, but it should be of the right kind. If the magazine likes experts, perhaps I should talk to five experts in order to quote two later, but I shouldn't bother interviewing many ordinary folks. On the other hand, if the magazine likes anecdotes, perhaps I should interview twenty ordinary people to use eight or nine later, but not bother to chase down a scientist. Yes, it's smart to have more research than you need, but it's stupid to have bundles of the wrong kind.

While there are no hard and fast categories of kinds of research, there are some journalistic conventions. Usually your options are to study people, expertise, places, things, statistics, chronology and visual (or other sensory) detail. First, eliminate what you don't need. If you don't need visual detail, don't travel. Then with a list of what you *do* need—statistics, people or whatever—start searching for leads.

Here are a few tips (though keep in mind there's always more than one way to find something).

## People

What kind of people do you need? Celebrities? Ordinary folks? The best place to find people with specific interests is through organizations. *Encyclopedia of Associations*[1] is a guide to over 22,000 organizations from agriculture to fan clubs, science to hobbies. The book usually gives the phone numbers and addresses of national headquarters. For local chapters of associations, you can either look in a phone book or call or write the national organization.

Sometimes talking to local stores will produce names of area hobbyists. A hardware store might know the local woodworking genius, or a specialty grocery will know a nearby master of ethnic cuisine. Word of mouth is one of the best ways to find people. Let friends know what you're doing and wait. Some writers advertise in newspaper classified sections asking for people with a special interest to call or write.

Celebrities can be found through *Who's Who in Entertainment.*[2] This volume gives an address to write, usually the actor's agency. Be sure to allow lots of time for response and don't be surprised if it takes two, three or ten letters to get a reply. Another reference book giving information on agents and other entertainment leads is *The Working Actors Guide.*[3]

## Expertise

One of the first things you'll have to decide in designing your research strategy is who will be an expert for your purposes. An author or a scientist? A head of a government agency or leader of an interest group? A consultant? After deciding that, of course, where are these people? *The Encyclopedia of Associations* again is a place to start. Heads of associations usually know who the leading researchers in their fields are and how to get in touch with them. Asking professors at a university for names of experts in their field can produce good leads, although I sometimes find professors will say they themselves are the experts rather than give you a name an editor might respect. It's an awkward moment. How do you tell a professor he or she just isn't famous enough for *McCall's?*

Always, if a magazine puts great stock in experts, check out the credentials of your source. *Who's Who* entries will list degrees. If the source is not listed in *Who's*

*Who in America*, try a volume specific to the field. I don't know how many *Who's Who* volumes there are—many dozens. A few of the many in my own library included banking, education, ecology, art, history, Methodism, nursing, music, and politics. I think it's safe to assume that *Who's Who* has surveyed most fields of endeavor. Another technique for checking reputations of experts is to hunt down articles they have written and read accompanying bios. The more reputable the magazine, the less respect they have for degrees from marginal institutions (the kind that will admit even a parakeet if it will pay tuition). The Center for Science in the Public Interest in New York City can provide expert sources on opposing sides of major issues.

Another technique I use to find experts is to locate a very good, very current scholarly or business article on my topic and call the author. To get phone numbers or addresses of these experts, an additional source (besides *Who's Who*) is the *National Faculty Directory*.[4] Computer services such as CompuServ can also be a source of names through their specialty bulletin boards.

## Places

Visiting a place is not the only way to research it, but it is the most fun. You should, even if you do visit, check with a local Chamber of Commerce or tourism bureau (easily accessible in a phone book) for regional details. Two books to help prepare you for a visit include *Going Places: The Guide to Travel Guides*[5] and *The Traveler's Reading Guide*.[6]

One way to capture the flavor of a place is to provide details about its climate, terrain, flora, fauna, industries, natural resources and local culture—in other words, its geography. Background instruction in geographical research methods are in *A Guide to Information Sources in the Geographical Sciences*[7] and the *Bibliography of Geography*.[8] One of the best sources of geographic data, other than a good atlas, is geographical survey offices at large universities. The *Monthly Catalog of U.S. Government Publications* can also provide leads.

## Things

There's no better source than the *Library of Congress Subject Headings* (LCSH), a three-volume guide for finding anything and everything. Most people think of it as a guide to book catalogs, but what the LCSH provides is words for things, the key words you need for searching periodical indexes. These words are important even if you can't use books because your topic is too current for any to have been written. But the LCSH requires a peculiar kind of thinking to be used successfully. Rarely is any topic I research actually listed. Instead I have to think of a broader term or related term, or occasionally even a narrower term. A book I like to consult before I tackle the LCSH is Mona McCormick's *The Fiction Writer's Research Handbook*.[9] I don't write fiction, but I find her book's organization by things a great source for research ideas. For example, in her chapter on "dress" she recommended the LCSH headings "Clothing and Dress; Costume—History; Costume Design; Jewelry; Hats; and Jeans." I might not have thought of any of these if my topic were, say, "Fashion." Several abbreviations in the LCSH listing are important. "UF" stands for "Use For" and means the term listed is the approved term and the one you really wanted isn't. Such is life. "BT" stands for "Broader Term" and means you will probably find much more under these terms. "RT" is "Related Terms." Here you need to be careful. Remember efficiency counts. Is a related term indeed relevant for your topic or just an interesting tangent? "NT" stands for "Narrower Terms" and as with Related Terms, I'm judicious about indulging. Is it worth chasing down a topic narrower than my topic? Often it's not.

Broader terms are usually more productive for me than narrower terms but even then there are hazards. For example, when I did the article on corn, the editors asked for some additional information on the drought-resistant abilities of modern hybrids. I checked the LCSH and was delighted to see one of the subheads was "Corn—Water Requirements." But when I actually used that term in a search, I came up—you'll pardon the expression—dry. I went back to the LCSH and using the "when in trouble think broadly" theory, looked under "plants" and found "Plants—Drought Resistance" and "Plants—Water Requirements." When I went back to indexes with these terms, I found lots of material. Students who complain they can't find things in the library have usually gotten trapped into thinking too narrowly about their key words.

## Statistics

With more and more libraries converting to computerized data bases, this nightmare task is becoming easier. I use Congressional Information Service's (CIS) *Statistical Masterfile*, available on CD-ROM in our library to find current statistical reports. (CIS has a print index too.) Using *Statistical Masterfile* is tricky because its references are generic, not specific. For example, when I checked "Sleep" for the "sleeping in public" topic, it referred me to *Gallup Poll Monthly*. It didn't tell me which of the reports or issues to consult, but only gave me a lengthy description of what Gallup does (as if I didn't know). While this advise was frustrating—I would have preferred a page number—at least I could go to Gallup's own index and look for something on sleep and know it wouldn't be a wild goose chase because the *Masterfile* said there was something there. I just didn't know what.

Another useful source is *Statistical Abstract of the United States*. Its footnotes serve as a bibliography to government research. If you find a statistic that resembles what you want, the footnotes will give the source and the source may give you more. Once again, associations are great sources of statistics, but these may be tainted by the association's political agenda, so use with caution.

Finding a statistic doesn't mean using it correctly. Quoting a statistic without a base number is meaningless, for example. A 66 percent yes response rate melts into silliness if the base number (or how many people were interviewed) is three. A good book to help you avoid the various forms of statistical quicksand is Philip Meyer's *The New Precision Journalism*.[10] Another readable book is *News and Numbers* by Victor Cohn.[11]

## Visual Detail

What could be simpler? Just look, right? Yes, but if the subject is technical, you may not have enough knowledge to know what you're looking at. And these days almost every subject has a technical component. All four of our topics—milk, peonies, hair products and sleep—required that we dabble a bit in chemistry, biology or psychology. For background reading on technical subjects, I like the *McGraw-Hill Encyclopedia of Science and Technology*.[12] It's more sophisticated than an ordinary encyclopedia and has good bibliographies for further background reading. Don't try to wing it when gathering visual detail. If you don't know what you're looking at, get someone who does to go with you and describe the scene for you.

## Time Passage

Vivid writing often evokes events as if they were occurring now. The illusion that the author was witnessing time as it passed can give prose an unforgettable immediacy. But there are very few events a writer is lucky enough to actually observe. These events must be reconstructed, either through interviews (sometimes called oral history) or through conventional historical research. Historical research is its own peculiar discipline. Similar to journalism in its love of detail and accuracy, it differs from journalism in both its freedom—the historian may interpret—and its rigor—the historian must defend those interpretations. Historians must glance over their shoulders constantly to see if other historians approve. You can learn a lot from historians. Two books to get you started are Barbara Tuchman's *Practicing History*[13] and Robert J. Shafer's *A Guide to Historical Method*.[14]

Talking to history buffs is one of the best ways to get a feel for historical methods, and here the *Directory of Historical Organizations in the United States and Canada*[15] is a good way to find such people. A few general reference books include *National Register of Historic Places*[16] and *Historic Houses of America*.[17] Two indexes, *America: History and Life*[18] and *Historical Abstracts*[19] are good sources of background reading as well as names of experts.

## CONNECTING WITH REALITY

When you have found your leads, the next step in designing a strategy is to decide what research methods will elicit the best details. Again your freewriting and magazine analysis should contain the information you need to make efficient decisions. There really are only three methods: look, talk and read. Most of my work requires a mix of all three methods, but the emphasis varies with each story.

Sometimes I'll do mostly interviews, a little reading, a little looking. Sometimes I'll live in the library or live at the scene but not talk to many people. But always, I think over my strategy before committing. A writer who gets into the habit of always doing interviews, or always doing massive library research, soon goes stale. Again some tips.

## Look

The number-one reason editors send magazine reporters back for more research is failure to collect visual detail. The writer just didn't see enough. For a profile of a poet I did once, the magazine sent me back to look at her house. I was baffled because from my point of view her poetry was about the outdoors, not the house. But I'm just the writer here; I do what I'm told. I looked at the house. I described its attic window. The editors were happy.

Looking is part of research, but it's assumed to be so natural that writers don't realize they have to work at it. Some people use photography to help them see. I know a woman who carries a Polaroid camera with her. She takes pictures and shows them to the people she's interviewing for conversation icebreakers. Other writers use ordinary snapshots to remember details as they write. Of course, some writers are accomplished photographers who illustrate their own stories.

I don't like using a camera. I don't see as well when I photograph. The camera records everything in the viewfinder but I don't want everything. I want the *telling detail*, that one most important something that reveals what a place or a person is truly about. A writer learns that economy of detail is the foundation of powerful prose. If I'm busy looking through a camera, I might get so much detail I miss the one I need.

For me, sketching and painting have been ways to build skill in seeing. Perhaps it is the concentration drawing requires that helps. For example, to be able to draw a hand, I have to notice that fingers are composed of three varying-sized rectangles hinged together or that a back is really a pie-shaped wedge. A face is not the happy circle children draw but a series of ovals and rectangles, triangles and squares bunched together to distort the light. After I began taking drawing courses, my writing became richer with detail. I was simply able to see more. Even today, I will always take time to look at a subject or scene *as if* I were going to draw it. I may not have time to actually sketch, but the effort of looking at a scene that way helps me see detail.

Whether you observe with the help of camera or sketchbook or simply look without aids, I think one thing is universal for writers—you must take notes. No one's memory is reliable. No one sees very well. Partly this is because you are frantically busy when working on a story. You're talking to people, thinking constantly, puzzling through your confusions and rushed for time. The more harried your research, the less likely your perceptions are to be accurate. More than once, if I felt my notes on visual detail were sloppy, I've returned to the scene to look again and sometimes discovered, to my embarrassment, that what I remembered and what was didn't match. Visual detail makes writing strong. Looking is the source of that detail; and yet if anything is going to humiliate the writer for its inaccuracy later, it will be what is seen. Quotes, numbers, these are easy to get right. But seeing? All of us are blind. Be careful.

## Talk

For a magazine reporter, listening is more important than questioning because flavor, character and detail are important in magazine writing. An interview has to encourage a person to reveal these kinds of details. The best way to encourage people to talk is for you to be quiet. Don't rush in with a new question at every pause. Let people have a minute or two to think. Let a silence hang in the air once in a while. Or say, "For example?" now and then. Or just lift your eyes to make eye contact. Any of these behaviors could trigger specific recollections from the source. People usually talk in generalities and abstractions at first. To elicit those rich once-upon-a-time details takes very gentle handling on your part and patience—lots of patience.

It also requires ego control. A mistake I see young reporters make over and over again is to care what the source thinks of them. You want to make a good impression; you want the source to think you're smart. Resist this need. You're there to get a good story. The source does want to respect you and will say things like "You're familiar with the Miller report, aren't you?" or "You remember when that was on the news, don't you?" Nine out of ten reporters—egos flaring—will say, "Oh, yes." Even in the unlikely event that you have read the Miller report or do recall the news story, your answer should be, "No, tell me about it." If you allow your ego to appear when the source, usually unconsciously, confronts you with your own ignorance, then you lose forever an opportunity to hear what the source had to say.

One of the conventions taught in journalism school is that the interviewer should be objective. A reporter must appear to be dispassionate, uninvolved, you're taught. I disagree—at least for magazine work. Display of natural emotion stimulates conversation. Your laughter when something is funny or sad face when something is not is a reward for the talker. It makes the source want to talk more. A reporter whose interview style I recommend any magazine reporter study is that of Susan Stamberg on National Public Radio. She's usually heard on Sunday mornings. An admirer of hers once said, "She's like your big sister, asking the questions you really want to ask." I admire her for the intensity of her listening. She laughs, she empathizes, she exclaims. Because of this, sources trust her even when, as she always does, she asks discomfiting questions.

Most guidebooks on interviewing I have read also talk about the importance of being prepared. The beginner assumes being prepared means having a list of questions. I suppose there's nothing wrong with that, except a reporter who is too dependent on a list of questions is not going to think of good follow-up questions. A simple reality of journalistic interviewing is that the best question is the one you didn't think of. To better prepare to think of that hard-to-think-of question in the middle of an interview, I recommend being absolutely clear in your own mind what your focus is. (This should be clear from your freewriting or serendipity exercises.) And be absolutely clear in your own mind who your audience is. (This should be clear from your magazine analysis.) These two bits of information, if you keep them sharply in mind as you talk, will allow good follow-up questions.

One last tip. Make sure your last question is always "If I have any more questions, may I call you later?"

## Read

As with interviewing, there are dozens of books on how to use a library. The trouble with most is that they are not guides to the library you have to live with. For example, my favorite guidebook, Mona McCormick's *The Fiction Writer's Research Handbook*, recommended in its food chapter that writers use the *World Encyclopedia of Food*.[20] When I worked on my linzer torte essay, my library didn't have this resource. What they did have was a wonderful book, *The Food of the Western World*.[21] McCormick's handbook helped me realize such a directory might exist, so guidebooks are worth checking; but don't get overly concerned in looking for a specific reference book, including the ones I list here. Use guidebooks to help you imagine reference tools rather than find them. You may need this help because the variety of reference works available, even in a medium-sized library, is beyond imagining—at least beyond my imagining. To illustrate, in one afternoon of shelf-hunting, I found a dictionary of angels, a guide to hardware history, a list of socially responsible corporations, a history of the early years of science fiction (from the second century A.D.) and an encyclopedia of famous disasters (including elephant stampedes). None of these had I handled or known about before.

There are more zany reference books than boring ones in any library. But the point is, they're there. If you can imagine a need, you might be able to find a book to help you. But don't be too specific in your needs. While there is a dictionary of angels, I didn't find an accompanying dictionary of demons.

Research handbooks tend to recommend that you follow specific procedures when using a library. You are supposed to start with tools that give broad overviews such as encyclopedias and dictionaries. Then you're supposed to look at bibliographies and periodical indexes and then go to specialized resources, such as dictionaries of quotations, statistical records, government documents or archives. This is all very nice, but it should be obvious by now that magazine research is better determined by your market and your topic, not by some formula from a book. Once again—I know I've said this before—efficiency counts. Match your efforts to your strategy. If the magazine you're writing for always quotes people from live interviews, an exhaustive search from every encyclopedia or dictionary and bibliography is a waste of your time. Two or three encyclopedia entries would probably give you enough background. On the other hand, if the magazine always quotes scientific research, you are wasting your time reading 653 *popular* articles.

When your strategy does call for library research, and most magazine work does, shortcuts save you time. (See also the two case studies that follow later for additional ideas.)

Tips:

**Encyclopedias.**    Rather than go to a regular encyclopedia such as *Americana* or *Britannica*, I like to go to *First Stop: The Master Index to Subject Encyclopedias*.[22] This book has a key word index in the back that tells you which specialized encyclopedias will have entries on a listing. Specialized encyclopedias usually have more detail and more thorough bibliographies.

**Dictionaries.**    Almost every field has a specialized dictionary. You'll probably need to have one of these handy while reading the specialized encyclopedias. One dictionary I always consult at the beginning of a research project is the twenty-volume *Oxford English Dictionary*. This book gives much more than definitions—it goes into the origins and usages of words. Sometimes in the origins I find much food for thought.

**Bibliographies.**    Poke a graduate student and you will find a human being who at least once has had to do a bibliography. It's one of those useful things grad students do—meaning if you can't find a bibliography on your specialty, you just don't know how to look. The secret once again is identifying key words. Once you have a broad enough key word, check a book catalog or periodical index for the subcategory "bibliographies" (as in "Plants—Bibliographies" or "Flower Gardening —Bibliographies," but, alas, not "Peonies—Bibliographies.") The bibliographies will list the titles of every book and article on your topic the author could find.

The trouble with all bibliographies is that they're out of date before they're published. However, a way around that, if you find a very good scholarly article (not popular; this won't work with popular articles), is to use a reference work called a *Citations Index*. It's sort of a reverse bibliography; that is, it lists all articles since your article was published that footnote it. There are indexes for both natural and social science. Thus, if you have a 1986 biology piece on peonies, the *Citations Index* will list anything since then that referred to that 1986 article as a source. With highly technical material, sometimes this *Citation Index* may be the only way to find current information. For most topics, however, a good search of a periodical index will turn up what you need.

**Indexes and Data Bases.**    My library is completely converted to computer indexing for both its card catalog and periodical indexes. It does still receive print forms of some, such as *Readers' Guide* or *Art Index* or *Business Periodicals Index*, but the data base (CD-ROM) forms of these indexes are so much faster that I rarely see anyone using print anymore. And they provide much more information. For example, Tracey didn't actually count those 653 articles on hair in *Readers' Guide*— the computer told her. Data base entries also automatically suggest related key words.

Data bases take practice to learn to use but in the long run save time because they allow targeted search strategies, often called "Boolean" searches after the mathematician George Boole (1815–1864). It's a simple concept. First you search an index or thesaurus (usually listed on the data base) to decide what key words it responds to; then using commands shown on the screen instructions, you set up a research formula. For example, one such formula would be PEONIES [AND] ART. The computer starts searching, tells me how many articles refer to peonies, how many to art and how many to both. I can then decide, often just from the numbers, whether my search is too broad or too narrow. Tracey's milk search used a Boolean combination of MILK [AND] OVARIAN [AND] CANCER.

I do not know how many data bases exist. In my library, there is an on-line encyclopedia; several data bases for business; several for science; one each for biology, agriculture, nursing and medicine; several for news and public affairs; one for literature; several for social sciences; several for art; and one for history. And just as I was typing this paragraph, the library announced they had bought a new one for philosophy. Some extremely specialized data bases are also available in my library— for example, the *Hazardous Materials Information System* and the *County & City Data Book*. These are all accessible to anyone. Besides these, the library has access to many more data bases through its phone lines. Using these, however, involves a fee and the searches often must be done by a librarian.

***Quotations.***    I don't recommend relying too heavily on dictionaries of quotations for research. Editors tend to prefer original quotes to published ones. But I sometimes can get a feel for a topic from them. For example, in the *Home Book of Humorous Quotations*,[23] under "Sleep," was this quote: "Most people spend their lives going to bed when they're not sleepy, and getting up when they are." This gave me ideas for the "sleeping in public" topic. Most quotation books tend to be filed together, usually in the literature section.

***Government Documents.***    A good-sized library will have some government documents, particularly those intended for consumers. For example, I found a pamphlet on growing peonies in our government document collection ("Home and Garden Bulletin #26"). But only a few libraries are government document repositories, meaning that everything the government produces is sent to that library. It's worth a trip to a repository sometimes to get at this material. For example, a repository will have microfiches of all congressional hearings. Hearings include not just the actual testimony but any documents the experts brought to the hearing because witnesses often ask that their papers be read into the record. No senator ever reads this stuff; but I do. From my point of view, if I'm trying to find the leading experts, the most current information and the points of disagreement or controversy, a hearing will provide all three. The experts come, they quarrel and they put their recent research in the record. I once based a story for children on the future of the space program entirely on a Congressional hearing. Buried deep within papers with esoteric titles like "Biological Effects of Artificial Gravitational Systems" were some perfect details for children. The experts wondered if goats or chickens could adapt to artificial gravity. While they didn't agree, I felt I could at least raise the question in my story. Another detail that I was certain would fascinate children came from that same report, namely, that objects would spiral to the "ground" when they fell. My audience was children, but my source of information was the dry text of a hearing transcript.

***Special Collections.***    Many libraries in addition to general collections will have a collection unique to themselves. Scholars often make special trips just to study these collections. *Directory of Archives and Manuscript Repositories in the United States*[24] lists all special collections and archives in this country. You might check it when beginning a topic. There may be a library within reasonable traveling distance that will provide rare documents you can find nowhere else. Profiles and historical topics can be especially enriched through use of special collections.

## TAKING NOTES

Once again, guidebooks are specific with their advice. You should organize your note cards just so; you should use a certain size notebook. If you need that sort of advice, fine—read the books. But I've never paid much attention to them because every story of mine is different, requiring a different way of taking notes. Just as I reinvent my basic research strategy every time, I also reinvent how I'm going to take notes before I get too deeply into a project.

But I do have three hard and fast rules about notetaking: one, don't take too many notes; two, don't take too few notes; three, take notes on my notes. This last is most important. When I take notes on my notes, sometimes I jot them down as I'm taking them. Sometimes I add notes later. Either way, these extra notes help me decide later what my article is, guide me toward more research or, better yet, help me stop researching. One thing I have learned the hard way is to be sure that I can tell the difference later between my comments and the facts or quotes I am recording. My thoughts, of course, don't have to be attributed, but everything else does. The late Alex Haley, author of the best-selling *Roots*, found himself in some nasty copyright suits for plagiarizing after his book came out. His explanation was that he had so many notes he wasn't sure after a while what was him and what was research. Such things should not happen, but I can understand how they do. E. B. White once wrote that writing was like duck hunting—thousands of thoughts fly overhead and you're lucky to bag even one. In the midst of research when you're rushing to keep up with your own thinking, it's easy to forget that your mission is first to get the facts right.

When I'm taking notes by hand, I use double-entry note paper, facts on the right, my thoughts on the left. When I'm typing notes on a computer, I put [brackets] (not parentheses) around my thoughts and later try to highlight my thoughts with a marker just as added insurance. When I'm taking notes on cards or small slips, which is rare now that I've been spoiled by computers, I put my thoughts on separate sheets and staple them to the facts they accompany. Technique doesn't matter but practice does. Your thoughts are as important as your facts.

To organize notes for writing, some people are very mechanistic, using file folders and careful codes. I separate my notes by chapter or major subtopic, but beyond that I just read and reread the notes many times. Then I set them aside for a few days and I deliberately don't look again at the notes as I write. This helps me find my own language and get free of the jargon of the original. It also helps clear my thinking. Trivial details drop; important ones stay. After I've written a draft, I review my notes and correct my errors.

About the "too many, too few" notes dilemma: too many notes is more likely to be the problem, thanks to the easy access of copy machines. It's too easy to copy. I try to avoid copying because when I do, the information is on copy paper but not in my head. If I type the notes from the original source, I learn them. If I must photocopy, then at least I highlight the text to try to memorize it, but that's never as effective as typing. Research assistants think I'm too cheap to spend a nickel for a copy, but I'm not. I buy the best tulips, good clothes and fresh baked bread. Would such an extravagant person begrudge a nickel to the university library? I take notes for the benefit of my mind and for no other reason. If my mind is not engaged in the process, I'm wasting time, paper—and nickels.

I do find note taking varies with the type of story I'm doing. For a profile, where one person is going to provide most of the information, I always tape the interviews plus take notes as I'm talking. For a general information story, which will have many interviews but only a quote or two from each source, I find hand-written notes are sufficient. For in-depth stories on a topic, in which a source might talk to me for an hour or more, I find a laptop computer is adequate.

The advantage of notes by hand is that they are distilled: I've sorted out what I really want as I'm listening and don't have to wade through a massive tape or printout to get the details. The advantage of the laptop is that it allows me to be faster, get more detail, and get more flavorful quotes from the source, while again distilling out much extraneous material. Also, since I touch type, it allows me to maintain eye contact with the source, which I can't do while making handwritten notes.

The advantage of tape is that it gets everything, every nuance, every "um," every failure of subject–verb agreement. No one can accuse you of being inaccurate if you have a tape to back you up. The disadvantage of tape, of course, is that you have to sort the wheat from the chaff later. Plus the demon of tapeology is more potent than all other technodemons—even the computer one, a mere imp by comparison. I've only had my laptop fail to store once, and I solved that by not turning off the computer until I got back to my study to retype the notes. Only once has it run out of battery power. It beeped; the source said, "What's that?" And I said, "It means this interview's over." But as for tapes, talk to a writer, any writer, me included, and you're in for an hour or two of ear-bending weeping. Tapes that shred, tapes that stick, batteries that fail, machines that explode. The tape recorder is a cursed machine.

Some research guidebooks I've read often mention that sources find tape recorders or laptops disquieting and this is a disadvantage in using the machines. I've never encountered this. I don't know if I've been lucky or if the preinterview procedures I go through help. I always spend a few minutes making small talk to put the source at ease. I share my enthusiasm for the topic, telling the source some of the interesting things I've learned, or what I'm feeling. My excitement, if genuine (and if I ever stop feeling genuine interest in my topics, I plan to quit writing), becomes contagious. The source has usually become so interested in the coming conversation, he or she has forgotten about the machine before the first question is asked. I always treat the source as if the interview is with me, not with a tape recorder or a laptop. If I work to put the person at ease, then the machines don't matter. Sometimes I talk about the tape recorder or laptop as part of my preinterview small talk, but only if talking about the topic hasn't worked.

## SOME FINAL THOUGHTS

No attempt to discuss research methods could ever be complete. No list of reference books or tips for interviewing could begin to exhaust the topic. There is too much variety of materials and techniques out there. More significantly, each researcher is different. I think if you recognize the value of your own mind, if you commit to accuracy (meaning check everything twice) and if you know your audience, you'll do fine. Think of research strategy as calculated laziness. Work like crazy to get what you do need; ignore what you don't need. And always, think every step of the way. If time is worth three dollars a minute, time thinking is time well spent.

## NOTES

1. *Encyclopedia of Associations*, Gales Research, Detroit, various dates.
2. *Who's Who in Entertainment*, Marquis Who's Who, Macmillan, Wilmette, Ill., various dates.
3. *The Working Actors Guide*, Paul Flattery Productions, Los Angeles, various dates.
4. *National Faculty Directory*, CMG Information Services, Gale Research, Detroit, various dates.

5. Greg Hayes and Joan Wright, *Going Places: The Guide to Travel Guides*, Harvard Common Press, Boston, 1988.

6. Maggy Simony, editor, *The Traveler's Reading Guide*, Facts on File Publications, New York, 1987.

7. Stephen Goddard, editor, *A Guide to Information Sources in the Geographical Sciences*, Barnes & Noble, Totowa, N.J., 1983.

8. Chauncy Harris, *Bibliography of Geography*, University of Chicago Department of Geography, Chicago, various dates.

9. Mona McCormick, *The Fiction Writer's Research Handbook*, New American Library, New York, 1988.

10. Philip Meyer, *The New Precision Journalism*, Indiana University Press, Bloomington, 1991.

11. Victor Cohn, *News and Numbers: A Guide to Reporting Statistical Claims*, Iowa State University Press, Ames, 1989.

12. *McGraw-Hill Encyclopedia of Science and Technology*, 7th ed., McGraw-Hill, New York, 1992.

13. Barbara Tuchman, *Practicing History*, Knopf, New York, 1981.

14. Robert J. Shafer, *A Guide to Historical Method*, Dorsey Press, Homewood, Ill., 1980.

15. *Directory of Historical Organizations in the United States and Canada*, American Association for State and Local History, Nashville, Tenn., various dates.

16. *National Register of Historic Places*, National Park Service, Washington, D.C., 1989.

17. *Historic Houses of America Open to the Public*; by the editors of *American Heritage*, American Heritage, New York, 1971.

18. *America: History and Life on Disc*, ABC-Clio Inc., Santa Barbara, Calif., various dates.

19. *Historical Abstracts*, on Disc, ABC-Clio Inc., Santa Barbara, Calif., various dates.

20. Coyle, L. Patrick. *World Encyclopedia of Food*, Facts on File, New York, 1982.

21. FitzGibbon, Theodora, *The Food of the Western World*, Quadrangle/New York Times, New York, 1976.

22. Joe Ryan, editor, *First Stop: The Master Index to Subject Encyclopedias*, Oryx Press, Phoenix, Ariz., 1989.

23. A. K. Adams, *Home Book of Humorous Quotations*, Dodd, Mead, New York, 1969.

24. National Historical Publications and Records Commission, *Directory of Archives and Manuscript Repositories in the United States*, 2d ed., Oryx Press, Phoenix, Ariz., 1988.

# *Research Case Studies*

Neither of the two case studies below was done for a real article. Both Tracey and I were "just practicing." Yet even for practice, we still needed a target magazine in order to make research decisions. We both imagined magazine audiences rather than target real ones because analyzing magazines is covered in preceding chapters. These cases are about analyzing research problems, and we wanted to stay focused on that.

## RESEARCH CASE STUDY: HAIR PRODUCTS

What follows are my notes, as fully as I can recall, of my own research on the hair care topic. They are idiosyncratic; my thoughts (and confusions) are here. None of this resembles a final article. The notes may be personal, but they and my discussion of them in each section can give you ideas for developing creative strategies of your own. For purposes of the case study, my target magazine has a young career-oriented audience of men and women who are concerned about, but not obsessed by, their appearance; the magazine's editors like classic form and a wide variety of authority bases, including anecdote.

### Freewriting

*What I Know.* Mousse is sticky. Clarifier dissolves chemicals and minerals on hair. Hot oil feels good. Heat curls hair. Hard water damages hair.

*What I Don't Know.* Is hair "dead"? Is there a relationship between cost and quality of shampoos? Are the environmental claims about the safety of hair sprays valid? How to use any of these products? How to choose any? The hair shaft: its makeup, its needs. Comb, brush and dryer handling. Here I am, blessed with thick, straight hair and I've done nothing with it most of my life, except wash it and go. How have others suffered?

*What Readers Want to Know.* Whether there's hope. Can using products make a difference? (I'm reminded of the *Cathy* cartoon where she kept a room of hair care products, none of which she liked, but none of which she could throw away, either.) Safety issues: When is a product useful and when does using it abuse the hair? Is there a difference between long and short hair care? Is there such a thing as easy hair care? Individual products: what each can and can't do. When does a hair problem require a doctor, not a salon? Are there differences in caring for youthful, middle-aged and older hair? Product claims: what's valid? what's hype?

*Assumptions.* That my magazine may shy away from an honest piece because of advertisers. That I'll have to study hair itself to discuss the products. That the reader is confused. That readers are diverse in their hair needs. That psychology (reader need for magic products to build self-esteem) is part of the topic. That I know so little about hair products I can't even start without help.

## Strategy: Phase One

The freewriting, which took less than an hour, shocked me. Psychology? Technology? Ethics? Clearly I was in over my head. I wouldn't dare try the library yet. Instead I called my hairdresser, Steve Keiffer. He was eager to help or, as he told me later, "There is so much nonsense out there." To prepare for my conversation with him, I went to a drugstore and copied the names of any product that struck me as funny. This took fifteen minutes:

Mega, Ultra, Super and Extra Hold hair sprays

Glossing hair spray

Keratin conditioner

Curl Activator

Sculpting and Mega mousse

Mega, Modeling and Finishing spritz

Flexible, Modeling and Styling gel

Styling foam

One-step shampoo

Grapefruit and Papaya conditioners

Then I talked to Steve for an hour. In the notes that follow, words in brackets are my own thoughts—not his. It is important in any research—even in interviews—to note thoughts as well as facts—but keep it clear which is which. Some of the notes I added later, some as I typed. I took my notes with a laptop computer.

[I explained this interview was for background only and that we weren't to discuss brand names.]

### How do you keep up to date on new products?
The companies send us materials, and they send us chemists who talk to us every three or four months. Also, there are trade journals; they're not technical, but they give us new product information.

### [I described my walk through the drugstore.]
Basically the hair care industry is overpopulated with products.

### Is there some product everyone should use?
Products today have become specialized by type of hair. It's become a prescription thing: dry scalps use one kind of product; oily scalps use another. It's an individual prescription-type situation. [Translation: No?].

### [Then I went down my list of products.]
*Hair spray—Mega, Ultra, Super & Extra Hold?*
The differences in hold are percentages of lacquers and polymers; this could be a difference of one-half of one percent. There's even one spray called "freeze"; when it's on the hair it stays put; the hair even feels brittle because the spray has coated the hair so significantly. It keeps hair from expanding. Hair has to be able to expand.

*Glossing hair spray (& what is gloss)?*

A lacquer, but maybe it doesn't have polymers. It's a coating, something like automobile paint; no, no, don't write that; it's not LIKE auto paint, but the same idea, like a wax job.

*Silk & keratin?*

Silk is a word to describe how your hair is supposed to feel with the product, but keratin is a real chemical. The cuticle layer on hair is small [meaning won't absorb?] and keratin slickens it down. It's something you don't want to do to your hair more than once or twice a week because of effect on scalp. [I don't understand at all— read up on keratin later.] The body produces most of the things that are in shampoo [does he mean the additives? Surely soap isn't produced by the body]. Some people have a deficiency in some of these, but it's rare.

*Spritz? & finishing spritz?*

That's a gimmicky word for hair spray. Finisher is a conditioner—a lightweight rinse; perhaps it doesn't have as much protein as a regular conditioner. Finishing products are THE big thing now. When I started in business, shampoo and conditioner were the only products—maybe some people used a little hair spray. That was it.

*Curl activator?*

A product for African hair to help put elasticity back into it. It should be rinsed out every day to prevent oil. [buildup?]

*Moisturizing oils?*

I'd need to see the product. Most are for African hair. Caucasian hair will not accept oils because of its many layers. Blacks have fewer layers. The molecular structure of oil is big. For blacks the oil helps the cuticle open more? [Not sure I got that right]. Hot oil treatments are not good for Caucasian hair. It won't penetrate; it is good for the scalp, but has no benefit for the hair.

## It feels good though

Well, if you want to feel good take a little olive oil, some cotton balls and rub on the scalp; then wrap your hair in a plastic bag for a while and let natural body heat do the job. Maybe you'll smell like a salad for a while.

*Sculpting mousse and Mega mousse?*

[laughs] I've never heard of mega mousse. Mousse is like hair spray; some brands use numbers. Again it's a change in the percentage of polymers.

*Gel?*

A holding product that is heavier than mousse or hair spray. It has the same ingredients but some of the water has been removed and replaced with a glycerine base, which means [laughs] when you use it you want to get your hands out quick or they might get stuck. Also, products that heavy pick up environmental impurities like dust and smoke.

*Conditioner? What is it?*

B-complex vitamins mainly and amino acids, which the body also produces. Conditioners supplement what should be taken into the body anyway [through nutrition?] and only drop off due to poor diet or pregnancy. A healthy body only needs to use conditioner once or twice a week, no, not even that often. There is only so much protein the body can use; it can't break it [the protein?] down, so it lies on the scalp and won't rinse off, leading to scalp problems, which most people think is dandruff but is actually just scaling. Then you need a clarifying shampoo to remove it [the protein?] Clarifiers will remove other chemicals picked up from the environment or minerals in water. Most conditioners are abused; they're good for once in a while, but people feel if they have a few tangles they have to put lots of conditioner on. Too much protein will FRY the hair.

### So what you've been telling me is it's best to use as little of these products as you can?

I've gotten a lot of thanks from clients for not pushing products. If they've got a genuine hair problem, yes, I'll suggest a product. But if their hair is normal, and 75 percent of people are, then I figure whatever they're doing is fine. All these products are legitimate; I'm not saying they're bad products, but it's back to the prescription thing; I believe in giving people what they *need*. But kids, they use so much; they're overwhelmed by the advertising. It all seems geared for 13- to 15-year-olds. Boys too; there's one line of products for boys that is so complex it takes charts for the kids to choose what they want. I think that is the biggest bunch of nonsense, but the kids will insist on having the products. No one product or line of products is the answer for everyone.

#### Body-building products?

Conditioners protect the hair from heat from blow drying or curling irons. The conditioner swells the hair by about 25 percent [and the rest just lies there?]. When heat is applied the remaining conditioner is evaporated [instead of oils from the hair?]. But any conditioner will do this [not just body-building ones?]. As for body building, if hair is extremely dry, and dry hair is rare, it will look frizzy and limp, then more conditioner is absorbed and builds body.

#### One-step shampoos?

I've never tried them. Never believed the claims. Shampoo is an astringent. It has to clean the scalp. Conditioner coats the scalp. [I mention then that I'll have to talk to someone else about these. He's not to be deterred, however.] I think someone ought to enter an FDA challenge—women have lower pH than men. You don't want to go above or below that pH. Below is more acidic and causes oiliness. Above causes drying. One-steps logically ought to drop the pH so low it would build up oil rather than remove it. Cosmetically it might look great but the hair's not clean. [I mention again I still need other opinions on this.]

#### Grapefruit conditioner

[I told him I laughed out loud when I saw that.] No. Grapefruit conditioner stimulates the scalp. [I'm surprised—it's the first product he's seemed to respect.] It's very acidic, like a menthol feel.

### You mean coolness?

Yes. Like a feeling of coolness. It opens pores and raises nerve endings. It's a feel-good product. It does cleanse, and it's not something to use all the time, but it feels good and opens the hair follicles more. You couldn't clean hair with just grapefruit juice, but it's nice.

*So you're saying it's fun and if used sparingly, couldn't hurt?*
Yes.

*Papaya?*
A natural source of B-complex vitamins. If you're not getting it elsewhere [in your diet?] then put it [meaning products in general?] directly on the hair.

*[Digression: We talk about hair vs. skin absorption.]*
Stuff absorbed by hair won't be picked up by the body, but anything absorbed by the scalp could be, which is why Monoxidal [spelling?], the baldness treatment, had to be by prescription—some feared that heart patients or low blood pressure patients could be affected.

*When does a person need a doctor instead of a salon or a hair care product?*
There's no such thing as a bad *hair* condition, but also a bad *scalp* condition is rare. Psoriasis is a severe skin disorder and a person definitely needs a doctor for that. As for dandruff, there are two basic types, oily and dry, and both can be treated by a professional hairdresser. Those are diseases too, but incurable. However, 95 percent of the time, what people think is dandruff is just dry skin. If it is dandruff most of it can be treated by the salon, but if it is severe, you may want a doctor; there are some internal medicines available for it.

*[I started to end the interview—he had more thoughts.]*
You know another thing—the new "no alcohol" gimmick in products. People come in insisting on alcohol-free products. This is nonsense. Alcohol can make the skin pliable, not dry. Why do you think hospitals use it—it cleans without skin damage.

## Strategy: Phase Two

With this interview I felt I had a good start. Total time so far: three clock hours. Total calendar time: two days. I paused, of course, to think—first entering "thought notes" into the text of the interview as you've seen and making more notes for myself as follows:

*What Were Steve's Main Points?* That people overuse products; that no product is "bad," just misused; that everyone's needs are different; that understanding hair and body chemistry is important to matching product to need; that polymer, keratin and protein are key words; and that yes, there's a lot of hype out there that exploits a person's low self-esteem.

*What Did I Miss?* Most of the chemistry he explained was over my head, and yet that is probably the key to understanding this topic. Also I'm still not clear on what conditioners are and how they work.

*Any Other Thoughts?* Steve is opinionated. As a person, I trust him because in the time I've known him he's never pushed products at me. But opinions are not facts. As a journalist, I've got to double-check everything he's said even if I believe him. I especially need to check out his opinions on one-steps and alcohol-free products.

This thinking made it clear—I had to get objective sources. Where could I find neutral people? The consumer magazines? The business press? Science periodicals? Phase two for hair care must be not to gather facts but to find sources to interview. Now at last I went to the library. I found the same things Tracey did, that there were 653 articles on hair styling, 70 on hair care products; as well as dozens more articles on beards, eyebrows and wigs, even one on polymers, plus 868 on beauty. But unlike Tracey, I wasn't looking for facts, but *sources*. Instead of being overwhelmed by the numbers I looked for patterns. For example, in consumer magazines (in the *Readers' Guide* data base), did any *titles* strike me as objective? My expectation was they would not be. And my instinct was right; most titles were like these:

> "Holding a Hairstyle in Place Has Never Been Easier with the Many New Gels, Mousses, Spritzes and Sprays" by Laura McCarthy, *Vogue*, March 1991, p. 328.
>
> "The Gel Generation," *Mademoiselle*, May 1989, p. 52.
>
> "Get a Grip on Your Hair: New Ways to Shape, Style, Control," *Glamour*, January 1989, pp. 148–153.

Only one article I saw seemed to be cautioning readers, but even this didn't suggest avoiding products altogether.

> "Misuse Can Cancel Out Many Benefits of Today's Hair Tools" by Laura McCarthy, *Vogue*, August 1989, p. 160.

Would the business press (in *Business Periodicals Index*) be more objective? The answer—definitely yes, or at least more honest about the hype side of hair care. *Progressive Grocer* had a number of articles on how to jazz up displays to stimulate impulse buys. *Chemical Marketing Reporter* and *Drug and Cosmetic Industry* frequently surveyed ingredients in products:

> "Silicones in Hair Care Products" by Michael S. Starch, *Drug & Cosmetic Industry*, June 1984, p. 38. (Subjects covered: hair care products, silicones.)
>
> "Cationic Salts in Hair Conditioners" by Albert Shansky, *Drug & Cosmetic Industry*, May 1984, p. 42. (Subjects covered: hair care products, salts.)
>
> "Keratin in Cosmetics (Shampoos and Conditioners)" by Geoffrey Brooks, *Drug & Cosmetic Industry*, October 1983, pp. 38–40. (Subjects covered: hair care products, keratin, shampoos.)

Marketing stories were perhaps bluntest of all:

> "The Hair Care Market: Responding to Niches, Naturals and Combos" by David A. Davis, *Drug & Cosmetic Industry*, April 1991, p. 20. (Subjects covered: Hair care products industry/competition market segmentation.)
>
> "Hair Wars" by Howard Rudnitsky and Jay Glasen, *Forbes*, December 6, 1982, p. 132+. (Subjects covered: Hair care products.)
>
> "Shampoo Marketers Use Their Heads (shampoo-plus-conditioner concept)" by Robert McMath, *AdWeek's Marketing Week*, November 11, 1991, p. 33. (Subjects covered: Hair care products/Marketing shampoos/Marketing.)
>
> "Hair Care Makers Going All Natural" by Gretchen Busch, *Chemical Marketing Reporter,* July 23, 1990, p. SR 34+. (Subjects covered: Hair care products/ Marketing.)

So I had some sources, but—important point here—these *articles* are not the sources. Their *authors* are. These trade magazines cover the industry regularly so may not be as vulnerable to advertiser pressure as are fashion magazines. Phone calls to these reporters could produce good interviews. I had no interest in reading the hundreds of articles, but I was very interested in finding two or three business journalists to *talk* to. And now I had them.

Science periodicals were perhaps the most objective of all, but they also were indifferent. One title was specific, "Deadly Ingredient Banned from Hairspray" (in *New Scientist*, January 23, 1986, p. 24). But all others were medical, zoological or anthropological articles. So I wouldn't chase down their authors.

Next I checked our reference collection. A 1989 book by Ruth Winter, *A Consumer's Dictionary of Cosmetics Ingredients* (Crown, New York, 1989), billed itself as "complete information about the benefits and desirable ingredients found in men's and women's cosmetics." When I read entries, however, I read a very cautious writer. Occasionally she would remark that a product was toxic or nontoxic. Sometimes she would cautiously comment that a product was not proven to work; but other than that, she kept her opinions to herself. Is the cosmetics industry so powerful that no one dares speak against it? What was I getting into?

I next went to the *Encyclopedia of Associations* and found eight national organizations, all of which I wrote asking for pamphlets on hair care products. I also asked them to recommend chemists who might be willing to speak to me. Steve had also promised to give me some of the handouts he had in his collection and introduce me to a traveling chemist when one visited his shop. He also mentioned he used to teach workshops and had a lot of materials left from that.

Still on the trail of interview sources, I checked the *Monthly Catalog of Government Publications* and found some hair references in the *FDA Quarterly Activity Report*.

Now I felt I was ready for background reading. I checked *First Stop* for specialized encyclopedias. Under the key word "hair," they listed five:

*Encyclopedia of Aging*

*Encyclopedia of the Biological Sciences*

*Woman's Encyclopedia of Myths and Secrets*

*Encyclopedia of Chemical Technology*

*McGraw-Hill Encyclopedia of Science and Technology*

These answered most of the "what I don't know" questions, cleared up my confusion about some of the chemistry and hair composition and gave me ideas for questions. This exercise also reinforced my intention of staying focused on challenging hair product claims.

Finally I checked the *Statistical Masterfile*. The most promising source here was the annual *U.S. Industrial Outlook for 250 Industries with Projections*. I'd check it, but the FDA reports would probably be more useful than these.

## Comments

At this point the basics were done. I knew the issues, I knew where the quicksand was and I had leads. The rest would be a matter of just digging. Total time so far: five hours, twenty-five minutes, or $255 in play money.

I don't know unless I follow through, but the digging part will probably be another ten to fifteen hours ($900). This means that the creative part is a fourth of total research time. But without that creative part, I might spend double the digging time ($2,400) trying to make sense of those fourteen hundred hair and beauty articles.

## RESEARCH CASE STUDY: SLEEPING IN PUBLIC
**By Tracey Modic**

After my near disaster with the research for our hair products story, Professor Westfall and I sat down for a conference. I was a little nervous about launching another project so quickly, but Westfall reminded me that I had already learned from my mistakes. She re-emphasized the importance of freewriting, prewriting and designing a creative research strategy and assured me that following this method would save time in the long run. I must admit that I was still reluctant about trusting my instincts. But Westfall insisted.

### Freewriting (notes verbatim)

What I know:

- falling asleep is caused not just by exhaustion but also by boredom, inability to pay attention or lack of concentration.
- sleeping in public is embarrassing for both the sleeper and the presenter who is slept on.
- President Reagan was often criticized for sleeping during Cabinet meetings—possibly through the entire Iran–Contra affair.
- sleeping during the day is often the result of not sleeping at night (insomnia).
- most people want to avoid sleeping in public.
- some people really are boring speakers who are easy to fall asleep on.
- listening ability (hence the ability to stay awake and alert) is often cited by employers as an important component of interpersonal communication in the office.
- human sleep goes through four stages; REM (rapid-eye movement) sleep is the last one; the full cycle lasts about 45 minutes.
- doctors used to advise 7–8 hours of sleep per night. But lately they say that some people can get by on less sleep than others.
- you can't make up for lost sleep; the body somehow adjusts to missing a night.

What I don't know:

- why are some people more prone to fall asleep at inopportune times than others?
- how can a speaker grasp the attention of listeners—and keep it?
- how much sleep is enough? how much is too much?
- does a regular sleep pattern really make you more healthy?
- how important is sleep to mental alertness or job performance?
- how can a person whose sleep pattern is very irregular get back on schedule?
- are naps beneficial, or do they interfere with your regular sleep schedule? how long should they be and when should you take them?
- are there gender differences in how much a person needs and when s/he should get it?
- what role does stress play in sleep problems?

- how is a "sleep disorder" different from "having trouble sleeping"? Is either a serious medical problem?
- do sleeping pills work? what about alertness aids with heavy doses of caffeine? are they safe?

What readers want to know (in first-person view of reader):

- how can I avoid falling asleep in class or at work?
- how much sleep should I get per night? how much is too much?
- how can I tell when I've had a decent night's sleep?
- how can I avoid feeling tired when I don't get enough sleep?
- how can I pay attention better and stay more alert in class/at work?
- how can I keep the attention of listeners/students/colleagues?
- should I take naps when I feel tired, or is napping at a certain time of day more beneficial?
- are sleep aids/alertness aids safe and effective?
- are sleep problems (or problems staying awake) anything to worry about? when should I see a doctor?

After freewriting, I decided the best audience would be career-oriented college students and professionals aged 20–35. These readers view sleeping in public as an embarrassing problem and are interested in finding solutions. These readers want quick answers. Focused on upward mobility and hard work, they believe that they can cure themselves of their sleep problems, and they distrust the medical community.

In order to satisfy these readers, I decided that the article should take on a straightforward, how-to format. The story should answer reader questions by offering simple steps toward improving sleep habits, prescribing the ideal number of hours of sleep, recommending over-the-counter sleep aids and suggesting specific ways to stay awake.

The freewriting exercise also generated a list of key words such as SLEEP, INSOMNIA, REST, PRODUCTIVITY, ATTENTION and STRESS that would later prove valuable in research. But first I needed to analyze the competition—and find out if someone had already beaten me to my story.

## Competition Analysis

Armed with my list of key words and subject headings—now expanded to include SLEEP DEPRIVATION, SLEEP AIDS, BOREDOM, ALERTNESS and HEALTH—I turned to the *Reader's Guide to Periodical Literature* to assess the competitive damage.

The entry SLEEP yielded 105 entries, while SLEEP DEPRIVATION yielded 15. These listings confirmed my audience analysis; titles ranged from the *New Republic* and *Men's Health* to *Glamour* and *Working Woman*. But none of the citations from the past three years covered sleeping in public or workplace sleep problems. Under ATTENTION, I found a cross-reference to ALERTNESS AND VIGILANCE TESTING, where I discovered articles in *Prevention, American Health* and *Science News*. These stories outlined recent psychological studies on lengthening the human attention span. All of them would be useful for research later. But not one answered the specific questions my readers might wanted addressed. Popular magazines had virtually ignored the issue of sleeping in public. My topic was awake and kicking.

In addition to helping me sort through the *Reader's Guide,* the ALERTNESS and VIG-ILANCE TESTING subject headings had introduced me to two new psychological buzz-words. At this point, I turned to the Social Science Index, where I hoped to uncover further evidence of scientific research into my topic. I performed a Boolean search linking the terms SLEEP [AND] PERFORMANCE LEVEL. Five entries in psychological journals were available. SLEEP [AND] ATTENTION yielded an additional entry, as did SLEEP [AND] VIG-ILANCE, SLEEP [AND] MOTIVATION and SLEEP [AND] STRESS. Now I knew that my story idea was viable; no popular magazines had covered it, and the relevant journals were full of background information. I was almost ready to begin my research. But I still needed to develop a strategy for reading, interviewing and reporting that would provide me with just enough information to write an effective story. It was time for "efficiency," as Professor Westfall would say.

## Designing a Research Strategy

At this point, Westfall and I discussed the difference between "items" and "procedures" in research. Items, she said, include the fundamental elements of evidence—people, things, expertise, statistics and so on—that lend credibility to a story, while procedures represent the methods employed toward discovering these items. Our task was to determine what mix of items and procedures would generate the best story for the market we had targeted.

Right away, I determined that people were the most important element for this story. Anecdotes and quotes play a critical role in the market for 20- to 35-year-olds, especially where embarrassing issues are concerned. In magazines such as *Forbes* or *Working Woman,* only first names are used in describing "office nightmares" so that an intimate relationship with the reader is maintained. The implied setting for this type of story is gossip at the copy machine.

I decided that our readers should be encouraged to feel comfortable with their "sleep problem" by realizing that it happens to the best of us. In order to inspire the reaction, I needed lively quotes and anecdotes from colorful people who weren't afraid to admit to their own lapses in concentration. Procedure number one, I decided, was to track down some good sleep stories.

First, I chose to place a classified advertisement in our campus daily newspaper asking for people with interesting sleep stories to call me. This method of finding sources had proven effective before when covering topics of interest to students. Writing a clever ad would be a first step toward uncovering humorous tales from sleepy students and frustrated professors. Next, I chose a sunny day to wander the College Green and conduct "person-on-the-street" interviews. Finally, I turned to the library in search of real-world professionals who would share their tales of office woe.

I'm no expert in corporate communications. In fact, I had no idea where to find real-world businesspeople to interview other than by flipping through the telephone book. My librarian, however, referred me to three volumes: *O'Dwyer's Directory of Corporate Communications, O'Dwyer's Directory of Public Relations Executives* and the *National Directory of Corporate Public Affairs* (Columbia Books, Washington, D.C., published annually). In each of these books, major corporations were listed alphabetically, along with their addresses, telephone numbers and the names of public relations contact people. The volumes were also cross-referenced geographically. I was thus able to find several companies located within my area code; setting up the interviews would be easy now that I knew where to call.

Supporting my assumptions with expertise was the next item on my agenda. Procedure number two, I decided, was to find experts and interview them. Because our audience is college educated, I determined that we would need at least a token authority to grant our story credibility. Also the problem-solving approach I visualized would require the advice of a qualified professional. An industrial psychologist seemed to me the most useful kind of expert. He or she could explain the effect of sleep deprivation on office productivity and recommend steps for staying alert. I returned to the library in search of such an expert.

I knew from our earlier competition analysis that several entries about sleep and performance level existed on the Social Science Index. I retrieved these entries and wrote down the authors' names. Then I could look up their addresses and telephone numbers in *World of Learning,* contact them and ask them to grant interviews. I also consulted the *Encyclopedia of Associations* for the address and telephone number of the American Psychological Association (APA), the professional organization of contemporary psychologists. This group publishes a variety of journals, directories and newsletters and serves as a clearinghouse for literature in the field. Naturally, the staff at APA could recommend several industrial psychologists who would be willing to speak with me.

Now that I had uncovered people and expertise, I needed statistics and background information to round out my research. Procedure number three, I decided, was to journey yet again through our library—this time in search of detail. The middle-class, managerial reader profile suggested a concern with numbers and specifics. I jotted down questions that only a journal article or case study could answer: How common was the problem of sleeping on the job? What were other companies doing to prevent it? How much productivity (read: money) could be lost because of it?

Previous competition analysis had turned up six journal entries. Subjects ranged from the effect of sleep loss on psychological variables to the psychological aspects of sleeping in various positions. Although I needed only a few token statistics to balance out my anecdotes, I needed a more generalized background about the nature of sleep itself. For this, I turned to the library reference room—but not without consulting two important handbooks.

The first, *Walford's Guide to Reference Material,* is published by the Library Association of London. It lists the names and abstracts of major specialized encyclopedias, dictionaries and other reference volumes. The second, *The New York Public Libraries Bibliographic Guide to Psychology,* is part of the NYPL series cataloging all reference materials that pass through the NYPL system during a given year. Both proved indispensable in referring me to specialized volumes.

In the *International Encyclopedia of the Social Sciences,* for instance, I found entries on sleep causes and processes, sleep loss and biological functions, fatigue at skilled tasks, the effect of sleep on learning and performance, sleep disorders and sleep therapy. A similar wealth of information was available in Richard L. Gregory's *Oxford Companion to the Mind.*

Procedure number three was complete, and my story was beginning to take form. The groundwork was laid for a fascinating article about sleeping in public; I was prepared to satisfy a clearly defined market. All that remained was to follow through—but not without taking time for a nap.

# 11

# *Beyond Intuition*

Since I began this book, *Savvy*, *Memories*, *New York Woman* and *Wigwag* have folded. *Psychology Today* folded but was later relaunched. *Spy* teetered on the brink of collapse for a while but then found new financing. Later one of *Spy*'s editors left to take over *Vanity Fair* and Tina Brown, the sometimes outrageous former editor of *Vanity Fair*, was hired away to edit the stodgy *New Yorker*, much to the astonishment of her colleagues. *Victoria*'s rapid growth slowed. Dozens of new titles, such as *Zoo Life*, *Blushing Bride* and *Chile Pepper* (the magazine of spicy foods), were launched. These all have yet to prove themselves in the rough-and-tumble media world. Newspapers and book companies too were bought and sold, launched or folded, in the three years I worked on this book. In recession or expansion, no industry is more volatile than media. Those who choose to play the game accept risk and change as givens.

It's been the central argument of this book that the foundation of professional writing and editing is analysis—deliberate, nonintuitive, slog it out, tedious, time-consuming analysis. Amateurs can write intuitively from the heart, but professionals reach beyond intuition to analyze audiences, their own prose and the work of others. Because of the constant changes and wide variety of publishers, analysis is essential for designing a publishing strategy. Specifically, being able to describe an audience, detect a focus, evaluate form, diagnose structure, perceive authority base and mimic voice are the strategic analytical skills that unlock publishers' doors. Ability to deliver through good tight writing and well-researched facts keeps those doors unlocked.

Most of the examples in the text have been taken from magazines, but analytical skill is useful for sizing up a newspaper or book publisher too. Newswriting in the past generation has been in flux because of the ferocity of newspaper economics.

Consequently, papers have become more hospitable to free-lance writers and non-news-service articles. At the same time, the homogeneity of newspaper writing has lessened. Fifty years ago, a news story in San Francisco would read much the same as one in St. Louis. Today, that is no longer a given and the writer who would write for both cities cannot assume newspaper formulas of old-time journalism textbooks still apply.

Book publishers are less focused than magazines or newspapers in that their lists might contain books for many audiences and range widely over subject matter. But they, too, need to be approached analytically. The writer who sizes up a company by examining its trade list (consult the *Publisher's Trade List Annual* or *Literary Marketplace* for this kind of information) is more likely to publish. Don't try to send a cookbook to a company that specializes in horror fiction unless it's a very bad cookbook. Once again, analysis defines the pro. Only an amateur would approach a company without first researching its philosophy.

## PRACTICAL MARKETING

Mastery of the plodding, time-consuming analytical skills described in this book is the heart of the writing process and consumes perhaps as much as 90 percent of its time. The key mistake amateurs and beginners make is not to give enough time or energy to this side of the craft. The professional begins by sizing up the target, whether it is a magazine, newspaper or book company, so as to detect uniqueness. What sorts of titles does a given book company specialize in? What is a newspaper's survival strategy? What distinguishes a magazine from its rivals? The professional ponders these questions with clinical detachment, struggling to describe a medium's agenda in value-free language.

Next, the professional applies the same discipline to his or her own work. Criticizing a draft to adapt it to the needs of the target market while at the same time maintaining one's own voice again requires detached and thorough analysis.

The goal of all this analysis is not the prose itself but a letter or a book proposal. It is customary to query editors before submitting manuscripts. A query saves editors' time and protects you. Would you remodel someone else's kitchen without first negotiating design and price? Then why should you give away your writing before securing your contract? The analysis is your source for ideas for constructing an irresistible query. Queries are often harder to write than the article or book itself. Nothing is more eagerly described in advice books than formulas for winning queries, but a pro, skilled in analysis, would never be foolish enough to trust a formula.

### Tips for Writing Magazine Queries

Lee Jolliffe, now a professor at the University of Missouri, wrote her doctoral dissertation on magazine queries. One of her observations in it was that of the score or more writing-advice books in print, none agreed unilaterally. Some advised attaching clips to the query; some didn't. Some advised calling editors; some specifically warned against this as a bad idea. Even the wisdom of writing a query letter was not universally endorsed by the books.

I do endorse letters; don't call. In those letters, of course, use your analyses to frame your proposal. Analyze the market until you know it so well you can ape its style in your letter. You should also redo analyses from time to time. If it has been six months since you have approached a magazine, do a new one. There has probably been a change of editors or format in the interim.

Whatever you do, don't send a manuscript. It probably won't be read by an editor. An intern or office receptionist might glance at it, but not an editor, unless the company is small or the editor inexperienced. In the letter, don't wheeze or whine. Don't waste time with empty pleading: "I would like to propose an article . . ."; "I think your readers would be interested . . ."; "I have been interested for some time in . . . " Instead start immediately to explain the focus of your topic. Remember focus sells your idea, not topic alone. A topic can be done in a thousand ways; the editor needs to know clearly and simply your intended approach. So, if not in the first sentence then in the first paragraph, spell out the focus.

From there, a good second paragraph would tantalize the editor by giving a few intriguing facts from your proposed story. Concrete details sell better than abstract ones. Instead of saying, "I will travel to visit windmills," say, "Today only one in twenty windmills pumps a well." Specifics are more likely to impress an editor than vague promises of future trips or interviews. Yes, this means you have to do some research to write a query letter, but you don't have to do all of it—just enough to fill a letter.

The remainder of this letter can be anything you deem relevant. Do you have the cooperation of people you plan to interview (especially if they're celebrities)? And do you have any special credentials to help you do the story? Don't underestimate the power of personal experience as a credential.

Enclose a self-addressed, stamped envelope (often called an SASE) with your query. Keep the letter to one page. Also keep in mind the letter is a sample of your writing. If your market encourages voice, and your voice is important to the success of the article, be sure your letter uses the same persona you intend to use in the final article.

Having said all that, let me point out that advice books devote most of their chapters to tips like this. I have written only four paragraphs of tips and ten chapters about analysis. My real advice, then, is to ignore the tips, mine included, if your analysis tells you you should. Be sure you're basing your opinion on careful, strategic analysis though. I have written letters where I talked about my experiences in the first paragraph instead of the third as I advise above. I have sometimes quoted specifics from the story in my opening and not revealed my focus until the last paragraph. Sometimes I've written a headline on my letter. Other times I have not. And yes, although almost every book on marketing tells you to keep your query letter to one page, I have occasionally written longer letters. There are no rules. Each topic, magazine, editor and writer is unique. Only analysis can tell you what to put in your letter. Should you mention your other writing credentials? I don't know. Some magazines might be impressed by your column in a weekly newspaper and others might dismiss you because of it. Should you get yourself a personal letterhead? I don't know. Some magazines might be impressed by this businesslike touch; others could care less. Trust your analyses; don't trust a guidebook.

## Tips for Writing a Book Prospectus

The same principles apply for book proposals. Trust your analyses over guidebooks. Approaching a publisher with an idea for a nonfiction book takes more work than writing a magazine query, but focus, concrete details, style and brevity all are important here, too. An analysis, not some copied formula, should reveal to you how to structure your proposal.

Some extra steps are needed to prepare a book prospectus, however. One, you need to actually write a market analysis yourself. For a magazine query, you must evaluate a market for your own needs, but you don't need to pass this information on to the editor. For books it's just the opposite—you should share your market perceptions with your target publisher because your competition analysis reveals your thinking more clearly than a book description alone. A market analysis essentially compares your book with similar titles or contains your notions about the audience. Are there special groups of readers out there who should be interested in your topic? (Chapter 2 of this book gives you techniques for researching an audience.) If rival titles have covered the same ground, is your book a new approach or an update? (A new approach is easier to sell.)

Don't be negative when comparing your book to rivals. It's more diplomatic (not to mention more effective) to argue that your book is different, not better. On the other hand, don't claim a book is totally unique. There is nothing new under the sun. You have rivals. Study them. The competition analysis is where you argue your case. If a lot has been done on a topic, I like to select four or five very good books, ones I respect, and compare my proposed book to them. Defending my book at the expense of others doesn't prove my idea is better. Praising rivals does.

Another part of a good prospectus is a sample chapter. Just as in the magazine query, a chapter is stronger if the facts it contains are concrete, vivid, strong. Therefore, I avoid using an introductory or concluding chapter for the sample. Those usually are too theoretical to stand alone out of context. The middle of the book has the meat so I usually research and write a midbook chapter.

Elements I consider essential in a book proposal are

A title (and subtitle).

A one- or two-page statement explaining why this book is needed.

A one-paragraph synopsis of the book.

A chapter list. Include one- or two-paragraph descriptions of each chapter in this list.

The competition analysis. This is as much an essay defending your book as a look at rival books.

Potential markets or audience for the book.

Sample chapter or chapters.

Research strategy (but guard your secrets.)

A resumé.

Once again, this tidy list is deceptive. I have written book proposals without one or more of the above. Only the sample chapter was universal. I think a chapter is essential for making a sale, but whether I use anything else from this list depends on my analysis. How long should a prospectus be? Most average around fifty pages; but again let analysis determine the length, not some formula. What order should the elements be in? The order listed above is good, but again, not always. Must it be sent to only one publisher at a time? Maybe. Maybe not. What publisher should get the proposal? *The Publisher's Trade List Annual* can give you clues but not answers. If I'm doing a book on gardening and my target company has five garden books, does that mean they specialize in garden topics and so are a good target or that they are saturated with gardening and so are a bad target? Again, only long hard analysis will reveal the answer. Each problem is unique. Every solution distinct.

## THE EDITOR–WRITER RELATIONSHIP

Analysis techniques have been discussed in detail in the preceding chapters. Not specifically discussed, however, but alluded to in many places, is another arena where willingness to carefully analyze can improve publishing success. This is the editor–writer relationship. Theodore Bernstein in his classic, *Watch Your Language*, compared the editor–writer relationship to that of a mongoose and a snake. It is an apt image, one I've thought of many times whenever I'm baffled by an editor or frustrated by a dense writer. What does that editor want? Why can't my writer follow instructions? The mongoose–snake image summarizes our situation perfectly. We are both predator and prey as we try to communicate.

Editors and writers do become fast friends. They are alike, after all, in their love of language and curiosity about the world. But they differ, too. A writer is closer to experience, on the scene. An editor is closer to an audience. It's a subtle distinction but one fraught with potential for conflict. The writer wants to describe reality exactly. The highest compliment for a journalist is to say, "You were exactly right." But an editor wants to fascinate a reader. There is no greater compliment for an editor than for a reader to say, "I couldn't put that story down; I identified with it."

As writer, I personally am puzzled when a reader tells me this. "Thank you," "I think," but why is it important that you relate to the story? Aren't you curious about people other than yourself?" An editor likewise may be baffled by the writer's favorite compliment. What's so important about it being perfectly exact if the reader is bored? This difference means the two, writer and editor, will often disagree on what to emphasize, what facts are relevant, what language is appropriate. The mongoose and the snake eye each other, two polite but passionate predators. Whose will will prevail? Who will be prey; who will be predator this time?

If both editor and writer are willing to use analysis and give it the time it deserves to develop their communications, the potential for frustration is lessened. I've known only a handful of editors and writers who even seem to realize this is needed. Language about reality is slippery; language about writing even more so. Even with a stack of grammar books, thesauri, dictionaries and encyclopedias at hand, no editor or writer will share the same vocabulary. If they are to communicate at all, they need to agree on words to describe what they're trying to do.

Together they need to analyze the audience, the topic, the medium, the writer's voice and the editor's style of thinking. They both need to respect what a difficult task communication is. I am to this day baffled by what my editor wanted when he told me that my "Cold" article was to be about mystery. I studied his magazine and tried to talk with him, but I still haven't a clue. When poor communication leads to a failure, everybody loses—writer, editor and readers.

At the beginning, the burden of communication rests with writers, since they are so numerous. An editor's daily mail contains dozens of ideas or queries from writers and would-be writers. The more time writers spend on analysis to try to guess the approach an editor prefers, the more likely they are to break through an editor's shell and get a hearing.

Once a writer–editor relationship is established, though, the burden shifts. If editors want to keep writers productive, they must be able to put their needs in concrete language. An editor needs to get beyond intuition, just as a writer does. If both writer and editor do not get beyond intuition, the mongoose–snake pattern will prevail. Both are interesting animals, I'll grant, but I wouldn't keep either as a pet.

## RECOMMENDED FOR THE PROFESSIONAL BOOKSHELF

If I could have only one of the following, I would take the Kirk Polking book. I own all of them, however—and use them.

Blue, Martha. *By the Book: Legal ABCs for the Printed Word*. Northland Publishing, Flagstaff, Ariz., 1990.

Fry, Ronald W., editor. *Magazines Career Directory*. Career Press, Hawthorne, N.J., 1987.

Goldin, Stephen, and Kathleen Sky. *The Business of Being a Writer*. Harper & Row, New York, 1982.

Holsinger, Ralph L. *Media Law*. McGraw-Hill, New York, 1991.

Peterson, Franklyn, and Judi Kesselman-Turkel. *The Author's Handbook*. Prentice-Hall, Englewood Cliffs, N.J., 1982.

Polking, Kirk, and Leonard S. Meranus, editors. *Law and the Writer*. Writer's Digest Books, Cincinnati, Ohio, 1985.

# Working in Groups

Writing and editing are skills best learned alone. The writer in training should write. The editor in training should edit. But a classroom is most effective when it exploits the energy of the group. How can the teacher use the group's dynamics to teach solitary skills? The following exercises, arranged by chapter, are meant to stimulate student interaction, so the students can help one another learn. But they are not meant to substitute for solid writing or editing practice.

## WORKING IN GROUPS: CHAPTER 2

1. Divide the class into pairs. Have one student in each pair describe a reader of a magazine using just the ads as clues. Have the other student describe the same magazine's audience using just the editorial for clues. In group discussion, ask for student opinions on how the descriptions are similar, different, accurate and inaccurate. Does looking at only ads or editorial distort the reader concept?
2. With students working in pairs again, have them compare two competing magazines which occupy the same niche. (Part of the challenge is to be sure they identify niche companions accurately; disqualify teams that compare, say, *Forbes* with *Esquire* or *McCall's* with *Glamour*.) Ask the students to compare niche strategies of each magazine. How does each signal its readers and advertisers, that is, how does each say it's a little bit better than the other? How are coverage, graphics and covers different? Which magazine is winning in its niche? (Be sure students back up their opinions on this last with data from SRDS or Audit Bureau of Circulations—ABC.)

3. Ask students to select a magazine they don't admire and bring it to class. What changes would they make—short of changing the basic subject matter—to make it more appealing to them?

4. Ask students to bring both a magazine they like and one they don't like to class. Arrange the magazines so students can see both groups. Ask, were students uncomfortable buying a magazine they didn't like; why? Are there any in the don't-like group that are also in the like group? Have the students defend their acceptance or rejection. (If a student feels threatened because he or she likes a magazine others dislike, then I usually jump in and defend the student—the point is to show students how their tastes are interfering with their observations.) Have students try to describe psychographic qualities of the class from the magazines they chose. (I usually offer a counter description, since their portrayals of themselves tend to be outrageously flattering.)

5. Using a saturated market, such as the Seven Sisters, ask students to "fight" over an advertising client. I assign a magazine to each team, give them a big-name product, such as Cheerios, and tell them the company has decided to buy space in only two of the magazines this year. Their success at being chosen rests on their ability to describe, accurately and appealingly, the readers of their magazines. Sometimes I bring in an independent judge to choose the winning teams.

6. Pair an advertiser with an unlikely magazine, Kellogg with *Esquire* or Smucker with *Victoria*. Have students devise arguments to convince the advertisers that readers of these magazines could be attractive targets.

7. Ask students to examine current and old copies of a magazine to detect repositioning. The visual changes will be fairly obvious, but what has changed in the writing? Are the social issues different, the viewpoints, the overall tone? Does the role of the writer change, becoming stronger or weaker as a presence in the magazine? Does the relationship with the reader change? How?

8. Ask students to devise cover roughs for a real or imaginary magazine. Then ask them to test their covers using one of the test methods in Appendix 2.1.

9. A major assignment: Ask students to prepare a complete demographic and psychographic portrait of their target magazines. Emphasize that they must explain their ideas by citing clues from the magazine and by quoting articles about the company from business journals or reference books. Be sure they use correct demographic terms (Appendix 2.2). For an editing class, an additional part of this assignment could be to ask them to calculate the percentage of its potential reader universe the magazine has captured.

## WORKING IN GROUPS: CHAPTER 3

1. Take any one of the sample articles (listed at the beginning of the book in Demonstration Articles, after the Contents) and have students devise as many new focuses as they can think of, including some appropriate for business,

science, sports, women's, men's, children's and health magazines. (I take *SRDS* volumes, open at random and assign each student whatever market category comes up.) What implications does each focus have for content, research strategies and writing style of each article? Would the student feel comfortable developing the alternative focuses? Why or why not?

2. Study the list of raccoon articles (p. 56). If a magazine appears more than once, how did the focus for the topic change? How frequently did the magazine use the topic? Why? Do any magazines seem unlikely ones for the raccoon topic? Why? Are there any magazines that should have been covering the topic missing? Are the lengths of the articles significant?

3. Ask students to take a topic they plan to write about and prepare a focus report. Ask them to look at index entries in *Readers' Guide, Business Periodicals Index*, and perhaps *Newspaper Abstracts*. (A Boolean search or word search is more thorough than simple subject search—see Chapter 10.) What angles have other authors used toward the topic and will this limit what the student can do with it? Are there any markets that have been exhausted by the topic? Are there any angles that have been overdone? Conversely, are any missing? How long has it been since anyone used the angle the student wants to do? Is the target magazine ready to try the topic again? How will the student change his or her focus because of this exercise?

4. Have students examine already published articles in a magazine (ideally from one they plan to target as a writer). Ask each to propose new focuses for the same topic that would still be appropriate for that magazine. How long do they think the editor should wait before running the new angles? How long should the new articles be? What sort of research or writing styles should be used? What sort of graphic treatments and sidebars should accompany them?

5. Ask students to come to class having all read the same article. Divide students into groups and ask each group to reach a consensus among themselves about which are the focus, refocusing and transformation statements. Have each group put their decisions on the board. The groups will probably agree and disagree. Have the class as a whole discuss the differences, with each group defending its interpretation of the focus of the article. Then have the class return to their groups and rediscuss the article; do they want to change their interpretations? Whether the class reaches a consensus or not, discuss how students read. How do they think the writer signals them about the meaning of the piece? How many readings does it take before students can see the signals? Do the focusing statements they see form any pattern? Is the pattern unique to this writer?

6. Take an article with a weak focus, such as "Eva's Ghost," and have students propose solutions.

7. Have students write heads and decks for their article drafts or the sample articles in this book, with the rule that the focus must be in the head and the topic in the deck. Then reverse the rule, with the topic in the head and the focus in the deck.

(It might be useful to have them first examine published heads and decks to see how professional editors use focuses and topics in heads.)

## WORKING IN GROUPS: CHAPTER 4

1. Divide the class into groups and have each group propose a topic and focus appropriate for the linzer torte article for one of the three magazines analyzed in this chapter. Have the class discuss the differences in their proposals, explaining why they think their idea is right. Avoid voting for the "best" proposal, though— let them see the "rightness" of all proposals.

2. Divide the class into groups of four each—one magazine title per group. Have each student take an aspect of form (purpose, effect, subject, genre) and identify the dominant forms in each category for their magazine. Then ask the group to put together a description of the mix and range of the magazine and present it to the class.

3. Have a student or a group prepare charts and graphs for a magazine they dislike. Ask them to discuss how their perceptions of the magazine after the analysis are different from their perceptions before.

4. Pick a scene or topic or incident and have each student write a short paragraph reflecting a single "form." Example: Take the class to a garden or coffee shop; have them draw slips you have prepared with forms written on them (e.g., "bizarre, wry, thoughtful, informative, summary, the Nineties"). Have a good mix of subject-, purpose- and effect-based forms. Try to avoid "textbook" language on these slips. In discussion, talk about the ways the form shaped the students' perceptions, styles, even audiences. Explore how one setting could produce such diversity of writing. Sometimes students will ask you privately to define the word on the slips for them; resist this. But later talk about the discomfort that freedom to interpret causes. (This exercise is a great icebreaker for an early session.)

5. Have each student do a forms analysis of the same issue of the same magazine. Then have them compare analyses. The point of this exercise is to show students how different yet how right each subjective reading is; the intent is to give them confidence that their own perceptions are useful. They tend to want to take the teacher's or editor's or other "smarter" students' words over their own, but their own is the only one that matters since they must do the writing.

6. There are enough facts about linzer tortes scattered through this chapter for students to write a short piece. Have students first write in any voice they choose about linzer tortes or raspberries. Then ask them to write for a specific target. In discussion, talk not only about differences between the two drafts but also about the frustrations of form restrictions. This is a good exercise for teaching revision as well.

## WORKING IN GROUPS: CHAPTER 5

1. Hand out a short article in class and have students first map it and then compare maps.

2. Have students work in pairs to map each other's article drafts. What changes do the maps seem to suggest?

3. Begin by asking students to devise an ideal or target map for "The Cold." (This might be done in groups.) Then ask students to try to edit the piece to match the map. Is it difficult to edit toward a map; why or why not? Is mapping best as an editing or writing tool? Do the changes weaken or strengthen the piece?

4. Ask each student to keep a map of each draft of their pieces as a record of changes from version to version and turn in the maps with the final draft.

5. Have students analyze the leads of two niche rivals. Are there similarities, differences between the rivals' styles?

6. Have students map two or three short pieces by a single author. What variety does that author show in structuring each piece and what patterns seem to repeat from piece to piece? Is structure a component of that author's style?

7. Have students select a single article from a magazine they like and map it. Ask students who think they have unusual maps to draw them on the board. Then ask them to explain their maps to the class and recommend revisions. (I thought students would be shy about this public an exercise, but giving them power to "edit" real magazines, instead of their friends, unlocked something. They seemed to enjoy this.)

8. Divide students into groups of three and have each group map three issues of a magazine. Does the group discover any patterns? How crucial are these patterns to the identity or personality of the magazine?

## WORKING IN GROUPS: CHAPTER 6

1. Have students select magazines they don't particularly admire and analyze their dominant authority bases. How are these bases appropriate for the readers of the magazine?

2. Ask students to relocate an article or book chapter that once persuaded them or changed their opinion about an issue. Ask them to reexamine the article for authority bases. Is the article as strong to them now that they can read for authority base? Why or why not? A variation: ask them to bring in a textbook from another course and read it for authority base. Tell them to especially look for weak authority cues.

3. Ask students to take an article they have already written, analyze its dominant authority base and rewrite it using another authority base. For example, if the

piece used personal observations as the dominant base, change it to an expert piece, or change an expert to a generic *you* and so forth. Students usually only need to do a few paragraphs to get the idea.

4. Ask students to take a short article from a magazine and rework it into an authority base pattern appropriate for a rival magazine. This is a tough exercise; you may prefer to have them work in teams. If everyone in this class does this exercise for the same two magazines, be sure to compare versions. The diversity possible will be surprising.

5. If you have students solicit writers' guidelines or if you have a collection of them, have students compare the guidelines with the actual editorial of the magazine. Have them critique the guidelines for clarity and accuracy. Then have them write a new set of guidelines for the magazine.

# *Index*

Adjectives
  in tightening, 162
Adverbs
  in tightening, 162
*Advertising Age*, 23, 24, 31
*Adweek*, 22
*America: History and Life*, 193
*American Demographics*, 14, 25, 30
Analogy
  as form, 65
  and voice, 148
Analysis
  as form, 63
Anderson, Curt, 81
Anonymous sources. *See* Unnamed sources
*Apartment Life. See Metropolitan Home*
*Archives. See* Special collections
Aristotle, 63
Articles
  as authority base, 129–131
  ideas for, 175
  research methods for, 6, 193–199
  *See also* Audience research
*Art Index*, 197
Assertions, 133
*Atlantic Monthly*, 14
Attribution, 98, 111, 117, 118, 130, 229
Audience, 11, 12, 13–18, 19, 189, 196, 215. *See also* Readers
  editing for, 24
  writing for, 24–25
Audience research, 61
  methods, 29–31
  uses, 17–18

*Audubon*, 71
Author experience
  as authority base, 122–123
Authority base, 111–143
  definition, 111

Baker, Sheridan, 97
*Bakery Production & Management*, 72
*Basically Buckles*, 20
*Bedford Bibliography for Teachers of Writing*, 85
Beginnings
  as element of structure, 94
Bernstein, Theodore, 219
*Better Beagling*, 21
*Better Homes and Gardens*, 3
*Between Fact and Fiction*, 117
Bias
  in audience research, 30
  in descriptions, 122
Bibliographies, 197
*Bibliography of Geography*, 191
*Bird Watcher's Digest*, 93
Blount, Roy, Jr., 21
*Blushing Bride*, 215
*Bon Appetit*, 19
Book prospectuses, 218
Boolean searches, 198
Brown, Tina, 215
*Business Periodicals Index*, 72, 179, 197, 208
*Business Week*, 18

Catalogs
  as authority base, 126

*Cat Fancy*, 13
Cause and effect
  as form, 65
CD-ROM, 72, 198
Chaos, 4–5, 88
Charts
  for analyzing form, 71, 73–74
*Chile Pepper*, 215
*Citations Index*, 197
City magazines, 126
Classification
  as form, 64
Clauses
  in tightening, 163, 164
Close reading, 4
Cohn, Victor, 193
*Columbia Journalism Review*, 21
Comparison
  as form, 65
*Composition/Rhetoric: A Synthesis*, 59
*Concise Oxford Dictionary of Literary Terms*, 59
Concordances, 180
*Conde Nast Traveler*, 24, 91
  map, 106
Congressional Information Service, 192
*Connections*, 22
*Consumer's Dictionary of Cosmetics Ingredients*, 209
Contrast
  as form, 65
*Control of Nature*
  analysis of, 147–149
Cooke, Janet, 139
*Cosmopolitan, 91, 127*
*Country America*, 22
*Country Journal*, 42, 48, 120
  map, 107
*County & City Data Book*, 198
*Creative Loafing*, 21
Credentials
  of experts, 127
Credibility, 112, 119
Crisp, Wendy, 11
Critical perception, 3, 4. *See also* Value judgments

Dale, Edgar, 89
Data bases, 197–198. *See also* Indexes
Definition
  as form, 64
Demographics, 15
Demographic terms, 32–33
Demographic trends, 24–26
Derrida, Jacques, 121
Description. *See also* Sensory detail
  as form, 63
Dictionaries, 197
*Dictionary of Modern Critical Terms*, 59
*Directory of Archives and Manuscript Repositories in the United States*, 199

*Directory of Historical Organizations in the United States*, 193
Discipline, 6, 7
Documents
  as authority base, 129–131
*Doll Reader*, 21
Drawing
  as research tool, 194

Editor–writer relationship, 219–220
Editors
  and authority base, 141–143
  and tightening, 159, 168–169
Effects
  as form, 67–68
Efficiency
  in research, 189, 196, 212
Elements of structure, 88–101
*Elements of Style*, 146
Elements of voice, 145–146
*Elle*, 96–97, 99–100
*Emerge*, 22
*Encyclopedia Americana*, 179
*Encyclopedia of Aging*, 209
*Encyclopedia of Associations*, 72, 190, 213
*Encyclopedia of Chemical Technology*, 209
*Encyclopedia of the Biological Sciences*, 209
Encyclopedias, 197
*Encyclopedic Directory of Ethnic Newspapers*, 72
Endings
  as element of structure, 99
Epistemological splash
  authority base, 120–121, 133
Epstein, Edward Jay, 117
*Esquire*, 19, 44, 91, 94–96
Evidence, 183–201 *See also* Research
Example
  as form, 64
Experience
  as form, 63
Expert
  as authority base, 136
Expert has a soul
  as authority base, 127–129
Explanation
  as form, 63

Fact checking, 119, 139
Facts
  and voice, 146–149
*Fame*, 26
*FDA Quarterly Activity Report*, 209
Fenn, Donna, 24
Fiction
  compared to nonfiction, 111
*Fiction Writer's Research Handbook*, 191, 196
*Field & Stream*, 45
*First for Women*, 22
*First Stop: The Master Index to Subject Encyclopedias*, 197

Focus, 37–48, 88, 189, 196
  definition of, 38
  in query letters, 217
Focusing statements, 40, 47, 48, 69, 94
Focus patterns, 40–47
*Folio*, 22, 72
*Food of the Western World*, 196
*Forbes*, 24
Foreshadowing, 40, 47, 94
Form, 57–86, 88
  definition of, 59
Fowler, Roger, 59
Free play, 178–179. *See also* Prewriting;
      Freewriting
Freewriting, 186–189, 203, 210–211. *See also*
      Prewriting
*Frisko*, 22

*Gale Directory*, 72
Gallup organization, 18
*Gallup Poll Monthly*, 192
*Garbage*, 22
Garbology, 13, 31. *See also* Audience research
Generic *Them*
  as authority base, 125–126
  double, 140
Generic *We*
  as authority base, 141
Generic *You*
  as authority base, 132
Genre forms, 68–70
*Gentlemen's Quarterly*, 3, 19
*Glamour*, 19, 24
*Going Places: The Guide to Travel Guides*, 191
Gould, Stephen Jay, 135
*Gourmet*, 14, 19
Government documents, 198–199
Graphs
  for forms analysis, 71
  for mix analysis, 81
Grey Advertising, 18
*Guide to Historical Method*, 193
*Guide to Information Sources in the
      Geographical Sciences*, 191

Hair products
  research case study, 203–209
Haley, Alex, 199
*Harley Women*, 21
*Harper's*, 70, 81, 87, 132
*Harvard Business Review*, 142
*Hazardous Materials Information System*, 198
Hearsay
  as authority base, 137
*Historic Houses of America*, 193
*Historical Abstracts*, 193
Historical context
  as authority base, 133–134
*Home Book of Humorous Quotations*, 198
*Hook, Line & Sinker*, 22

Hooks, 94
Hour glass form, 69

I'm not a doctor but I play one on TV
  as authority base, 139–140
Ideas. *See* Articles, ideas for
Indexes. *See also* Data bases
  for article research, 197–198
Information
  as form, 63
*InfoTrac*, 72
*International Directory of Little Magazines
      and Small Presses*, 72
*International Encyclopedia of the Social
      Sciences*, 213
Interviews, 195–196. *See also* Preinterview
      techniques
  sample of, 204–207
  sources for, 207–208
Intuition, 8–9, 13, 18, 61, 215, 220
Inverted pyramid form, 69

Jolliffe, Lee, 216
*Journalism Quarterly*, 14, 17
J. Walter Thompson Agency, 18

Kaplen, Alexander, 26

*Ladies' Home Journal*, 3, 19
*Laugh Track*, 22
Leads. *See* Beginnings
*Lear's*, 132
*Library of Congress Subject Headings*, 191
Lists. *See* Catalogs
Literary critics, 147
*Literary Marketplace*, 216
*Lively Art of Writing*, 97
*Living Word Vocabulary*, 89
Lounsberry, Barbara, 148, 149

*M*, 26
*McCall's*, 19, 72
  analysis of charts, 84–85
  profile of, 73
McDonnell, Terry, 26
*McGraw-Hill Encyclopedia of Science and
      Technology*, 209
McPhee, John
  analysis of voice, 147–149
  works by, 154
*Mad*, 81
*Mademoiselle*, 19
*Magazine Age*, 19
*Magazines for Libraries*, 72
*Magazine Week*, 72
Magna Carta, 180
Mapping
  for analyzing structure, 101–108
Marketing
  of articles, 216
Mead, Margaret, 128, 130, 136

*Memories*, 24, 215
Metaphor
  and voice, 148
Methods description
  as authority base, 135–136
*Metropolitan Home*, 23
Meyer, Philip, 193
Middles
  as element of structure, 97
Mind reader
  as authority base, 123–124
Mix of forms, 70–71
*Modern Baking*, 72
*Modern Maturity*, 23
Modic, Tracey, 183, 210
*Monitor*, 16
*Monthly Catalog of Government Publications*,
  191, 209
*Mother Earth News*, 41
Murray, Donald, 88

Narration. *See* Once upon a time
*Nation*, 38, 43
*National Directory of Community Newspapers*,
  72
*National Directory of Corporate Public Affairs*,
  212
*National Enquirer*, 4, 13, 14, 84, 127
*National Faculty Directory*, 191
*National Geographic*, 130
National Public Radio, 195
*National Register of Historic Places*, 193
*Nation's Business*, 23
*Natural History*, 47
*New England Journal of Medicine*, 180
*New Journalism*, 124
*Newlywed*, 22
*New Precision Journalism*, 193
*News and Numbers*, 193
*NewsBank*, 72
*Newsweek*, 70
Newswriting, 215
*New York*, 124
*New Yorker*, 14, 38, 43, 71, 81, 215
*New York Public Libraries Bibliographic Guide
  to Psychology*, 213
*New York Times*, 72, 147
*New York Times Index*, 72
*New York Woman*, 215
*Next One Hundred Years*, 127
Niche, 12, 19–23
  editing for, 24
  predictions, 22–23
  writing for, 26–27
Nonfiction authors
  noted for voice, 153
Note taking. *See* Taking notes
Number
  as authority base, 125

*O'Dwyer's Directory of Corporate
  Communications*, 212

*O'Dwyer's Directory of Public Relations
  Executives*, 212
O'Rourke, Joseph, 89
Object/conjecture
  as authority base, 131
Official records
  as authority base, 134
*Ohio*, 130
*On Writing Well*, 146
Once upon a time
  as authority base, 120
  as form, 64
*Organic Gardening*, 44
Outlining, 88
*Outside*, 21
Overtightening, 170–172
*Oxford Companion to the Mind*, 213
*Oxford English Dictionary*, 180, 182, 197

*Parade*, 14
Paragraphs
  as element of structure, 92–93
Payne, Lucille, 97
Perception. *See also* Sensory detail
  and voice, 149–152
Periodical indexes. *See* Indexes
Persona, 145, 217
Persuasion
  as form, 65
Photo essay
  as form, 69
Photography
  as research method, 194
Phrases
  as element of structure, 89
  in tightening, 163
Plato, 63, 67, 70, 73
Point/quote
  authority base, 131
*Popular Mechanics*, 87
  map, 106
*Practical Stylist*, 97
*Practicing History*, 193
Predicates
  in tightening, 160
Preinterview techniques, 201. *See also*
  Interviews
Prepositional phrases
  in tightening, 164
*Prevention*, 180
Prewriting, 6, 88. *See also* Freewriting
Process. *See* Writing process
*Professional Builder*, 126
Profiles, 200
Pronouns
  in tightening, 161
Psychographics, 12, 15–17
*Psychology Today*, 215
*Publisher's Trade List Annual*, 216, 219
Pulitzer Prize, 139
Purpose forms, 62–66

Quackenbos, G. P., 67
Qualifiers
  as authority base, 119–120
Query letters, 4, 141, 216–217
Quotations
  books of, 198
Quotes
  direct, 116–119
  indirect, 129

Range, 71
Readability, 89, 119
Reader abuse
  as authority base, 138
*Readers' Guide*, 38, 72 179, 188, 197, 198, 208,
  211
Readers, 67, 94, 151, 186. *See also* Audience
Records
  as form, 66
Reference books, 196–199
Refocusing statements, 40, 47, 48, 99
  as element of structure, 100
*Regional Interest Magazines of the United
    States*, 72
Repetition, 165–168
Reporting
  as form, 66
Repositioning, 12, 23–24
Research.
  case studies, 203–212
  in query letters, 141, 217
  types, of, 190–193. *See also* Evidence
Research methods for articles. *See* Articles,
    research methods; Audience research
Results description
  as authority base, 137
Revision, 146, 151
Rhetorical forms. *See* Purpose forms
*Rolling Stone*, 142
*Roots*, 199
Roundy, Jack, 149

SASE. *See* Self-addressed, stamped envelope
*Savvy*, 7, 11, 142, 215
*Science News*, 132, 136
*Self*, 19–20
Self-addressed, stamped envelope, 142, 217
Sensory detail. *See also* Description; Perception
  as authority base, 121–122
  as research method, 194–195
Sentences
  as elements of structure, 90–91
Serendipity, 175–182
  definition, 175
Service magazines, 126
*7-Days*, 26
Shafer, Robert J., 193
Shakespeare, William, 181
Sidebars
  as form, 69
Sleeping in public
  research case study, 210–213

*Smart*, 26
Smith, Kathy, 149
*Smithsonian*, 130
*Snow Goer*, 20
*Soldier of Fortune*, 3
Sound
  and voice, 151
*Southern Living*, 41
Special collections, 199
Spectra
  for forms analysis, 74–81
*Sports Illustrated*, 62, 71
*Spy*, 70, 72
  analysis of charts, 81–82
  profile of, 72–73
SRDS. *See* Standard Rate and Data Service
SRI International, 16
Stamberg, Susan, 195
Standard Rate and Data Service, 20, 71
*Star*, 14
*Statistical Abstract of the United States*, 192
*Statistical Masterfile*, 192
Structure, 4, 6, 87–108
  definition of, 87
Style. *See* Voice
Subject forms, 61–62
Subtopics
  as element of structure, 93–94

Taking notes, 176, 194, 199–201. *See also*
    Thought notes
*Technology Review*, 46
*Teddy Bear Review*, 21
Telling detail, 194
Theme, 149
Third person point of view. *See* Mind Reader
Thought notes, 184, 186–188, 204–207. *See
    also* Taking notes
Tightening, 146, 159–173,
  tricks, 172–173
Topics, 38, 94, 97, 152, 175, 186, 189
  in query letters, 217
Trade magazines, 208
Transference. *See* I'm not a doctor . . .
Transformation, 40, 47, 48, 99
  as element of structure, 100
Transitions
  as element of structure, 98, 100
*Traveler's Reading Guide*, 191
Trillin, Calvin, 42
Trust me
  as authority base, 133
Tuchman, Barbara, 193
*Turkey & Turkey Hunting*, 20
*TV Guide*, 13
*Twins*, 20

*U.S. Industrial Outlook for 250 Industries
    with Projections*, 209
*U.S.A. Today*, 26
*Ulrich's International Periodicals Directory*, 71

Unnamed sources
  as authority base, 138–139

VALS, 16–17
Value judgments, 3, 4, 118, 122. *See also*
    Critical perception
*Vanity Fair*, 26, 215
Verbs. *See* Predicates
Victoria, 72, 215
  analysis of charts, 82–83
  profile of, 73
Visual detail. *See* Sensory detail
Voice, 4, 6, 8, 145–152
  in query letters, 217

*Walford's Guide to Reference Material*, 213
*Wall Street Journal Index*, 72
*Washington Monthly*, 24
*Washington Post*, 139
*Watch Your Language*, 219
Weber, Ronald, 148
Weiner, Jonathan, 127
White, E. B., 11, 146, 199
Whittle Communications, 17
*Who's Who in America*, 190–191

*Wigwag*, 26, 215
Wilson, Phyllis Starr, 20
Winterowd, W. Ross, 59, 67
Wolfe, Tom, 124
*Woman's Encylopedia of Myths and Secrets*,
    209
Words
  as element of structure, 89
*Working Actors Guide*, 190
*World Encyclopedia of Food*, 196
*World of Learning*, 138, 213
Writer–editor relationship, 219–220
*Writer's Market*, 72
*Writer Teaches Writing*, 88
Writing
  and authority base, 140–141
  and tightening, 159
Writing process, 4, 5–8

Yankelovich, Skelly & White, 16
*Your Prom*, 20

Zinsser, William, 146
*Zoo Life*, 215